AFRICA PROJECTED

From Recession to Renaissance by the Year 2000?

Edited by
Timothy M. Shaw
and
Olajide Aluko

MACMILLAN

© Timothy M. Shaw and Olajide Aluko 1985

All rights reserved. No part of this publication may be reproduced or transmitted, in any form or by any means, without permission

First published 1985 by
THE MACMILLAN PRESS LTD
London and Basingstoke
Companies and representatives
throughout the world

Printed in Hong Kong

British Library Cataloguing in Publication Data
Africa projected.
1. Africa—Economic conditions—1960–
I. Shaw, Timothy M. II. Aluko, Olajide
330.96'0328 HC800
ISBN 0–333–34064–7

Contents

List of Tables and Figures

TABLES

FIGURES

List of Abbreviations

ACP	African, Caribbean and Pacific States (in Lomé Convention)
AHG	Assembly of African Heads of State and Government
ANC	African National Congress (South Africa)
ATRCW	African Training and Research Centre for Women
BHN	Basic Human Needs
BRALUP	Bureau of Resource Assessment and Land Use Planning UDM
BW	BRALUP Workshop on Women's Studies and Development, UDM, September 1979
CAR	Central African Republic
CEAO	West African Economic Community
CID	Centre for Industrial Development (EEC)
CODESRIA	Council for the Development of Economic and Social Research in Africa
DAC	Development Assistance Committee (OECD)
DRR	Disparity Reduction Rate
EAC	East African Community
ECA	(UN) Economic Commission for Africa
ECOWAS	Economic Community of West African States
EDF	European Development Fund (EEC)
EEC	European Economic Community
FAO	Food and Agriculture Organisation
FLN	National Liberation Front (Algeria)
FLS	Front Line States
GATT	General Agreement on Tariffs and Trade
GNP	Gross National Product
GSP	General System of Preferences
IBRD	International Bank for Reconstruction and Development (World Bank)
IDAFSA	International Defence and Aid Fund for South Africa
IDS	Institute of Development Studies, UDM
IMF	International Monetary Fund
LDCs	Less developed countries

LLDCs	Least developed countries
MNCs	Multinational corporations
MPLA	Popular Movement for the Liberation of Angola
MRM	Mozambique National Resistance Movement
MSA	Most Seriously Affected Countries
NICs	Newly Industrialising Countries
NIEO	New International Economic Order
OAS	Organisation of American States
OAU	Organisation of African Unity
ODA	Official Development Assistance
ODC	Overseas Development Council (US)
ODI	Overseas Development Institute (UK)
OECD	Organisation for Economic Co-operation and Development
OFN	Operation Feed the Nation (Nigeria)
OFY	Operation Feed Yourself (Ghana)
OPEC	Organisation of Petroleum Exporting Countries
PAC	Pan-African Congress (South Africa)
PQLI	Physical Quality of Life Index
SADCC	Southern African Development Co-ordination Conference
SADF	South African Defence Force
SADR	Sahrawi Arab Democratic Republic
SAIRR	South African Institute of Race Relations
SSR	Self-sufficiency ratio
STABEX	Export Earnings Stabilisation System (EEC)
SWAPO	South West African Peoples Organisation
TNCs	Transnational Companies
UDM	University of Dar es Salaam
UMOA	West African Monetary Union
UN	United Nations
UNDP	UN Development Programme
UNITA	National Union for the Total Independence of Angola
UNITAR	UN Institute for Training and Research
UPE	Universal Primary Education
UWT	National Women's Organisation of Tanzania
WHO	World Health Organisation
ZANU	Zimbabwe African National Union
ZAPU	Zimbabwe African Peoples' Union

Notes on the Contributors

Olajide Aluko is Professor of International Relations and Dean of the Faculty of Administration at the University of Ife in Nigeria. With a PhD from the LSE, Dr Aluko is one of Africa's leading students of international affairs. Besides books on *Ghana and Nigeria, 1957–1970, The Foreign Policies of African States, Essays in Nigerian Foreign Policy*, and *Nigeria and Southern Africa*, his many articles have appeared in *African Affairs, Issue, Millennium, Quarterly Journal of Administration* and *Nigerian Journal of International Studies.*

Cyril Kofie Daddieh is a Killam scholar in the doctoral programme at Dalhousie University preparing a thesis on food and agriculture in Ghana. He holds a BA from Ripon College and a master's degree in international affairs from Carleton University. His reviews have appeared in *International Journal* and *International Journal of African Historical Studies*, an essay on the Ivory Coast in Shaw and Aluko (eds) *The Political Economy of African Foreign Policy* and an article on African diplomacy in *International Political Science Review.*

Orobola Fasehun is with the Ministry of Foreign Affairs in Lagos. Dr Fasehun holds a PhD from Rutgers University and has been a Lecturer in International Relations at the University of Ife. His essays on Nigerian foreign policy and the OAU have appeared in *Afrika Spectrum, Journal of Modern African Studies*, Shaw and Ojo (eds) *Africa and the International Political System* and Shaw and Onwuka (eds) *Africa and World Politics*. He is co-author of *The OAU after Twenty Years* and *Nigeria: Africa's major power.*

Ravi Gulhati is Chief Economist for the Eastern Africa Region at the World Bank, Washington, DC. He holds a PhD from Harvard University and is the author of several books and articles. Among his publications are 'Industrial Strategy for Late Starters: the experience of Kenya, Tanzania and Zambia' and 'Rapid Population Growth in Sub-Saharan Africa'.

Richard A. Higgott is Lecturer in Social and Political Theory at Murdoch University in Western Australia, having previously been a lecturer at the Universities of Western Australia and Tasmania and a Fellow at Harvard University. Dr Higgott is author of *Political Development Theory: the contemporary debate*, co-editor of *Southeast Asia: the political economy of structural change*, and contributor to *Africa Contemporary Record, Australia in World Affairs, Journal of Modern African Studies, Journal of Commonwealth and Comparative Politics, Review of African Political Economy, Studies in Comparative International Development, Politics*, and *Social Analysis.*

Florizelle B. Liser is an international economist with the Office of the US Trade Representative, specialising in developing country trade issues. Ms Liser has a master's degree in International Affairs from the School of Advanced International Studies (SAIS) of Johns Hopkins University in Washington, DC. She was closely associated with the development of the Physical Quality of Life Index, has co-authored publications on this Index, and has prepared the statistical annexes to several volumes of the Overseas Development Council's annual publication, *The United States and World Development: Agenda*. Ms Liser has often focused on the issue of basic human needs, particularly in Africa, and is a contributor to Shaw (ed.) *Alternative Futures for Africa.*

Marjorie Mbilinyi is Professor of Research in the Institute of Development Studies at the University of Dar es Salaam, where she has taught since 1968. A citizen of Tanzania, Dr Mbilinyi has concentrated her research on education and on women's oppression. Among her many publications on the changing sexual division of labour is *Women and Development in Tanzania.*

John Ravenhill is Lecturer in International Relations at the University of Sydney in Australia. Holding a PhD from the University of California, Berkeley, Dr Ravenhill has worked at the University of Virginia and contributed articles on North–South relations and African international relations to *Africa, Africa Contemporary Record, African Studies Review, Africa Quarterly, International Journal, Journal of Commonwealth and Comparative Politics, Journal of Modern African Studies* and *World Development.*

Amadu Sesay holds a PhD from the LSE and is Lecturer in International Relations at the University of Ife. His essays on West African foreign relations and continental politics have appeared in *Africa Quarterly, Afrika Spectrum, Politique Africaine* and Shaw and Ojo (eds) *Africa and the International Political System*. He is co-editor of *The Future of Regionalism in Africa* and co-author of *The OAU after Twenty Years.*

Timothy M. Shaw is Professor of Political Science and Director of the Centre for African Studies at Dalhousie University in Nova Scotia; he has also taught at the Universities of Ife, Zambia and Makerere in Africa, and Carleton and British Columbia in Canada. Dr Shaw holds a PhD from Princeton University and has published articles on African political economy in a variety of journals, most recently in *Alternatives, International Journal, Journal of Modern African Studies, Millennium* and *Third World Quarterly*.

Roger Southall is a visiting professor in the Institute for International Development at the University of Ottawa, having taught previously at the National University in Lesotho. With a doctorate from the University Birmingham, Dr Southall has authored *Parties and Politics in Bunyoro, Federalism and Higher Education in East Africa*, and *South Africa's Transkei: the Political Economy of an 'Independent' Bantustan*, along with essays in *African Development, African Affairs, Africa Contemporary Record, Canadian Journal of African Studies, Journal of Modern African Studies, Journal of Southern African Studies, Labour, Capital and Society* and *Race Relations News.*

E. Diane White is an economist at the World Bank, focusing on agricultural development in Africa where she has lived and travelled extensively. Ms White holds a master's degree in International Affairs from SAIS in Washington, DC. She previously worked in the commercial banking sector, with the US Treasury and State Departments, and as a research assistant at the Overseas Development Council where she focused on the basic needs issue.

I. William Zartman is Professor of Political Science and Director of the African Studies Programme at SAIS in Washington. A leading student of African, especially North and West African, affairs, Dr Zartman is author of *The Politics of Trade Negotiations between Africa and the EEC, International Relations in the New Africa*, and *Ripe for Resolution: Conflict and Intervention in Africa*, and editor of *Man, State and Society in the Contemporary Maghrib, The Negotiation Process: Theories and Applications, Elites in the Middle East*, and *The Political Economy of Nigeria.*

Algiers
Tunis
TUNISIA
Casablanca
MOROCCO
Tripoli
ALGERIA
LIBYA
Cairo
EGYPT
MAURITANIA
MALI
NIGER
CHAD
Nouakchott
Khartoum
SUDAN
Dakar
SENEGAL
GAMBIA
Banjul
Bamako
UPPER VOLTA
Niamey
N'djamena
DJIBOUTI
Ouagadougou
GUINEA BISSAU
Bissau
GUINEA
BENIN
NIGERIA
Addis Ababa
ETHIOPIA
Conakry
IVORY COAST
GHANA
TOGO
Freetown
SIERRA LEONE
Monrovia
LIBERIA
Abidjan
Accra
Lome
Cotonou
Lagos
CAMEROON
CENTRAL AFRICAN REPUBLIC
Bangui
SOMALI REPUBLIC
Yaounde
Bata
Libreville
EQUATORIAL GUINEA
GABON
CONGO
UGANDA
Kampala
KENYA
Mogadishu
Nairobi
ZAIRE
Kigali
RWANDA
Bujumbura
BURUNDI
Brazzaville
CABINDA
Kinshasa
Zanzibar
Dar-es-Salaam
TANZANIA
Luanda
Lilongwe
ANGOLA
MALAWI
Lusaka
ZAMBIA
MOZAMBIQUE
Harare
NAMIBIA
ZIMBABWE
Tananarive
MALAGASY REP.
Windhoek
BOTSWANA
Gaberones
Pretoria
Mbabane
Maputo
SWAZILAND
Maseru
LESOTHO
SOUTH AFRICA
Cape Town

Preface

The initial thinking about the planning for a workshop on 'Alternative Future for Africa', from which the present collection is one result, occurred when we were colleagues for the academic year 1979–80 in the Department of International Relations at the University of Ife in Nigeria. Given (i) the developmental crisis confronting the continent of Africa, (ii) the imperative of informed projections and enlightened policy prescriptions for both African and non-African actors and (iii) the creation of an international joint seminar fund in the office of International Relations of the Social Sciences and Humanities Research Council of Canada (SSHRCC) we decided to apply for a grant to facilitate our collaboration and concern.

The result was a workshop on the campus of Dalhousie University in Nova Scotia, Canada, in May 1981. All the chapters included here were presented either then or at a couple of one-day follow-up sessions later that year. They have all been revised by authors in the light of the discussions at Dalhousie and continuing debates. As co-organisers and co-editors we are deeply appreciative of collegial and institutional support, particularly from the Centres for African Studies and Foreign Policy Studies at Dalhousie and the Department of International Relations at Ife. Clearly the timely and generous award from SSHRCC was crucial for this venture. Doris Boyle and Elaine Otto, as always, contributed essential skills to the editorial process.

This volume is intended to be one contribution to the continuing debate on Africa's future. Given the continent's inheritance of dependence and underdevelopment, projections based on established trends are hardly auspicious. The latest International Monetary Fund world report summarises the current condition of the non-oil developing countries of the continent, a decline exacerbated by the contemporary crisis in the global capitalist system:

> real per capita income has stagnated during the whole period, 1978–81. In a number of sub-Saharan African countries, indeed, per capita output declined . . . the adverse consequences of the recession in the

> industrial countries were much more severe than had generally been foreseen. The weak demand in industrial countries for primary commodities induced shortfalls in African export volumes that were largely unexpected, but have turned out to be substantial.[1]

The prospects for most of Africa's countries and peoples based on short- as well as long-term trends are depressing. However, as several contributors suggest, the future is not just the extension of such circumstances or cycles. Rather, the crisis may produce its own dialectic, its own antithesis. Notwithstanding existential difficulties and ideological differences, optimism is not to be denied altogether.

Africa's future may be transformed because of, and not despite, such current contradictions. Appropriately, one of Africa's leading historians has pointed to the prospect of limited change rather than lineal continuity; as Ade Ajayi has suggested:

> the very frustrations of the past point to the need for fresh approaches . . . The vision of a new society in Africa will need to be developed *in* Africa, born out of the African historical experience and the sense of continuity of African history. The African is not yet master of his own fate, but neither is he completely at the mercy of fate.[2]

The tone of this book is neither fatalistic nor optimistic. Rather, it points to some possible promising scenarios despite the prevalence of pessimism: Africa *has* a future.

TIMOTHY M. SHAW and OLAJIDE ALUKO

Halifax and Ife

NOTES

1. IMF, *World Economic Outlook: A Survey by the Staff of the IMF*, Occasional Paper No. 9 (Washington: IMF, 1982).
2. J. F. Ade Ajayi, 'Expectations of Independence', *Daedelus*, 3(2), Spring 1982, 8.

Part I

Projections, Prospects and Possibilities

1 Introduction: are the 1980s characterised by crisis and/or conjuncture?

TIMOTHY M. SHAW

'It is now *fashionable* to be a pessimist – "*apres nous le deluge*" might almost pass as a new (inter)national motto for the '80s' – Michael Korda, 'The Fashionable New Pessimism', *Newsweek*, 14 June 1982, 4.

'The implementation of the strategies proposed in either of these (World Bank and OAU) documents will have a profound effect on the African continent. Hence it is the duty of concerned African scholars not only to be familiar with these two documents, but also to undertake serious detailed analyses in order to make a constructive contribution to the strategy which, in his/her opinion, will bring about social and economic development beneficial to the majority of African people. In this debate for the future development of the continent, the African scholar must be scientifically involved and committed. He cannot remain a so-called "neutral" observer.' – Abdalla S. Bujra 'Editorial note: special double issue on the Berg Report and the Lagos Plan of Action', Africa Development 7 (1/2), January/June 1982, v–vi.

'The recommendations of the World Bank's report (on Sub-Saharan Africa) (which began preparation in 1979) have to a significant extent been overtaken by the events of the Western recession. Consequently, the World Bank is left proposing a very risky strategy, without being able to offer increased aid to smooth the transition or as a safeguard if the strategy fails.' – 'Briefing paper: Africa's economic Crisis', *Overseas Development Institute* (London, September 1982) 6.

If the decade of the 1960s was characterised by optimism and that of the 1970s by uncertainty, the 1980s are dominated by widespread and unrelieved pessimism. This shift of mood has been shared by Africa as it moves from its first two decades of independence into the last part of the present century. The symbolic sense of hopelessness has been expressed by Dr Adebayo Adedeji, Executive-Secretary of the Economic Commission for Africa: 'we are facing a crisis of exceptional proportions and persistence'.[1]

If the current crisis is serious for the advanced industrialised states, resulting in unprecedented levels of unemployment, interest rates and production declines, it is catastrophic for the impoverished African states, particularly the least developed ones. The relentlessness of the recession in Africa has resulted in even the 'success stories' of the 1970s suffering major setbacks – commodity producers like Botswana, the Ivory Coast, Kenya and Malawi, and oil producers like Algeria, Libya and Nigeria have all endured dramatic decreases in growth rates since the beginning of the new decade. The average African has been fortunate if his/her real income has remained the same rather than declined under pressure of inflation, unemployment, population, etc. The general and debilitating features of the crisis, at the national as well as personal level, have been succinctly stated in a recent ODI publication:

> Firstly, governments are finding it increasingly difficult to finance recurrent expenditure, investment programmes, and the necessary maintenance of infrastructure. Secondly, for most countries there is an increasing shortage of consumer goods, capital equipment and essential spare parts. Thirdly, price inflation has been significant throughout the decade . . .
>
> In many countries there is an increasing incidence of corruption, violent crime and a loss of confidence in government generally. Poor economic performance has contributed to these wider problems, and in turn these difficulties have further weakened the region's economies.[2]

The apparently exponential character of the crisis in Africa has generated a series of responses, both short- and long-term, projective and prescriptive which are the focus of this collection.

The exacerbation of the African condition has produced, then, a set of projections and prescriptions: analytic and strategic reactions. So while the new decade has been characterised by economic and psychological depression it has resulted in predictive and political discourse. Aside from general futures studies and global diplomatic debates, the major African proposals are contained in the ECA *Lagos Plan of Action* and the IBRD *Accelerated Development in Sub-Saharan Africa*, both prepared and released at the turn of the decade. Reflective of diverse origins and genres these documents offer divergent recommendations which remain the focus of an ongoing debate about their intentions and implications.[3] The present volume, and the seminars from which it is one result, is offered as another contribution to this debate, one which reveals the resilience and persistence of African determination and innovation. But before overviewing the current state of the debate, and of the political economies with which it is concerned, I turn first to the background to the crisis. After presenting the origins and directions of the situation, I conclude by examining the issue of whether the present constitutes a crisis and/or a conjuncture.

MARGINALISATION AND DIFFERENTIATION

Notwithstanding the pre-colonial civilisations of Benin, Egypt, Sokoto and Zimbabwe, the eighteenth and nineteenth centuries witnessed the intensification and acceleration of the underdevelopment of Africa. The continent's place at the periphery of the world system was confirmed by the extension of formal colonialism. This subordinate position in the global division of labour was not changed by either the post-war economic recovery of capitalism or the post-war political revival of nationalism. Although some African economies grew in the 1950s and 1960s their inheritance at 'independence' was still fragile. This essential vulnerability was revealed when the Bretton Woods economic order began to decay in the early 1970s under the impact of America's decline and OPEC's ascent. Although a minority of African economies was able to take advantage of the new situation – for example, Ivory Coast and Kenya, Libya and Nigeria in the commodity and oil-producing sectors, respectively – for the majority the past decade represents the beginning of a nightmare of high import costs, including the high price of money, and low export values, implying foreign exchange shortages. As the World Bank's *Agenda* indicates:

> for most African countries, and for a majority of the African population, the record is grim and it is no exaggeration to talk of crisis. Slow overall economic growth, sluggish agricultural performance coupled with rapid rates of population increase, and balance-of-payments and fiscal crises – these are dramatic indicators of economic trouble.[4]

Minimal and uneven economic growth constitutes the intervening variable – between external dependence and internal underdevelopment – which causes and explains Africa's ineluctible trend towards marginalisation and differentiation. Overall, Africa's position in the world system today is more peripheral than at any time since World War Two: its contribution to global exchange, production and profit is of decreasing importance. Only as a source of instability and as a locus of debt – two factors which reinforce each other in the special case of Zaire – does it retain some salience. As an exporter of raw materials, other than certain 'strategic' mineral or energy supplies, and as an importer of manufactures, other than in one or two newly industrialising countries (NICs) such as Algeria, Nigeria and South Africa, its status is marginal. And given global trends this peripheral position is likely to continue until either the global depression lifts or 'another development' strategy is adopted.

Despite the continent's overall marginalisation, however, a few countries and classes have experienced above-average growth either because of their relatively privileged position in global production or because of their relatively superior capacity for exploitation. A minority of NICs and of bourgeois fractions have been able to take advantage of the global and continental condition for their own purposes whereas the majority of states and fractions, even relatively privileged ones, have suffered relative loss of income. This differentiation, leading to new hierarchies of states and peoples, is not only a problem in terms of present politics, it also constitutes a potential difficulty as such interests are less critical of current crises than most. As I will suggest later under the heading 'Projections and prescriptions', the relatively advantaged countries and classes are less prepared to espouse the continent's collective response as reflected in the *Lagos Plan of Action*. However, before examining this debate, I turn to some basic features of the African crisis.

RETRENCHMENT AND RE-EVALUATION

The fundamental cause of the current condition is dependence on the world system. This dependence was exacerbated following independence by the adoption of an essentially outward-looking development strategy by most of the continent. And the logic of 'trickle-down', which was always circumscribed in practice, came to an abrupt end with the demise of the post-war Bretton Woods era of expansion. Contraction eliminated any residual rationale for an exogenous orientation, even among the most successful of the 'open', commodity-based economies. As the World

Bank *Agenda* admits, if the first decade or so of independence was a relative 'golden age' not everyone participated:

> Between 1960 and 1979, per capita income in 19 countries grew by less than 1 per cent per year, while during the last decade, 15 countries recorded a *negative* rate of growth of income per capita. And by the end of the 1970s, economic crises were battering even high-growth countries like Kenya, Malawi, and Ivory Coast – where per capita GNP growth had averaged an annual 2.7 per cent between 1960 and 1979 – compelling them to design programs, supported by the Bank, to restructure their economies. Output per person rose more slowly in Sub-Saharan Africa than in any other part of the world, particularly in the 1970s, and it rose more slowly in the 1970s than in the 1960s.[5]

This inauspicious inheritance was the cause of unpromising projections for the continent as a whole, projections which began to worry decision-makers as the 1970s closed. Unattractive scenarios based on established trends produced a set of retrenchments – austerity, not growth, became the watchword – and led to the urgent reconsideration of past policies and failures. The seriousness of the situation resulted in widespread foreign exchange crises: the unavailability of spare parts, the smuggling of scarce goods, black markets in currency and so further declines in production and productivity. Output declined further so shortages and prices increased: import substitution reverted to straight importation and the policy of outward-lookingness was replaced by the reality of inward-lookingness. Disengagement or 'delinking' became popular by default.

Given these dramatic changes in the second half of the 1970s, a re-evaluation of developmental assumptions and directions was clearly an imperative. Among the first efforts at reconsideration were a UNITAR/CODESRIA conference on 'Africa and the Future' (Dakar, 1977), the Monrovia OAU Symposium on 'Future Development Prospects in Africa' (Liberia, 1978)[6] and an OAU seminar on 'Alternative Patterns of Development and Life Styles for the African Region' (Addis Ababa, 1978). These essentially non-official consultations provided a constituency and framework for the major landmark in the continent's intellectual or ideological turn-around: the April 1980 economic summit in Lagos which produced the *Lagos Plan of Action*. By contrast to this indigenous re-evaluation, the African Governors of the World Bank requested in the autumn of 1979 a 'special paper' on the crisis confronting Sub-Saharan

Africa. Drafted by an American 'development economist' in the old school, Elliot Berg, *Agenda* was presented to the continent in October 1981. By contrast, the *Lagos Plan* was extensively debated and revised in Africa itself (see opening quotation by Abdalla Bujra) being accepted by the OAU Heads of State in August 1980. In subsequent debates comparing and evaluating the two prescriptions, the indigenous origins of the *Lagos Plan* are an important consideration. As Bujra notes:

> The Lagos Plan of Action was thus a culmination of a long intensive process of discussions and preparations by African scholars, experts and government officials, principally through the umbrella of the OAU and ECA. The Plan contains the fundamental ideas and sentiments concerning the future economic development of Africa, as perceived by the Africans.[7]

So if the reality of the new decade was negative – as Adedeji warned 'the 1980s promise to be a decade of extraordinary toughness compared with the 1970s and 1960s'[8] – one result (i.e. alternative prescriptions) was positive. Given the apparent inappropriateness of past, let alone future, World Bank policies, Africa came to formulate and advocate its own development strategy: the *Lagos Plan* and declaration for a continental Common Market by the year 2000. This embodied two novel concepts in contrast to the outward-orientation of *Agenda*:

> the Lagos Plan of Action rests on the principles of self-reliance (i.e. reliance on indigenous raw materials and other factor inputs) and self-sustainment (i.e. dependence on internal rather than external needs or demand stimuli).[9]

By contrast, the *Agenda* was drafted by and oriented towards foreign interests. As Samir Amin asserts in his advocacy of the *Plan* and rejection of *Agenda*, the latter

> is an outward-oriented and not a self-reliant strategy, a policy of adapting to the requirements of transnationalisation, a strategy which means renouncing any intention of constructing a diversified national and regional economy which, through its own internal dynamics and autonomy, would be capable of acting as a partner in an interdependent world system rather than being a mere excrescence of the transnationals.[10]

The debate over *Plan* and *Agenda* is not merely about two documents and directions, important and divergent though these may be; it is also a disagreement about world views and definitions of development, a timely, albeit belated attempt by Africa to strive for epistemological and psychological, as well as economic and political independence.

PROJECTIONS AND PRESCRIPTIONS

The development of a distinctive African reaction to the continental crisis has been assisted by (i) the detractions of the World Bank's *Agenda*, (ii) the challenges of the continuing recession and (iii) the realisation that no satisfactory NIEO was about to be negotiated. First, and typical of the African rejection of the World Bank's diversionary (Agenda) was a report on 'Implementation of the Lagos Plan of Action' for the ECA Conference in Tripoli in 1982 which, *inter alia*, supported the *Lagos Plan* as a necessary 'alternative to past approaches which have led the continent to the unenviable position in which it finds itself today' and expressed concern 'that the agriculture-based and export-oriented strategy which the Bank recommends detracts a lot from the central philosophy of the Lagos Plan of Action.'[11]

Second, reflective of the ECA's determination in the face of IBRD subversion and the recession's continuance, Adedeji has advocated a 'hard' long-term option based on 'the realisation that the world economy is faced with a serious disequilibrium which calls for fundamental structural changes'. This option calls for more change over time than suggested by the Bank so that Africa increases its development and reduces its vulnerability:

> Firstly, we must accept the inevitability, for some time, of delinking our economies from that of the international economy if we are to be able to undertake the kind of fundamental restructuring which would enable us to cope with the evolving crisis as well as lay down a firm foundation for national and collective self-reliance as envisaged in the Lagos Plan of Action. Secondly, we must declare a war for economic survival in each member state and adopt a siege approach to development . . . Thirdly, we must intensify our efforts to strengthen intra-African co-operation.[12]

Third, Lagos represents a re-evaluation of past development foibles and failures based on the reluctant recognition that no NIEO was about to be negotiated in any global dialogue. Moreover, established developmental assumptions were under challenge in the North as well as the South:

> the call for a NIEO . . . was an unequivocal endorsement of the patterns of development and life-styles of the developed market economies. And this was at a time when citizens of these countries were increasingly questioning the rationality and continued sustainability of such patterns of development and life-styles. Thus the call for a NIEO still fails to recognise the basic issues mirrored in the development and economic growth of African countries.[13]

This sense of unreality and irrelevance has increased as the World Bank continues to espouse an outward-looking orientation for Africa despite (i) the apparent failure of such an approach in most states to date, and (ii) the great unlikelihood of such a direction in a period of sustained recession. In response, a sense of confidence within the ECA nexus has grown in proportion to the Bank's demise: the Commission has continued to define, refine, and develop its perspective and several discussions in Africa and elsewhere have offered further advice and nuance.[14]

Support for the *Lagos Plan* may be augmented even further by a sense of fatalism: the world system is so hostile and anarchistic that self-reliance may be something of an inevitability. Most African countries are increasingly peripheral and marginal: they cannot expect to be integrated into the global economy let alone realise development thereby. A few countries and classes in the semi-periphery may still possess some choice, although even oil-exporters are vulnerable until the cloud of recession begins to lift. For the majority, however, the 'global shocks' of the early 1970s may have constituted a healthy form of therapy or medicine: a trauma to pry them out of a sense of uncertainty. So although Africa's position in the global political economy is increasingly peripheral, its collective response to interrelated crisis and demise is to turn both to good advantage: a recession is a good time to disengage and a bad time to reintegrate, other than on very disadvantageous terms. In retrospect, then, the timing of the *Lagos Plan of Action* was excellent; that of the *Agenda* rather unfortunate, given the demise of the external order with which it advocated incorporation.

POLICY DECLARATIONS AND DEBATES

So the scope and sophistication of responses to Africa's increasing problems and unpromising prospects have increased significantly in the 1980s, with the primary debate being between the *Lagos Plan* and World Bank *Agenda*, that is between more inward-looking and more outward-looking orientations, respectively. The dialectical character of the two declarations was recognised by a meeting of the directors of African social science research institutes:

> The correct orientation and therefore significance of the Lagos Plan of Action is clearly highlighted when it is contrasted with the World Bank Report. The orientation of the two 'Plans' are opposite and contradictory, the Lagos Plan of Action advocating a form of development which would benefit the African people whereas the World Bank Report clearly and unambiguously represents the interest of foreign capital. The World Bank Report specifically expresses a very negative and demeaning attitude on the ability of African leadership and African institutions. The two documents must therefore be seen as representing sharply opposing points of view concerning African development.[15]

Despite the continued recession, the World Bank still advocates agricultural and export-led growth whereas the *Lagos Plan* has an immediate appeal for countries already experiencing 'withdrawal' from the world system. As the opening ODI citation indicates, the Bank's report is increasingly irrelevant whereas the *Lagos Plan*'s advocacy of self-reliance serves to legitimise and advance the trend towards delinking.

The OAU *Action* plan is also preferable because it relates directly to the question of the future, the focus of this volume. The ECA has recommended recently that the continent establish its own Institute of Futures Studies, something which I advocated in an introduction to an earlier collection on the subject.[16] Now that the continent has its own collective development strategy as well as foreign policy it can usefully design and consider alternative tactics and scenarios for implementation. Even if economic difficulties continue, this testing time has at least advanced Africa's diplomatic and developmental independence: the recession is a time for delinking rather than recoupling, with all sorts of potential, especially in political economy and psychology. To this extent, maybe Africa's timely adoption of self-reliance may prove the pessimistic projections of both the World Bank and Michael Korda (see opening citation) wrong: pessimism may yet come to be misplaced and displaced.

NOTES

1. 'The deepening international economic crisis and its implications for Africa. Statement by Professor Adebayo Adedeji at the opening of

the 17th session of the Commission and 8th meeting of the Conference of Ministers, Tripoli, April 1982.' (Addis Ababa: ECA, 1982) 4. See also J. F. Ade Ajayi 'Expectations of Independence' *Daedulus* 3(2), Spring 1982, 1–9. In his historical overview of Africa's expectations and frustrations, Ajayi suggests that 'the optimism of development plans of the 1960s has given way to increasing frustration in the 1970s and disillusionment in the 1980s' (p. 6).

2. 'Briefing paper: Africa's Economic Crisis' *Overseas Development Institute* (London, September 1982) 3 and 1.
3. See, for instance 'Special Double Issue on the Berg Report and the Lagos Plan of Action' *Africa Development* 7 (1/2), January/June 1982 and Caroline Allison and Reginald Green (eds) 'Accelerated Development in Sub-Saharan Africa: What Agendas for Action?' *IDS Bulletin* 14 (1), January 1983. See also Timothy M. Shaw 'Beyond any NIEO: ECA and IBRD Plans for African Development' in Ralph I. Onwuka and Olajide Aluko (eds) *The Future of Africa and the New International Economic Order.*
4. World Bank *Accelerated Development in Sub-Saharan Africa: An Agenda for Action* (Washington: IBRD, 1981) 2.
5. *Ibid*, 2–3.
6. For a summary of this meeting see Appendix C in Timothy M. Shaw (ed.) *Alternative Futures for Africa* (Boulder: Westview, 1982) 329–340.
7. Abdalla Bujra 'Editorial Note' (to 'Special Double Issue on the Berg Report and the Lagos Plan of Action') 1.
8. *Biennial Report of the Executive-Secretary of the Economic Commission for ECA, 1979–1980.* (Addis Ababa, 1980) E/CN. 14/798, 6.
9. ECA 'The Public Sector and the Implementation of the Lagos Plan of Action' (Addis Ababa, April 1981) E/CN. 14/807 and E/CN. 14/TPCW. 11/24, 1.
10. Samir Amin 'A Critique of the World Bank Report Entitled "Accelerated Development in Sub-Saharan Africa"' *Africa Development* 7 (1/2) January/June 1982, 24. See also Timothy M. Shaw 'OAU: the forgotten economic debate' *West Africa* 3375, 12 April 1982, 983–4.
11. ECA 'Implementation of the Lagos Plan of Action' (Addis Ababa, April 1982) E/ECA/PSD.2/12/Rev. 1, 1.
12. 'The Deepening International Economic Crisis and its Implications for Africa' 12–13.
13. ECA 'Implementation of the Lagos Plan of Action: Some Proposals and Recommendations for the Guidance of Member States' (Addis Ababa, April 1981) E/CN. 14/801, 2.
14. See, for instance, the papers presented at a Conference on 'Africa: Which Way Out of the Recession?' (Uppsala: Scandinavian Institute of African Studies, September 1982). See also continuing debates in international forums: 'At Toronto Meeting: Africa hopes for more, Despite US Foot-dragging' *African Economic Digest* 3(36) 10–16 September 1982, 2–3.

15. 'Report of the CODESRIA/ECA Conference of Directors of Social Science Research Institutes and Policy-makers on the Third UN Development Decade, the Monrovia strategy and the Lagos Plan of Action, Addis Ababa, March 1982', *Africa Development* 7 (1/2) January/June 1982, 199.
16. See 'Introduction: The Political Economy of Africa's Futures' in Shaw (ed.) *Alternative Futures for Africa* 1–16.

2 The State in Africa: Some Thoughts on the Future drawn from the Past

RICHARD A. HIGGOTT

INTRODUCTION

Like the poor in history, the state in political science is always with us. This is so even when, again like the poor in history, our attitude to the state is one of neglect. The attitude of the political science community towards the state has tended to be an excellent indicator of the prevailing political strategies, options and expectations that exist at a particular point in time. This is so in the study of political science generally and in the study of politics in post-colonial Africa specifically.[1] It is the intention of this chapter, therefore, accepting the exhortations of David Ricci that the political scientist learns the value of historiography,[2] to review our changing perceptions of the role and functioning of the state in the first couple of decades of our study of post-colonial Africa. The value of historiographical analysis for a book concerned with the future of Africa is largely self-evident, yet, at the risk of over-simplification, such value can be briefly spelled out.

The social sciences, it goes without saying, are not exact sciences. Predictions frequently turn out to be inaccurate and/or misleading. Attempts to remedy such shortcomings very often lead in the short term to sharp deviations or 'about turns' in the predominant modes of analysis existing at a given point in time. Such 'about turns', in their own turn, are often similarly flawed. In the longer run, however, this oscillation can settle down into some form of more meaningful analysis out of which understanding or the 'accumulation of knowledge' is pushed a stage further forward.[3] An analysis of the variety of perceptions of the role of the post-colonial state in Africa that have emerged over the last couple of decades presents just such a pattern of intellectual development. Our perceptions of the role of the state have oscillated in quite violent fashion as various 'fads' – some might call them paradigms – have risen and fallen with alarmingly short life-spans. The obvious case in point is the much-discussed rise and demise of modernisation theory over the first two decades of the post-colonial era,[4] and the much less discussed to-date but now similarly evident rise and demise of dependency theory over the last decade.[5] The interaction of these two broad competing perspectives over this period has seen the emergence of a much more sophisticated and realistic analysis of development *and* underdevelopment than was present in the early post-colonial period. Whether our superior descriptive capabilities will yet lead to improved prescriptive capabilities is somewhat more problematic.[6]

While such general concerns are not of primary import for this chapter, they need to be appreciated if we are to extract from recent general theory the specifics of that general theory's analysis of the state in the Third World and Africa specifically. An analysis of the role of the state suggests a similar pattern of violent oscillation, but one which appears to be slowing down somewhat of late and giving rise to the emergence of a more measured and constrained view of the role and functioning of the state in Africa. Optimistically we might be able to suggest that we are entering a phase of intellectual maturity, in contrast to the naivete of the preceding two decades, from which we may be able to offer some tentative suggestions as to how we feel the state in Africa may develop over the near- to mid-term future.

MODERNISATION THEORY, DEPENDENCY THEORY AND THE STATE

Model I: The Modernisation Perspective

Despite the optimism of the late 1950s and early 1960s political scientists were in fact aware of the fragile nature of the new African state. It was for this reason that analysis emphasised the issues of nation-building and national integration.[7] This early phase was, however, also characterised by the belief that these were essentially manageable problems, imbued as we then were with that optimistic first flush of the decolonisation era.[8] During this period the assumptions of political scientists about the role of the state, writing in the heyday of the behavioural revolution, were essentially sociological.[9]

The assumptions were sociological in several ways. First, the underlying *raison d'être* of the state in Africa was sociologically and empirically justified. Steeped in the history of the functional evolution of the European state we tended to ignore the essentially colonial and force-related origins of the modern African state and the manner in which the boundaries of these states were sanctified in juridical terms by their European masters.[10] Second, we assumed that the African state, inheritor of Western political institutions, would operate in the largely pluralist manner of the advanced industrial state on which its inherited or imposed institutions had been modelled. The state's role, in the fashion of the prevailing liberal democratic ideology of the period, would be that of neutral arbiter of the political game and the manager of some mildly reformist welfare state system of economic organisation.[11] The analytical outcome of such a set of assumptions was a focus on a variety of 'inputs' into the political system, such as interest articulation, interest aggregation and political socialisation functions rather than the 'outputs' from the political process.[12] While lip-service may have been paid to analysing the 'capabilities' of the political system the analysis of institutions and their impact on the polity was decidedly unfashionable in a period that was dominated by socio-psychological forms of analysis.[13]

Illusions were, of course, soon rudely shattered. The breakdown of the party system, the drift to one and no party states, the rapidly increasing incidence of military intervention and the failure of economic 'take-off' to occur saw academic aspirations dashed and the underpinnings of much modern social science swept aside. Down but not vanquished, the social scientist went searching for alternative explanations.

Model II: The Dependency Perspective

The search went two ways. One way saw the jettisoning of early notions of the utility of (and impossibility of successful implantation of) the institutions of the modern democratic state in Africa. This way instead posited the notion of the need for a strong state able to preserve 'order', seen in the normative sense of the absence of open conflict.[14] Such influences were to become very strong in the contemporary policy-making process in the African context and need to be reconsidered in some detail in our later discussion of future trends. More immediately, however, the most popular route followed in the wake of the inadequacies of our earlier conceptualisations was a route which saw students of Africa swallow – hook, line and sinker in some cases – that variety of early dependency theory generated in Latin America and served up in suitably popular (and populist) fashion for export by André Gunder Frank.

Explanations of the development of African underdevelopment began to abound in the early part of the second UN development decade in a manner similar to analyses of nation-building in Africa which had abounded at the beginning of the first.[15] The supposedly abiding nature of the development of underdevelopment of African states, or Third World states in general, has been criticised in sufficient depth elsewhere for me to pass over it.[16] Of greater importance is the very specific view of the state that emerged from within dependency theory and in particular its tendency to minimise the very real tensions that exist between efforts of African states to achieve domestic advance through international interaction on the one hand, and efforts to achieve some greater degree of national autonomy on the other. The popular, and the populist, nature of dependency theory in the first half of the 1970s tended to blind us to any view which saw these two aims as anything other than mutually exclusive. Rejecting the socio-psychological approaches of the modernisation theorist and working from a simple economic determinism, radical structuralism (to give dependency theory one of its other names) perceived African countries as largely incapable of producing an indigenous dominant class capable of serving other than foreign interests. The dominant class was perceived as an intermediary agent of foreign domination controlling the process of accumulation on behalf of these external interests and through its control of the state apparatus.

The corollary of this view of the dominant class was a conception of the state in the post-colonial societies of Africa as 'overdeveloped'. This view found expression in the African context, in, for example, John Saul's and Issa Shivji's work on Tanzania and in Colin Leys' early work on Kenya.[17] The overdeveloped post-colonial state was, in essence, one which exhibited a certain autonomy from the indigenous class structure *per se*, at the same time as it exhibited control over the production process. In this context the state was seen as a mediator between local and international capital and as a security agent for international capital.

Also central to the notion of the 'overdeveloped' post-colonial state was the large military, administrative and bureaucratic apparatus inherited from colonialism and responsible for expropriating and utilising a substantial proportion of the state's economic surplus.[18] The consequence of such activity, as Shivji for example would argue, was that the personnel of the state apparatus who took on those functions developed a specific class interest of their own. This group, essentially a class in the making, Shivji described as the 'bureaucratic bourgeoisie'. He saw them as a class

of well-paid administrators, military officers and/or party officials appropriating or controlling production with one outcome, at least, being the personal acquisition of private capital. As a class, the bureaucratic bourgeoisie was perceived as having a vested interest in preserving its client role with international capital.

If the over-optimistic view of the modernisation theory that dominated our thinking until the second half of the 1960s was naive, then the similarly pessimistic view of the dependency school that took over and held sway in many quarters until the mid-1970s must be counted as equally naive. Both views exhibit a strikingly similar flaw – namely a universality and teleology which reduced to the level of banality the developmental processes that were taking place, or not as the case may be, in Africa.

The period since the mid-1970s has, however, seen us begin to reject narrow, essentially reductionist, forms of analysis concerning the nature of class behaviour and the role of the state in Africa in favour of those forms of analysis which stress a complexity and diversity of options that is a more accurate reflection of reality. The early political scientist of political development looked primarily at the socio-psychological aspects of political behavior in the Third World at the expense of the underlying structural and economic influences that inevitably affect any policy-making process. The dependency theorist in a similarly perverse manner ignored these socio-psychological processes in favour of an approach which saw the economic structure as primary and the potential role of the individual actor as irrelevant. In general terms, both approaches treated the state in extremely cavalier fashion. The former theorists saw the 'political' as all and the economic as nothing, while the latter provided little prospect whatsoever for the autonomy of the 'political' from the 'economic'.

Model III: Marxist Refinements

The preceding, and necessarily brief, discussion of the perceptions of the role of the state that emanated from modernisation theory and dependency theory represents a rather crude caricature. During the second half of the 1970s, however, there developed a corrective to this view that needs to be taken into account in any efforts to explore the possible avenues of development in Africa in the 1980s. Particularly influential has been the auto-critique by Colin Leys of his early work on Kenya.[19] Rejecting the '*dependencia*' view of class and state in Africa Leys, amongst other Marxists, somewhat ironically joined with those more orthodox critics of dependency theory who have tried to establish an empirical critique of the development of under-development.[20] The essence of the argument was summed up as early as 1973 by the late Bill Warren:

> If the extension of capitalism into non-capitalist areas of the world created an international system of inequality and exploitation called imperialism, it simultaneously created the conditions for the destruction of this system by the spread of capitalist social relations and productive forces throughout the non-capitalist world.[21]

If we accept the validity of Warren's argument – that imperialism does not inevitably prevent the spread of indigenous capitalist development in peripheral formations, in contrast to dependency theory – then we need also to reject a subsequent tenet of dependency theory, namely, that increased political independence, in the nominal sense of decolonisation, is irrelevant as a means of facilitating capitalist development. The logical extension to an acceptance of this view is the rejection of a third tenet of dependency theory, namely, the assertion that the dominant class in Africa will, almost by default, be 'comprador' and in a patron–client relationship with international capital. As Richard Sklar has pointed out, such views of class in Africa, especially notions of the burgeoning of a bureaucratic bourgeoisie as a functional or structural class are:

> too narrowly conceived to comprehend the dominant class of a developing country that has a significant entrepreneurial sector in addition to a large and growing number of persons in professional occupations. Theoretically, a functional élite, such as the civil and military bureaucratic élite, by itself could form an élite-class (sic). But this limiting case does not exist anywhere to my knowledge. In all societies, the functionary element is part of a social class, not its sole constituent.[22]

No researcher, party to this debate conducted largely in the African context, was suggesting – to look at dependency theory's general strengths – that the dominant forces at work in Africa, or in the Third World generally, were other than expatriate. What they were not prepared to accept, however, was the restrictive nature of a class analysis based on the notion of the growth of a structurally-determined bourgeoisie, be it 'bureaucratic' or whatever. Such a position, as Leys indicated, could only deflect us from asking more important questions about a more numerous and more general dominant class and its relations to the post-colonial state; particular questions about the extent to which the dominant class undermined, as opposed to supported, external interests. As Leys, in his autocritique of *Underdevelopment in Kenya* argued:

> Instead of seeing the strength of the historical tendency lying behind the emergence of the African bourgeoisie I tended to see only the relatively small size and technical weakness of African capital in face of international capital, and to envisage the state as little more than a register of this general imbalance; rather than seeing the barriers of capital scale and technology as the register of the leading edge of indigenous capital in its assault on those barriers.[23]

What Leys, and others investigating Kenya were effectively doing, was reversing the view of the role of the state that had developed in the first half of the 1970s. The dominant class in Africa or fractions thereof, it was being argued, could in fact use state power for its own purposes and not just simply for the benefit of international capital. In retrospect such an interpretation would appear self-evident, yet to accept such an assumption, is not, *ipso facto*, to accept that the way is open for development in Africa centred on the resurgent economic nationalism of a growing bourgeoisie. Rather, as Anne Phillips has noted:

> The discovery that there *is* a national bourgeoisie in Africa, that it *is* capable of capital accumulation, that it is *not* necessarily restricted to 'comprador' activities such as commerce or construction, could after all mean no more than that Africa will be able to achieve the same form of underdevelopment as Latin America.[24]

Phillips might have gone on to add that such a process might also be restricted to quite specific areas of Africa. We need to be careful, in our extrapolations from work on Kenya, not to throw out the baby with the bathwater. Processes of capital accumulation (and the prospects for capital accumulation) based on factor endowments, the degree of colonial penetration and so on, are markedly different in states such as Kenya, Ivory Coast and Zambia, for example, from what they are in some other states; for example, many of the land-locked states of former francophone Africa. Consequently, we would do well to bear in mind at all times the variety of stages of development possible in Africa resulting from the variety of combinations of factor endowments and the degrees of colonial penetration.

Leys himself points to some of the advantages settler-colonialism bestowed on Kenya and its subsequent position in the East African context which, relatively speaking in African terms, paved the way for significant 'early industrialisation initiatives not to be found in other areas of the continent.'[25] The position of settler capital in Kenya also prevented the degree of penetration of international capital, in relative but not absolute terms, experienced in other states. The subsequent substitution, in the early years after independence, of the personnel of a growing national dominant class at the expense of settlers would appear to have obvious future parallels for a state such as Zimbabwe, given Zimbabwe's favourable endowments, very high levels of international penetration and recent history of innovation in the face of externally-created obstacles.

Very few other African states would, however, appear to exhibit a similar set of what Leys, albeit in somewhat laboured Marxian terminology, calls 'a "systematical combination of moments" conducive to the transition to the capitalist mode of production'.[26] However, there are clearly a substantial number of states, that, in contrast to say Kenya, Zimbabwe, or to a lesser extent Ivory Coast,[27] possess extremely small entrepreneurial and professional sectors, exhibiting low or even negative processes of growth and where, as a consequence, the personnel of the state bourgeoisie constitutes not a fraction but in fact the vast majority of the broad category of people we may call the dominant class. As has recently been demonstrated, in regard to one of Africa's poorest land-locked states, in some states, for the sheer want of any alternative, there is little or no prospect – at this particular point in time – for the development of a significant component of the dominant class outside the confines of what we might call a state bourgeoisie.[28] Further, again using Leys' terminology, it is perhaps more appropriate, in such contexts to minimise the role of the state as 'the leading edge of indigenous capital in its assault' on international capital at the expense of a view which sees the state as the 'register of a general imbalance' between domestic and international capital.

It behoves us therefore to recognise the important influence of the different historical and socio-economic considerations of respective peripheral states. Such a conclusion leaves the debate at a stage where it is difficult to attempt to formulate generalisations with any degree of certainty, apart from the need to see dominant classes in African states in holistic terms (despite their acknowledged fractions) as opposed to seeing the dominant class in a structural sense of being a specific functioning group, which had been the tendency from within the radical structuralist framework of the dependency theorist in the 1970s.

To urge this holistic approach is not, however, to assert a relatively straightforward process for the analysis of class formation in the Third World. Indeed, in an excellent recent review of the problems faced in analysing classes in the Third World in general but particularly appropriate to African analysis, Ian Roxborough points out that classes are, on the whole, more complex, weaker and incomplete than, for example, classes in advanced industrial societies:

> the political behaviour of any class, group or category is not an inherent function of the class itself, but rather a result of its interaction with other classes in the context of the overall political system. Therefore one cannot say 'the military will be radical', or 'the peasants will be conservative' or 'the marginals will be a source of revolutionary support' in general terms. One can only say, 'in such-and-such a political system with such-and-such characteristics, then an historically defined social class with such-and-such characteristics may be expected to behave in this or that manner'.[29]

As with class, then similarly with the role of the post-colonial state in the 1980s; we need to recognise the variety of stages of development and the subsequent range of options open. The post-colonial state is neither economically determinist nor politically voluntarist. The economic structure may well be the dominant factor, but it does not preclude the state, or rather the personnel of the state, behaving with varying degrees of political or ideological independence.[30] The major pitfall that needs to be avoided in the attempts by students of African politics to build up some kind of generalised hypotheses around the nature of the state in post-colonial societies is the danger inherent in the creation of one or possibly two abstract models of the 'state-in-general'. This pitfall has often not been avoided, especially by dependency theorists. It would seem methodologically absurd to make generalisations about the post-colonial state of which our data and knowledge in individual cases is almost always inferior to that which we possess about the state in advanced industrial societies, but about which we are far less ready to make similar sweeping generalisations.

Discussions about the nature of class domination and the role of the post-colonial state in Africa do of course have specific 'levels of analysis' criteria which need to be applied. To talk about a dominant class that interacts with the international environment requires a different perspective from an analysis which focuses on Africa's dominant classes' domestic relationships within their specific African social formations. In this context the class can, of course, look much less dominant than it does when it is involved in a process of international interaction. As Goran Hyden has pointed out in his recent study of some of the weaknesses of *ujamaa* implementation in Tanzania for example, it is possible for many sections of an African national community to 'opt out'. In this specific context Hyden suggests that the dominant class in Tanzania has not been able to bring the 'uncaptured peasantry' under its total control.[31] Such an analysis needs to stand as a potential constraint when examining the influence of the dominant class and post-colonial state in other specific African contexts.

To summarise the discussion so far we can say that during the first decade after independence, spurred on by the heady optimism engendered by the decolonisation process and the influence of modernisation theory, we perceived possibilities for 'take-off' in Africa. In the second decade, chastened by the 'false start', and the failure of modernisation theory, we saw only 'underdevelopment' – epitomised by the work of Samir Amin and the late Walter Rodney. Both modernisation theory and underdevelopment theory were essentially unilinear macro-theories and, as we are now somewhat belatedly prepared to acknowledge, largely inappropriate for dealing with specific disaggregated events 'on the ground' in Africa.

At the beginning of the third decade after independence, we are methodologically more sophisticated in our assessments. We are now in a situation where we are not prepared to say that capitalist development cannot occur in Africa, nor are we prepared to say that its eventual achievement is inevitable. Instead we cling cautiously to the necessity of analysing on a case by case basis the process by which some states have, and some states have not, undergone significant growth. With these cautionary remarks in mind the rest of this chapter is devoted to some tentative hypothesising about the way the political economy of Africa may develop in the short- to medium-term future and in particular the role that the state *may* play and the way in which class relations *could* develop in this period. Specifically, I would like to suggest the growth of an environment in Africa which might be appropriate for some variant of the corporatist analysis that has become increasingly popular in the Latin American context of late.

BEYOND MODERNIZATION AND DEPENDENCY: A CORPORATIST FUTURE FOR AFRICA?

The Corporate State, Resource Allocation and International Linkages

It would seem reasonable to expect the pattern of growing bureaucratic predominance in decision-making in Africa to continue. Similarly, the role of the state in directing entrepreneurial activities, especially as a channel of international capital, can also be expected to continue and indeed strengthen. On the basis of our preceding discussion it is not sufficient, however, to assume that the dominant groups operating the machinery of the state are going to exist in an unambiguously comprador relationship with international capital, nor in the international environment more generally; but rather with self-interest and a limited degree of autonomy. We should see this desire of African governments to control their productive sectors and natural resources and their attitudes to international capital from the perspective of a growing African economic nationalism, not the perspective of unadulterated patron–client relations so dear to the heart of the latterday dependency theorist.

The strength of this nationalism will, of course, vary along a continuum which will see the wealthier states such as Nigeria, Zimbabwe, Kenya and Angola at one end, with the poorer states such as land-locked, war-torn Chad, for example, at the other end. In this context the achievement of political independence has given a greater freedom of movement to Africa's ruling élites and improved the bargaining position these élites may have with external actors. Independence has given them the opportunity to diversify, or rather create, foreign relationships that did not exist prior to independence. While the former colonial power is still, for most African states, the major external actor, there has for all states been a weakening of these links with a subsequent establishment of newer ones. This is so even for some of the very weakest of Africa's states.[32] It would seem not unreasonable, therefore, to expect the continuation of a similar tendency in the future to that envisaged by Leys and Sklar, for example, at the end of the 1970s. Colonial legacies might still be the overriding factors for most African states, but they are by no means immutable.

However, to reject dependency theory's 'development of under-development' hypothesis is not to reject that overall *syndrome* of characteristics we might call 'dependency'.[33] A dependent, as opposed to interdependent, position in the international political economy is clearly a fact of life for all African states. It would in this context seem that there is a clear link between this dependence and the authoritarian nature of most African regimes. For most African states the maintenance of short-run governmental stability will continue to take precedence over long-run structural changes in the society, economy and polity – with all their ensuing tendencies for disruption and instability. The desire of ruling élites to achieve stability, more often than not perceived simply as the absence of open conflict, will see African leaders continuing to rely on the former colonial power, or the broader international system, for economic and military support. This would appear especially to be the case for those states that will be unable to meet growing domestic demands on their regimes for increased material well-being from domestically generated sources.

We should, as an indicator for the 1980s therefore, note the very crucial relationship which will exist between African governmental policy and the quality and quantity of resources (seen in a broad sense) available to the policy-maker. Things such as initial factor endowments (be they demographic, mineral or agricultural) the degree of colonial penetration and the resulting social and economic infrastructure do seem to be important in accounting for the gap that appears to be opening up between that rank of Africa's richer states and the second and third ranks of Africa's poorer states. In a recent work, William Zartman has identified three distinct groups of African states on the basis of their wealth, power and potential for growth.[34] Zartman's basic, and largely incontestable, point is that as independence recedes Africa's fifty or so states are going to be strung out along an increasingly long continuum of wealth, power and influence.

Contingent on these growing disparities, it would appear fair to assume that it is those states in which the resource base will continue to expand that will be best able to cope, in part at least, with increasing demands. As early as 1972, Henry Bienen had in fact suggested a tentative correlation between economic growth and those political élites that had managed to stay in power by running relatively successful patrimonial political machines capable of creaming off, or incorporating, the more vociferous sections of the opposition to their regimes.[35] Bonnie Campbell's work on Ivory Coast also tends to such a view. In those states where there is minimal resource growth it may well be that governments will have a much more difficult task in accommodating growing demands, with the subsequent resort to further repression. This is not to suggest, however, that those states that do undergo economic growth will inevitably move in the direction of liberal democratic organisation as envisaged by the earlier political scientists of political development.[36] Far more likely would appear a form of political organisation approximating to the organic statist or corporatist models of governance envisaged by Alfred Stepan and others in their recent discussions of Latin America.[37] We should, therefore, consider a few of the major characteristics of this model that may, to a greater or lesser extent, be appropriate to a variety of African situations.

Corporatism, Political Control and Regime Maintenance

It needs to be noted at the outset that 'corporatism' is an abstract model from which all states will deviate on matters of detail – assuming they are deemed appropriate for corporatist analysis in the first instance. Perhaps its major characteristic is its high concern for political stability accompanied at times by a paradoxical propensity for radical intervention in the political arena to bring about major structural change predicated on some ideologically-inspired conception of the common good. Corporatism is also essentially an economic system in which 'the state directs and controls predominantly privately-owned businesses according to four principles: unity, order, nationalism and success'.[38] In a corporatist model the degree of control of the economy will deviate from the abstract model in the direction of a liberal market organisational format on the one hand – what we might call 'societal corporatism' – to a more controlled and centrally planned economy on the other – or what we might call 'state-corporatism'. The basic tendency in Africa in the forseeable future seems pretty likely to be more an approximation of the former than the latter. It does not seem unreasonable on the basis of the evidence available to expect the growth of, or perhaps more appropriately, the continuance in growth of a form of state-corporatism in which there is a strong tendency to *over*control at the political level and *under*control (in a relative sense) at the economic level. This creates a basically authoritarian corporatism which cracks down hard on the large mass of Africa's populations at the same time as it provides a fairly unfettered degree of freedom to its entrepreneurial groups. Whether this kind of authoritarianism is justified in the name of capitalism or socialism, government will become increasingly the preserve of Africa's educated technocratic elites.

We do not have to subscribe to Shivji's somewhat extreme, and indeed simplistic, notions of a bureaucratic bourgeoisie to recognise that the major trend in Africa since independence has been, politically speaking at least, the increasing power of the bureaucracy at the expense of other actors and institutions in the policy-making process. There are no reasons, at the moment anyway, to suggest that this trend is likely to be halted, although it may well slow down over the next few years since, as I will suggest in a moment, its growth has not been accompanied by any noticeable commensurate increase in government capabilities to implement policy decisions.

Two other aspects of corporatism, as a general phenomenom, are in need of brief discussion. First, we must understand corporatism not only in the national context, but also in the context of the changing nature of post-colonial dependence and interdependence alluded to in the first section of this chapter. Second, and relatedly, we should note the functional rather than territorial nature of interest representation that tends to predominate under corporatism. The primacy attached to these two issues in corporatist analysis allows us to recognise that dependency relationships are clearly not the mechanical and largely spatial phenomena they were perceived to be by the early dependency literature generally, or in the specific literature on neocolonialism in Africa.[39] The state-centric nature of such analysis had led us into the accompanying, and equally banal, analysis of stratification that had prevailed during the heyday of dependency theory.[40] It can be seen that the functional nature of representation in corporatism, characterised by the role that the state plays in controlling a *vertical* process of group representation, contrasts sharply with the earlier view of the dependency theorist concerning the role of the state – in dependency theory dependence was spatial; in corporatist analysis it is socio-economic. The corporatist process of representation also contrasts sharply with the essentially pluralist views of modernisation theory. Unlike pluralism, under corporatism the number of groups is limited, they are non-competitive and sanctioned by the state. In the post-pluralist, post-dependency era we can now recognise the possibility for class conflict taking place *within* African states.

In one of the few attempts to date to utilise the concept of corporatism in the analysis of the political economy of Africa, Tim Shaw quite correctly cautions us as to the transitional nature of the social relationships that prevail under corporatism and the resulting degree of variation that is possible.[41] The major form of variation has been touched upon already and relates to that discernible gap that has developed, and is indeed continuing to grow, between Africa's poorest, or 'classically dependent' states, and its less poor, or 'semi-industralising' states, and the degree to which they are incorporated into the global political economy.[42] The degree of incorporation will lead to a variety of social formations in which there are a variety of roles and functions for the post-colonial state. Clearly we must pay considerable attention to this distinct array of options – even within the two categories I have just mentioned. I have argued elsewhere that what one might perceive as one of Africa's 'classically dependent' states, Niger, has demonstrated the ability for considerable diversification of policy options despite being controlled by governments that have drawn their international power almost exclusively from their control of the state apparatus (as distinct from ethno-aristocratic base for their domestic power).[43] In short, a state that approximates to an almost 'pure' comprador model demonstrates considerable room for manoeuvre. On the other hand recent questions have been raised about the potential of Kenya, that most written-about of African states,[44] to achieve the process of industrial transformation to semi-peripheral status that many scholars expect for it. As Langdon has recently pointed out, just to say that there is in some states a growing nationalist bourgeoisie capable of capital accumulation, as is undoubtedly the case in states such as Kenya and Ivory Coast, should not lead *ipso facto* to assumptions that a process of transformation is inevitable.[45] It is not possible here to rehearse that extremely interesting, albeit at times seemingly interminable, debate about the nature of capital accumulation and semi-industrialisation in Kenya. My intention is simply to raise a cautionary note as to the complexity of the relationships under discussion, and particularly to suggest the importance of a state's industrialisation strategies for an understanding of this complexity.

As has been shown in a variety of works relating to Latin America,[46] and as seems similarly appropriate to Africa, there is a fairly significant relationship between early import-substitution industrialisation and 'inclusive' political behaviour on the one hand and late and post-import substitution industrialisation and 'exclusivist' political behaviour on the other. In the African context this situation can be seen in the accomodationist political behaviour of a populist variety that prevailed in the early idealistic phase of the immediate post-colonial period and its gradual (rapid?) passing for a more confrontationist political behaviour of a zero-sum variety in more recent pessimistic times. This political behaviour 'on the ground' in Africa mirrors and is mirrored by the optimism of early modernisation theory and the pessimism of later dependency theory.

In these practical and theoretical contexts the emergence of the kinds of centralised control typical of 'corporatism' are in many ways the logical outcome of the inability of post-independence governments to satisfy the demands and expectations generated by the rhetoric of the decolonisation process. The inherited post-colonial state, with its pluralist structures was essentially incapable of dealing with the competing tendencies of populist legitimation on the one hand and the necessity for production and growth on the other. It is, therefore, not surprising that the imperatives of order and regime maintenance triumphed over the demands of the 'revolution of rising expectations'. In pointing to the similarities between Latin America in the 1940s and Africa in the 1970s, Shaw cites the characterisation of O'Donnell; both periods are epitomised by:

(i) the exclusion of a previously politically active popular sector; (ii) the reconstitution of mechanisms of capital accumulation in favor of large public and private organizations; (iii) the emergence of a new coalition whose principal members are state personnel (especially the military and civilian technocrats), international capital, and the segments of the local bourgeoisie which control the largest and most dynamic national businesses and (iv) the expansion of the state.[47]

While one obviously needs to be cautious, following in the wake of the gung-ho transference of Frankian notions of the development of underdevelopment to Africa in the early 1970s, O'Donnell's characterisation of corporatism in Latin America does seem to have a good deal of utility in trying to explain the contemporary African situation. Particularly useful is the insight he provides into the intensification of political conflict that accompanies the import-substitution industrialisation phase. As we have seen in Africa, those groups that profited from this phase tend to adopt a 'what we have we hold' mentality leading to the creation of a kind of insider/outsider dichotomy in which the insiders, consisting of that growing politico-technocratic élite, exhibit low levels of tolerance for the political demands emanating from the outsiders. This has manifested itself at both the level of the academic literature and, of course, at the practical political level in an emphasis on the importance of order and regime maintenance, accompanied by low levels of political participation, as the necessary prerequisites for efficient and rational policy implementation;[48] in short the kind of bureaucratic authoritarianism that we have come to associate with the study of Latin America over the last few years. The greatest similarity is to be found in those African states that are undergoing semi-industrialisation such as Kenya, Ivory Coast and to a lesser extent Nigeria.[49]

The mention of Nigeria does, of course, pose one question that cannot be left untouched in any analysis that suggests the utility of some of corporatist model, namely, what is the role of the military in this model? Is this model rendered inapplicable if the military is not the major political actor in government? Does the recent extensive and elaborate redemocratisation processes that Nigeria and Ghana (until Rawlings' 'second coming') have recently undergone devalue our model? In some ways the answer has to be a limited 'yes' but in other ways 'no' and the military dimension does in fact serve to show the flexibility of the model when compared with earlier modernisation and dependency conceptualisations. When writing about the prospects for military withdrawal from politics in Africa several years ago, Claude Welch suggested that in any withdrawal a major, if not the major, consideration would have to be that the incumbent military junta would be handing over to a civilian regime of comparable persuasion and interest.[50] In a recent paper on the redemocratisation process in Nigeria, Richard Joseph argues that this has in fact been the case.[51]

Far more likely than a redemocratisation process along the Nigerian path in Africa is rather a process of 'liberalisation'. Liberalisation, characterised for example by fewer political prisoners, less torture, a freer press, freer rights of transit and, of course, economic liberalisation is quite distinct from a process of democratisation which would have to include the re-legalisation of a plurality of trade unions, political parties and elections run along classic democratic lines. While the prospect of the former scenario taking place in any wholesale manner would undermine a corporatist model it is an extremely improbable eventuality. The latter scenario is, however, more likely but is capable of sitting quite easily within the corporatist model outlined earlier in this chapter. Liberalisation would not necessarily mean an end to the corporatist pattern of relationships between the state and a body of functional, non-competitive and officially-sanctioned interest groups in a way in which redemocratisation inevitably would.

It is also necessary not to underestimate the continued and continuing influence of the military, processes of redemocratisation notwithstanding. As in the Nigerian case for example, this process was, after all, carried out under military initiative and supervision and we must legitimately expect the military to continue to play a role – what one author has called a 'New Professionalism' or 'Participatory Professionalism'[52] in which the military will insist on playing an obligatory advisory role whatever the nature of the civilian regime that might have recently replaced it. This is, of course, an uneasy and unclear picture, but the recognition by the military in many states of Latin America and Africa of the growing antipathy towards it by the other partners in the politico-technocratic and military alliances that have been running many states of the Third World for the last couple of decades makes a lower key, though not necessarily less influential, role for the military more likely in the foreseeable future. It goes without saying that in the vast majority of states, however, the preferred military emphasis on regime maintenance and security, followed by 'development' with 'participation' running a poor third is likely to remain the rank order of government priorities. The military will continue to be primarily interested in the role of the state as regulator rather than the state as either producer or legitimiser.

One final facet of corporatism that becomes apparent from the preceding discussion is its essential preoccupation with what happens at the national level – or at the centre. Corporatism is very much concerned with the defence of the 'centre' from disruptive sub-national elements. While our growing concern with the corporatisation of state–society relations is an appropriate concern we must not fall into the trap of assuming the existence of an over-concentration of power at the centre. To be sure, the authoritarian component of corporatism is geared to the preservation of order but there is no automatic reason to assume a greater degree of social discipline in Africa in the next decade than we saw in the first two decades after independence.

While there might be marginal improvement, there would seem to be no reason to assume that control over the policy implementation processes (administration capability being the ability to get things done as opposed to being able to preserve order) in most African states is likely to increase in any dramatic fashion over the next few years.[53] There are many reasons for this, some of which have already been outlined – especially the importance of resources (broadly defined) or, more accurately, the lack of them. Perhaps more important, however, to use Myrdal's old but extremely evocative term, is the 'soft' nature of the African state. The notion of the modern administrative state of popular Weberian image is not apt in the African context despite the fact that the state holds a predominant position in society. Despite this position, however, control of the policy-making and policy-implementing process proves illusive, and will in all probability continue to prove illusive for some time to come. Perhaps one recent example will suffice.

Control over their communities by African governing-groups is not necessarily assured by either utilitarian or authoritarian incentives. Until recently we have been so concerned to highlight the growing power of the state in Africa that we have tended to ignore the potentiality of certain segments of the community to 'exit' or 'opt out' of the political process, to use Hirschmann's now justifiably famous phrases.[54] Recently, however, Hyden has shown us in quite vivid fashion how certain sections of the Tanzanian peasantry have been able to evade the control of central government. The state in Tanzania has been shown to lack the necessary control agencies actually to 'get at' the peasantry. As Hyden notes, we cannot take it for granted that 'those who control the state also control the society'.[55] While the state may be powerful enough to ensure the continued preservation of those who run it, it may not be powerful enough to extend their domain over the rest of society as quickly as they might like. Notions of 'development' couched in vague and normative terms will not be sufficient to ensure African policy-making élites the

co-operation of the rest of the community. Again as Hyden notes, 'development' when seen in historical perspective has always been at the expense of the peasantry; it is therefore only natural that they should try to resist it.

The relationship between government and peasantry is not as utilitarian as we might assume. Central bureaucracies in Africa often have very little to offer the peasantries of their societies and it is for this reason that coercion is equally often a major element of the relationship between bureaucrat and peasant. The basic aim of the personnel of the central state in all African countries is, and will continue to be, to close the exit option for public sector control for dissident and/or unreconstructed elements of the national community. Failure of rational explanation or utilitarian inducement to achieve the desired rates of co-operation will inevitably turn African governments to more authoritarian measures. Devolution, apart from where it might actually be necessary to prevent the break-up of the national state as in the case of Nigeria, is not likely to be high on the agenda of African governments in the foreseeable future. Africa's ruling groups are concerned with the consolidation of the state not its decentralisation. African states are not yet, nor are they likely to be for some time to come, what we might call empirical or functional states to the extent that they are *not* stable communities. Rather, they are characterised by an ethnic, cultural, religious and regional heterogeneity, and to such an extent that they exhibit few of the characteristics of 'effective government'.

CONCLUSION: THE PARADOX OF WEAKNESS AND CONSOLIDATION OF THE MODERN AFRICAN STATE

In discussing the variety of ways in which the role and function of the state in Africa has been perceived in the post-colonial period, this chapter has deliberately sidestepped the essentially philosophical nature of much contemporary analysis of the state as it has evolved in Western social and political theory from Machiavelli and Hobbes through a latter-day theorists of the state such as Miliband and Poulantzas. What does need to be borne in mind, however, from this philosophical tradition is the multifaceted nature of the state, be it industrial, post-industrial or post-colonial. The state is at one and the same time three things (at least!): it is a territorial entity, a set of institutions and an 'idea'. Not the least important of these three facets is the notion of the state as an idea;[56] but it goes without saying, this is the weakest of the three facets of statehood in Africa.

Yet the state in Africa continues to exist as a territorial entity despite the absence of this supposedly crucial third facet and further, it will continue to exist – for two major reasons which might briefly be considered by way of conclusion to this chapter. The first factor is the existence of the state as a set of institutions; that is the existence of the state as an institutional structure, a body of law (whatever variant) and the personnel that staffs the institutional structure, be it in the military, bureaucratic (public and private) judicial or legislative and political arenas. The second factor is the existence of the wider international system of states in which the new states of Africa find themselves.

In regarding the state as an institutional structure one issue that this chapter has almost studiously avoided is the notion of the 'autonomy' or 'relative autonomy' of the state as a political actor. In many ways, the interminable debates of the last decade on the nature of the autonomy of the state have largely exhausted the topic. Consequently it is not necessary to rehearse them again here, since indeed some kind of consensus seems to be emerging. We are now in a position where Marxists (be they structuralist or instrumentalist) and non-Marxist alike tend towards a general agreement that the state can and does exhibit a certain degree of autonomy from the policy-making process under certain conditions and circumstances.[57] This general agreement is much more important for our purposes than the normative nature of any disagreement about the role to which this autonomy is put.

In the African context, radical and conservative alike agree on the pivotal nature of the state in the political economy. There is a general consensus that it (the state) is what gives strength to African rulers. Because it does not represent any one specific class it can be harnessed to the services of any incumbent ruling group, be it a regime of non-commissioned officers in Liberia, aristocrats in Northern Nigeria, or white supremacists in South Africa. Control of the apparatus of the state gives that group instant position as the recognised intermediary between the international and domestic arenas. It allows incumbents to bargain with international donors and providers on the one hand and control (to a greater degree than other groups) the distribution of resources domestically on the other hand. For some incumbent groups control of the state can be their sole basis of power. For other groups – and these usually tend to be the more stable of regimes – control of state power is supplemented by other forms of support, be they regional, religious, ethnic, economic or other forms of loyalty.

It is the recognition of the power that accrues to those who control the apparatus of the state that will guarantee the state in the future.

As groups compete to control this apparatus they are in effect sanctifying the state as an institution and establishing the parameters of the game, even though the rules of the game might leave a lot to be desired. If we continue the analogy, the game is also likely to continue because it is difficult to opt out. Would-be separatist or irredentist movements that would prefer to start a game of their own find it difficult to do so because of the nullifying effect of the umpire, to wit the international system of states that has effectively decreed that the state of the game as it exists at the moment is the way it shall be – even if the rules are open to interpretation. It is in this context that this chapter has pointed implicitly, if not explicitly until now, to the basic paradox of understanding the role of the state in Africa. At one and the same time, the state in Africa exhibits both great weakness and great power. No one doubts that African state structures are the weakest in the world or that the hold that most African governments have over their populations has been at best tenuous and in some instances non-existent, or that administrative capability is derisory and political instability rampant. Yet no new states have been created by a successful secession of a region of an existing state, and no state has as yet disappeared through a process of incorporation by force into a larger one. There would appear to be no major reason for a dramatic change in this situation in the foreseeable future.

The state of the game has not, however, been permanently frozen. While we might ignore the more alarmist predictions of those who suggest the continent's imminent fragmentation into a 'before and flood' style anarchy on the one hand, or the Utopian – albeit now somewhat muted – calls of the early Pan-africanists on the other hand, there are some tendencies that should be taken seriously. We should note the quite strong competing, though not necessarily contradictory, tendencies towards supranational (if limited) co-operation on the one hand of organisations like ECOWAS discussed in later chapters of this book and the assertion (or perhaps re-assertion) of numerous subnational identities on the other.[58] While these tendencies should not be overestimated, neither should they be ignored. More significant than these tendencies, however, is the growing juridical integrity, in contrast to the somewhat more problematic empirical integrity, of the African state within the international system.[59]

While the transnationalisation of the world's political economy is an important phenomenon to recognise and while African states will continue to be penetrated and threatened by the international system they will also be upheld by it. In contrast to the European experience where empirical or functional statehood preceded juridical statehood, the formation of African states occurred in exactly the reverse manner – as scrutiny of maps of the continent only too clearly demonstrate. Thus despite all that has been said in this chapter about the weaknesses of the African state and despite the fact that all the problems and pressures with which we have become so familiar in the post-colonial period still remain, there is no reason why Africa's states should succumb to these pressures and problems in the next twenty years having staved them off in the first twenty years of independence.

NOTES

1. For the first time in its history, the American Political Science Association devoted its 1981 conference to a specific theme. After years in the pluralist wilderness the state appears to have re-emerged. The theme of the conference was 'Bringing the State Back into Political Science'!
2. David Ricci, 'The Reading of Thomas Kuhn in the Post-Behavioural Era', *Western Political Quarterly*, 30, 1977, 7–34.
3. For a discussion of this contention see Richard Higgott, 'Understanding Modernisation and Marxist Theories of Development: The Importance of Historiographical Analysis', *American Political Science Association*, New York, September 1981.
4. For general discussions see *inter alia*, Henry Bernstein, 'Modernisation Theory and the Sociological Study of Development', *Journal of Development Studies*, 7, (2), 1971, 141–60; André Gunder Frank, *The Sociology of Development and the Underdevelopment of Sociology* (London: Pluto Press, 1981); Dean Tipps, 'Modernisation Theory and the Comparative Study of Societies: a critical perspective', *Comparative Studies in Society and History*, 15, 1973, 199–226; and Richard Higgott, 'Competing Theoretical Perspectives on Development and Underdevelopment: A Recent Intellectual History', *Politics*, 13(1), 1978, 26–41.
5. For a discussion of this theme see *inter alia*, Henry Bernstein, 'Sociology of Development versus Sociology of Underdevelopment' in David Lehman (ed.) *Development Theory: Four Critical Studies* (London: Cass, 1979); John Taylor, *From Modernisation Theory to Modes of Production: a Critique of the Sociology of Underdevelopment* (London: Macmillan, 1979); and Richard Higgott, 'Beyond the Sociology of Underdevelopment: an historiographical analysis of Marxist and dependencia theories of underdevelopment', *Social Analysis*, 7, 1981, 72–98. Specifically on Africa see *inter alia*, Antony Hopkins, 'On Importing André Gunder Frank into Africa', *African Economic History Review* 2(1), 1975, 21–31, and 'Clio-Antics: A Horoscope for African Economic History' in Christopher Fyfe (ed.), *African Studies Since 1945: a Tribute to Basil Davidson*

(London: Longmans, 1976) 31–48; and Fred Cooper, 'Africa in the World Economy', *African Studies Association*, Bloomington, Indiana, October 1981.

6. The problems of turning our descriptively superior forms of analysis into acceptable policy proposals are discussed at length in my forthcoming book, *Political Development Theory: the Contemporary Debate* (London: Croom Helm, *1983*) especially the introduction.
7. See for example the voluminous body of literature produced during the 1960s under the auspices of the United States Social Science Research Council's Committee on Comparative Politics: e.g, Gabriel Almond and Bingham Powell, *Comparative Politics: a Developmental Approach* (Boston: Little Brown, 1966). The work of this SSRC Committee is extensively reviewed in Richard Higgott, 'From Modernisation Theory to Public Policy: Continuity and Change in the Political Science of Political Development', *Studies in Comparative International Development*, 15(4), 1980, 26–58.
8. See for example the discussion by Dudley Seers, 'The Meaning of Development', in Lehman (ed.), *Development Theory*, 9–30.
9. See Gabriel Almond, *Political Development: Essays in Heuristic Theory* (Boston: Little Brown, 1970) 274–5.
10. On such issues see the excellent paper by Robert Jackson and Carl Rosberg, 'Why Africa's States Persist: The Empirical versus the Juridical in Statehood', *American Political Science Association*, New York, September 1981.
11. The prevailing norms of the social sciences as they pertain to development issues are discussed in Robert Packenham, *Liberal America and the Third World: Political Development Ideas in Foreign Aid and Social Science* (Princeton: Princeton University Press, 1972), especially chapter 3.
12. Almond and Powell, *Comparative Politics*, chapter 1.
13. Packenham, *Liberal America and the Third World*, 200.
14. See the review of these changes in Donal Cruise O'Brien, 'Modernisation, Order and the Erosion of a Democratic Ideal', *Journal of Development Studies* 8(2) 1972, 351–78.
15. Most notably, Walter Rodney, *How Europe Underdeveloped Africa* (London: Bogle l'Ouverture, 1972); and Samir Amin, 'Underdevelopment and Dependence in Black Africa – Origins and Contemporary Forms', *Journal of Modern African Studies* 10(4) 1972, 503–24, and *Neo-Colonialism in West Africa* (Harmondsworth: Penguin, 1973).
16. See note 5.
17. John Saul, 'The State in Post-Colonial Societies: Tanzania', *Socialist Register, vol. 11, 1974* (London: Merlin, 1974) 349–72; Issa Shivji, *Class Struggles in Tanzania* (London: Heinemann, 1976) and Colin Leys, *Underdevelopment in Kenya* (London: Heinemann, 1974).
18. For a discussion see Claude Ake, 'Explanatory Notes on the Political Economy of Africa', *Journal of Modern African Studies* 14(1) 1976, 1–16.
19. Colin Leys, 'Capital Accumulation, Class Formation and Dependency

– the Significance of the Kenyan Case', *Socialist Register, vol. 15, 1978*, 241–66.

20. See for example, Tony Smith, 'The Underdevelopment of Development Literature: The Case of Dependency Theory', *World Politics* 31(2) 1979, 247–88; Pat McGowan and David Smith, 'Economic Dependency in Black Africa: An Analysis of Competing Theories', *International Organisation* 32(1) 1978, 179–235, and Pat McGowan, 'Economic Development and Economic Performance in Black Africa', *Journal of Modern African Studies* 14(1) 1976, 25–40.
21. Bill Warren, 'Imperialism and Capitalist Industrialisation', *New Left Review*, 81, September–October 1973, 39.
22. Richard Sklar, 'The Nature of Class Domination in Africa', *Journal of Modern African Studies*, 17(4) 1979, 544–5.
23. Leys, 'Capital Accumulation, Class Formation and Dependency', 251–3.
24. Anne Phillips, 'The Concept of Development', *Review of African Political Economy* 8, January–April 1977, 8.
25. Leys, 'Capital Accumulation, Class Formation and Dependency', 260.
26. Ibid, 261.
27. On the Ivory Coast see Bonnie Campbell, 'Ivory Coast', in John Dunn (ed.) *West African States: failure and promise* (London: Cambridge University Press, 1978).
28. I have argued this point in Richard Higgott, 'Structural Dependence and Decolonisation in a West African Land-Locked State: the case of Niger', *Review of African Political Economy*, 17, July–August 1980, 43–58.
29. Ian Roxborough, *Theories of Underdevelopment* (London: Macmillan, 1979) 87–8.
30. For a discussion see Ralph Miliband, *Marxism and Politics* (London: Oxford University Press, 1977) 106ff.
31. See Goran Hyden, *Beyond Ujamaa in Tanzania: Underdevelopment and the Uncaptured Peasantry* (London: Heinemann, 1980).
32. Higgott, 'Structural Dependence and Decolonisation'.
33. For a discussion of dependency theory from this perspective see Raymond Duvall, 'Dependence and Dependencia Theory: Notes Towards Precision of Concept and Argument', *International Organization* 32(1) 1978, 51–78.
34. I. William Zartman, 'Social and Political Trends in Africa', in Colin Legum, *et al, Africa in the 1980s: a Continent in Crisis* (New York: McGraw Hill, 1979) 84.
35. Henry Bienen, 'Political Parties and Political Machines in Africa' in Michael Lofchie (ed.) *The State of the Nations: Constraints on Development in Independent Africa* (Berkeley: University of California Press, 1972) 195–213.
36. See Higgott, 'From Modernisation Theory to Public Policy'.
37. Alfred Stepan, *The State and Society: Peru in Comparative Perspective* (Princeton: Princeton University Press, 1978) especially chapter 1. See also the two excellent collections of readings: James

Malloy (ed.), *Authoritarianism and Corporatism in Latin America* (Pittsburgh: Pittsburgh University Press, 1977); and David Collier (ed.), *The New Authoritarianism in Latin America* (Princeton: Princeton University Press, 1979).

38. Raymond Pahl and J. T. Winckler, 'Corporatism in Britain', in Timothy Raison (ed.) *The Corporate State – Reality or Myth?* (London: Centre for Studies in Public Policy, 1976) 6.
39. The quintessential work is, of course, Kwame Nkrumah's *Neo-colonialism: The Highest Stage of Imperialism* (London: Panaf Books, 1971).
40. For critiques of the inadequacies of dependency theory's class analysis see, *inter alia*, Bernstein, 'Sociology of Development versus Sociology of Underdevelopment'; Colin Leys, 'Underdevelopment and Dependency: Critical Notes', *Journal of Contemporary Asia* 7(1) 1977, 92–107; and Ian Roxborough, 'Development Theory in the Sociology of Development', *West African Journal of Sociology and Political Science* 1(2) 1976, 116–33.
41. Timothy M. Shaw, 'Beyond Neocolonialism: Varieties of Corporatism in Africa', *Journal of Modern African Studies*, 20(2), June 1982, 239–61.
42. Ibid.
43. Higgott, 'Structural Dependence and Decolonisation', and 'Niger' in Timothy M. Shaw and Olajide Aluko (eds) *The Political Economy of Foreign Policy in Africa: comparative analyses* (Aldershot: Gower, 1984) 165–89.
44. For a spectrum of the competing perspectives on the Kenyan industrialisation debate see the special issue of the *Review of African Political Economy* devoted to this topic: 17 August 1980.
45. Steven Langdon, 'A Commentary on Africa and the World Economy: Theoretical Perspectives and Present Trends', *African Studies Association*, Bloomington, Indiana, October 1981, 8–12.
46. See Stepan, *The State and Society* and David Collier, 'The Bureaucratic-Authoritarian Model' in Collier (ed.) *The New Authoritarianism in Latin America*.
47. Guillermo O'Donnell, 'Corporatism and the Question of the State' in Malloy (ed.) *Authoritarianism and Corporatism in Latin America*, 78.
48. Higgott, 'From Modernisation Theory to Public Policy', 38–43.
49. See Timothy Shaw's pioneering work on the comparative analysis of Africa and Latin America in this context: 'Inequalities and Interdependence in Africa and Latin America: Sub-imperialism and Semi-industrialisation in the Semi-periphery', *Cultures et Developpement* 10(2) 1978, 231–63. See also Peter Evans, *Dependent Development: The Alliance of Multinational, State and Local Capital in Brazil* (Princeton: Princeton University Press, 1979) 308–14.
50. For a discussion of this issue and others affecting withdrawal see Claude Welch, 'The Dilemmas of Military Withdrawal from Politics: Some Considerations from Tropical Africa', *African Studies Review* 17(1) 1974.

51. Richard Joseph, 'Democratisation Under Military Tutelage: Crisis and Consensus in the Nigerian 1979 Elections', *Comparative Politics* 14(1) 1981.
52. Alfred Stepan, 'The Military, Civil Society and Redemocratisation: Brazil, Uruguay and Chile', *Joint Seminar on Political Development*, Harvard University/Center for International Affairs and MIT/Center for International Studies, November 1981.
53. On the future problems of policy implementation likely to face African governments see Higgott, *Political Development Theory*, especially chapter 4.
54. Albert O. Hirschmann, *Exit, Voice and Loyalty: Responses to Decline in Firms, Organisations and States* (Cambridge: Harvard University Press, 1970).
55. Hyden, *Beyond Ujamaa in Tanzania*, 29.
56. Generally on the basis of modern state theory see Gianfianco Poggi, *The Development of the Modern State: a Sociological Introduction* (Stanford: Stanford University Press, 1978).
57. Rather than refer the reader to an exhaustive (and exhausting!) bibliography on this topic, I suggest Eric Nordlinger's excellent review, summation and assertion of the possibility for the relative autonomy of the state. See Eric Nordlinger, *On the Autonomy of the Democratic State* (Cambridge: Harvard University Press, 1981), especially chapter 1.
58. Timothy Shaw, 'Towards a Political Economy of Nationalism and Regionalism in West Africa', Nationalism Seminar, Harvard University, Center for International Affairs, November 1981.
59. The concepts of empirical and juridical integrity are given full treatment in Jackson and Rosberg, 'Why Africa's States Persist'.

Part II
Regionalism in the 1980s

3 Eastern and Southern Africa: Past Trends and Future Prospects

RAVI GULHATI*

The decade of the 1970s was full of severe strains. While there was progress on some fronts, it was made after overcoming formidable obstacles. More recently many of these countries have encountered a major deterioration in the international environment which has exposed more clearly than before the fragility of their institutional framework and weaknesses in economic policies. A number of countries have begun to take stock of their situation and to initiate a process of policy reform and structural change. To regain development momentum, it will be necessary to sustain these processes during the 1980s by a combination of local initiative and adequate support from abroad. Foreign-aid agencies need to review their policies and programme against the background of the prevailing economic situation and prospects of African countries. To facilitate policy reforms in Africa, donors need to make supporting adjustments in their programme.

PAST TRENDS

Most countries in Africa are at the bottom of the development pyramid. They have low per capita incomes and a very limited stock of human

---

*The author is a member of the World Bank Staff: the views in this chapter, however, are personal and should not be attributed to the employer. This paper was prepared in connection with a joint DAC/OPEC meeting on Africa held in Paris in June 1980. The data were updated in August 1983. I wish to thank Messrs Michel Devaux, Peter Hansen, Tribhuwan Narain and Ms Judith Beard for their assistance.

capital or physical infrastructure. Exports are dominated by one or two primary commodities, especially coffee, tea and copper, and because world prices fluctuate widely, there are substantial disturbances introduced from abroad in income, savings and public revenues. Natural calamities take their toll as well, adding to economic instability. As the capacity of these economies to adjust to disturbances is weak, development efforts are interrupted frequently by financial difficulties. The pace of progress during the 1970s was seldom smooth and there were marked inter-country variations. Nevertheless, the decade was characterised by the following general trends:

- Income growth in African countries lagged behind that of all LDCs. Furthermore, GDP expansion in low-income African (those with per capita income less than $300 per capita in 1977 prices) countries was slower than that of low-income Asian countries.
- Population growth in Africa was accelerating while trends in other LDCs suggested some slowing down.
- The current account deficit on the balance of payments of many African countries increased markedly in recent years and budget deficits were growing as well. There was double digit inflation in many countries.

Changes in GDP

Growth of income in Africa has lagged behind that of other LDCs. (Table 3.1). Population growth, however, is growing at a faster rate. Falling death rates, combined with continued high fertility, led to a substantial acceleration in the rate of population growth. It is likely that the peak in the pace of demographic expansion has not yet been reached in most African countries.[1] Several countries now have population growth rates exceeding 3 per cent per annum. For these reasons, the falling behind of African countries in terms of per capita income is even more pronounced than the lag in GDP. The average per capita income of low-income African countries in 1970 was $182 compared with $151 in Asia (1977 prices). By 1980, this margin in favour of Africa disappeared completely. The average per capita income in low income Asia today is higher than that of low-income Africa.

The following review is based on trends in Eastern and Southern Africa. The main explanation for lagging growth lies in the behaviour of the agricultural sector which looms large in many countries. The long-run growth rate of agriculture production exceeded 3 per cent per

TABLE 3.1 *Growth of GDP and population (Average annual per cent growth rates)*

	1960–70			*1970–80*		
	Africa	*S. Asia*	*All LDCs*	*Africa*	*S. Asia*	*All LDC*
GDP						
Low-income	4.1	4.2	4.2	3.0	4.2	4.0
Middle-income	5.0	n.a.	6.4	4.3	n.a.	5.5
Population						
Low-income	2.6	2.4	2.4	2.8	2.2	2.3
Middle-income	2.5	n.a.	2.5	2.9	n.a.	2.5

SOURCE *World Development Report 1979*, 13.

annum in three countries during the late 1960s and early 1970s (see Table 3.2). But there were four cases in which agricultural output grew by 1 per cent or less during this period. What is even more startling and worrying is that the pace of production slowed down almost everywhere

TABLE 3.2 *Changes in real GDP and agricultural output (Average annual percentage change)*

	GDP			*Agriculture*		
	1967–73	*1973–78*	*1978–80*	*1969–73*	*1973–78*	*1978–80*
Malawi	5.4	6.0	n.a.	5.9	2.7	1.4
Sudan	4.3	4.3	-0.8	4.0	2.2	-0.1
Rwanda	5.6	4.8	6.6	3.3	3.7	3.3
Burundi	4.1	4.1	4.5	2.8	2.5	1.7
Kenya	6.7	5.8	3.3	2.8	3.9	0.1
Madagascar	1.7	0.3	0.2	2.8	0.9	2.1
Zaire	7.1	-1.5	1.7	1.4	1.8	0.7
Tanzania	4.4	5.1	4.5	1.2	3.4	1.0
Somalia	1.8	5.3	n.a.	0.7	0.7	0.0
Ethiopia	4.0	1.1	4.8	0.4	0.3	1.5
Zambia	5.8	-1.4	-2.0	0.4	0.4	0.0
Uganda	3.3	-1.2	-9.6	0.2	-0.8	0.7

NOTE Countries are listed in descending order of their agricultural growth rate during 1969–73. To minimise the impact of erratic fluctuations, growth rates were calculated on the basis of three year moving averages at either end of the period of observation.

SOURCE *World Bank Data Files*.

during the middle and later 1970s. This deceleration is reflected both in food and cash crop production. Over the entire period, food production per capita seems to have declined in most countries, which has resulted in substantial increases in food imports. Eastern and Southern Africa witnessed a slowing-down in the rate of increase of food production at a time when the pace of population growth was building up.

The disappointing picture of agriculture is at the heart of the development problem in Eastern Africa. To make agriculture a dynamic sector requires a combination of ingredients – viable technical packages adapted to local conditions, timely availability of key inputs, effective extension services, a reasonable relation between prices paid and received by farmers, availability of incentive consumer goods – and it has not been possible to secure and sustain this combination in many places. In addition, droughts, floods and pests took their toll; their incidence was specially marked in 1973–5. The scarcity of project managers and technicians reduced the effectiveness of delivery systems operating over long distances and connected by weak transport networks. Most governments have tended to follow pricing policies aimed at keeping food prices low in urban centres and have not always been convinced that attractive prices will elicit increased production, despite substantial evidence to the contrary. Producer prices for export crops have declined in real terms in many instances. Marketing was handled increasingly by monopsonistic parastatals and several of these organisations failed to provide efficient services. Consequently, the period saw the emergence of black markets and smuggling on a substantial scale in many instances.

Industry was very underdeveloped at independence and, despite vigorous attempts on the part of governments to promote this sector, progress made so far was fairly limited. Tanzania made a major policy switch in 1967 in the form of the Arusha Declaration and Zambia followed with the Mulungushi Reform in 1968. In both cases, the role of state intervention through parastatals and in other ways was greatly expanded.[2] Similar changes took place during the early seventies in Somalia, Sudan, Madagascar and Ethiopia. Parastatals were plagued, in many cases, by conflicting instructions to earn profits but also to adhere to price controls, to operate on a commercial basis but also to meet government targets regarding job creation. Trade policy and exchange rate regimes tended to bias incentives in favour of production for the home market and, given discouraging trends in farm income for much of the period, this market was not growing very rapidly.

In line with trends in the agricultural sector, the overall GDP expanded fairly rapidly during the late 1960s (see Table 3.2). Two countries recorded rates of growth of 6 per cent per annum or more. At the opposite end of the spectrum, there were two countries in which aggregate production failed to keep pace with population. The second half of the decade witnessed a widespread slowing-down in economic growth, compared with the earlier period. Zaire, Zambia and Uganda experienced an absolute decline in GDP during 1973–8 and the Sudan in 1978–80. In addition to these countries, per capita GDP declined in Madagascar and Ethiopia. The timing of the setback in output shows considerable inter-country variability. The first oil price increase of 1973–4 is often taken as a watershed in the recent growth history of oil-importing developing countries. This event was clearly of importance in the region, but it was far from decisive. A factor contributing to the slowdown was the incidence of border conflicts, revolution and internal strife during this period. In 1972 Idi Amin came to power in Uganda and initiated major changes in policy. In 1974 Ethiopia underwent a revolutionary change in government. In 1975 the civil conflict in Zimbabwe escalated. The same year also saw a decline in copper prices which severely affected Zambia and Zaire. Drought affected several countries during the mid-1970s. Many countries reaped the benefits of the coffee boom of 1976–7 to variable degrees. Another disturbing factor was the disruption of the East African Community. Created in 1967 to facilitate economic development in Kenya, Tanzania and Uganda, the Community arrangements collapsed in 1977, compelling erstwhile members to search for substitute markets, and leading to the closure of the Tanzania–Kenya border. The second increase in oil prices at the end of the 1970s led to a substantial loss for these oil-importing countries.

Growing Financial Pressure

Although expansion of GDP slowed down, there was a marked widening of the current account deficit of the balance of payments in many countries. As a proportion of GDP this deficit exceeded 10 per cent in Madagascar, Mauritius, Zambia, Tanzania, Malawi, Kenya and Sudan. The growing imbalance in external accounts was the combined result of the following:

- a substantial deterioration in the terms of trade;
- a slowdown or decline in the volume of exports.

Between 1966 and 1974 the regional terms of trade index (1977 = 100) remained rather stable around an average of 153 (see Table 3.3).

TABLE 3.3 *Eastern Africa terms of trade*

	Export Price Index[a]	*Mfg. Import Price Index (Manufactured Exports)*	*Petroleum Import Price Index*	*Composite Import Price Index*[b]	*Terms of Trade*
1966	64.0	41.4	10.5	37.7	169.8
1967	54.1	42.0	10.5	38.2	141.6
1968	56.7	39.3	10.5	35.8	158.4
1969	63.5	39.7	10.5	36.2	175.4
1970	64.6	44.0	10.5	40.0	161.5
1971	57.3	47.6	13.7	43.5	131.7
1972	60.5	52.7	15.3	48.2	125.5
1973	89.8	63.4	21.8	58.4	153.8
1974	122.0	79.0	79.0	79.0	154.4
1975	87.7	91.1	86.3	90.5	96.9
1976	92.0	92.7	92.7	92.7	99.2
1977	100.0	100.0	100.0	100.0	100.0
1978	97.8	115.9	100.8	114.1	85.7
1979	125.7	131.2	156.3	136.2	93.7
1980	156.3	145.0	263.9	158.9	98.4
1981	125.6	136.7	281.2	154.1	81.2

[a]Weighted by share of exports in 1977: copper (29%), coffee (10%), sugar (8%), beef (5%), cotton (4%), etc.
[b]Weighted by share of imports in 1977: manufactured goods (88%), petroleum (12%).

SOURCE *World Bank Data Files*

Major disturbances until 1973 were caused by fluctuations in primary commodity export prices, while prices of imports followed a slow upward trend. Since 1973 the pressure on the balance of payments has been much accentuated by a very sharp upward trend in import prices of capital goods and oil, while prices of Eastern African exports continue to fluctuate. In 1975 the terms of trade fell by 37 per cent; this was the year when copper prices fell dramatically. The next major deterioration occurred in 1978 with the large decline in prices of coffee and tea. Petroleum prices rose on average by 55 per cent in 1979 and by a further 80 per cent during the following two years. The cost of importing oil pre-empted a growing proportion of total exports (see Table 3.4). The index of the terms of trade in 1981 was 81; a very low level indeed in the entire post-independence history of the region.

Changes in the terms of trade have had a major impact but they are not

TABLE 3.4 *Energy imports in relation to merchandise exports (per cent)*

	1970	*1978*	*1979*	*1980*
Sudan	–	24	–	32
Kenya	14	30	38	63
Tanzania	10	–	30	47
Ethiopia	10	20	26	42
Madagascar	6	16	10	–
Malawi	10	22	27	24
Zambia	–	11	13	–
Burundi	5	–	14	14
Somalia	–	–	–	12

SOURCE *World Bank Data Files*

the whole story by any means. The problem was accentuated by a sharp setback in the volume of exports (see Table 3.5). In at least six countries, the quantity of exports was declining during the seventies. The causes varied but prominent among them were over-valuation of the currency,

TABLE 3.5 *Changes in volume of exports and imports (Average annual percentage growth rate)*

	Exports		*Imports*	
	1960–70	*1970–80*	*1960–70*	*1970–80*
Malawi	11.6	5.7	7.6	3.5
Somalia	2.3	5.5	2.6	7.2
Rwanda	15.8	3.5	8.1	11.6
Zaire	-1.8	2.2	5.4	-12.0
Zambia	2.2	1.2	9.7	-7.3
Kenya	7.2	-1.0	6.6	-1.0
Madagascar	5.3	-1.2	4.1	-0.8
Ethiopia	3.6	-1.7	6.2	-0.2
Sudan	0.1	-5.7	1.2	3.5
Tanzania	3.4	-7.3	6.0	-0.3
Uganda	5.0	-8.5	6.2	-9.8

NOTE Countries are listed in descending order of their export growth rate during 1970–80

SOURCE *World Bank Data Files*

inadequate incentives for cash crops, infrastructure bottlenecks and the like. For example, the quantity of copper exported by Zambia and Zaire declined; their combined share in world exports dropped from 24 per cent in the early 1970s to 15 per cent at the end of the decade. Similarly, Sudan's share of cotton exports fell from 7 per cent to 4 per cent. Uganda's share of tea exports diminished from 2 per cent to 0.2 per cent and Somalia's share of banana exports shrank from 1.8 per cent to 0.8 per cent.

The widespread deterioration in the balance of payments compelled many countries to reduce very considerably the rate of growth of imports. (see Table 3.5). In at least seven cases, there was an absolute decline in the volume of imports. It seems that in many cases the curtailment of intermediate good imports was particularly sharp. This led to a severe reduction in the utilisation of existing capacity not only in manufacturing but also in transport, construction, agricultural extension services as well as in education and health.

The immediate reaction of many countries to the large deterioration in their external position was to draw down reserves and borrow abroad. Net foreign assets fell precipitously in 1975 and turned negative in several countries. Most countries did not have much access to the Eurodollar market but those few which could borrow commercially did so. Examples are the sharp rise in foreign debt of Sudan, Madagascar, Malawi, Zaire and Zambia. The servicing of this debt in subsequent years strained the balance of payments and in several cases arrears in payments accumulated for the first time. Six countries have had to negotiate a re-scheduling of their debt-service payments with the Paris Club between 1976 and mid-1983: Zaire four times, Sudan three times, Madagascar and Uganda twice and Zambia and Malawi once. Some of them have also re-scheduled debt due to private commercial bank creditors.

Financial pressures were also manifest in the government budget. Public expenditures have risen rapidly in many countries and they have tended to outstrip revenues. Recourses to the banking system by governments to finance budget deficits were important causes of inflation in many countries. Average annual price increases in 1976–8 exceeded 10 per cent in most countries and exceeded 50 per cent in two instances (see Table 3.6). The pace of inflation increased further in subsequent years in Uganda, Sudan, Somalia, Tanzania and Madagascar.

Indirect taxation constituted the bulk of public revenues and the value of imports, expressed in local currency, was an important base for such levies.[3] The foreign exchange constraint in the late 1970s dampened the rise in imports and the overvaluation of the currency

TABLE 3.6 *Average annual rate of inflation (per cent)*

Country	*1976–78*	*1979–81*	*Type of Indicator*[a]
Zaire	72.0	66.0	CPI
Uganda	62.0	100.0[b]	CPI
Ethiopia	19.7	8.0	CPI
Zambia	18.2	16.0	DDD
Sudan	17.5	28.0	CPI
Somalia	15.0	40.0	CPI
Kenya	13.5	8.7	GDP
Tanzania	13.0	18.0[b]	CPI
Burundi	12.3	16.0	CPI
Rwanda	10.1	11.8[b]	CPI
Malawi	6.8	7.0[b]	GDP
Madagascar	5.7	20.0	GDP

NOTE Countries are listed in descending order of their rate of inflation in 1976–8

[a] CPI = Consumer Price Index
DDD = Domestic Demand Deflator
GDP = GDP Deflator

[b] 1978–80

accentuated the erosion in this important tax base. In addition, many governments failed to revise prices for economic services at a time when inflation was picking up momentum.

On the expenditure side, several powerful factors have led to large increases. A very high value was attached to social services in the wake of national independence and an impressive quantitative expansion has taken place, particularly in the field of education. Eight countries (Kenya, Lesotho, Madagascar, Mauritius, Comoros, Swaziland, Tanzania, Zambia) have already achieved primary school enrolment ratios exceeding 90 per cent. The expansion of secondary education has been equally dramatic, although the initial base was much narrower than that at the primary level. Education outlays have risen much more rapidly than total government expenditures. Altogether social services (education, health, etc.) absorb 30–35 per cent of total public outlays in recent years in five countries and more than 20 per cent in the remaining countries.[4] More broadly, capital expenditures have risen substantially as governments formulated plans, identified projects and secured external funds from donors and foreign banks or suppliers.[5]

Attempts made by governments to control the budget deficit have frequently led to a growing imbalance in the composition of expenditures. If funds are scarce, a reasonable approach would be to assign priority to the full utilisation of already-completed projects and speedy completion of half-completed investments. New projects would be started, under these circumstances, only to the extent that funds remained after meeting priority needs. But this reasonable approach does not seem to have been followed in practice in many cases. A strong preference has been shown instead for starving existing roads of maintenance funds, existing vehicles of spare parts and the existing school system of key inputs.[6] In addition, there are many examples of ongoing projects which have failed to obtain local budget funds required for effective implementation. And while completed and half-completed investments have been starved of funds, governments have started new projects, frequently in collaboration with foreign-aid agencies. Present benefits from already completed projects and expected benefits from half-completed projects which are within grasp in a matter of a year or two have been sacrificed in order to start new schemes whose pay-off would not materialise for five or six years.

Attempts to control public expenditure did not lead governments to reduce jobs in the public sector. On the contrary, there has been a tendency to create new posts and thereby offset the slack in employment opportunities in the private sector. This compensatory reaction is understandable, given government sensitivity to urban unemployment among secondary-school graduates, but the impact of more employees on the payroll (combined with less funds for supplies and provisions) on the productivity of the public sector and the morale of the civil service was debilitating.

Scarcity of High- and Medium-level Manpower

The foreign exchange and the budgetary position has been very tight. Superimposed on these financial pressures has been the acute scarcity of skilled and experienced manpower in the public sector. This has affected adversely the functioning of the administrative machine. Tasks such as macro-economic management, tax collection, licensing of foreign exchange and agricultural extension services are subject to costly delays and lapses. The malaise affects also the network of parastatals which have heavy responsibilities in operating the infrastructure, agricultural credit and marketing as well as industrial establishments in many countries. The unavailability of key personnel is also a critical bottleneck in the implementation of development projects.

The manpower gap remains a conspicuous feature of the scene in Sub-Sahara Africa. The number of secondary school graduates has risen substantially, and a small trickle of professionals have also emerged; but the situation remains critical. Members of colonial services who remained to work in Africa after independence have been replaced by indigenous personnel to a large extent. Expatriates under foreign technical assistance programmes have provided a measure of relief but their use is subject to a growing number of restrictions. Recent years have seen an outflow of skilled and semi-skilled workers from countries such as the Sudan and Somalia who are attracted by high wages and salaries in the Gulf countries.

Setback in Capital Accumulation

Gross domestic investment in real terms expanded at an average rate of almost 10 per cent per annum during the late 1960s.[7] The median rate of investment to GDP rose from 16.5 per cent in 1966–8 to a peak of 24.4 per cent in 1974–6. These levels could not be sustained and the median investment ratio declined to 20.9 per cent in 1977–9. This was the result of the deterioration in the terms of trade, as well as the weakening of domestic resource mobilisation. Investment would have fallen even more had it not been for a rapid rise of external assistance which rose by 17 per cent per annum in real terms during 1976–9.

Declining investment rates were accompanied by rising incremental capital output ratios (ICORs). The median ICOR increased from 4.3 in 1967–73 to 5.2 in 1973–9. The attempt by many countries to raise rapidly the level of overall investment, to industrialise and modernise their economies at the expense of agriculture and to expand the public sector at a rate which far exceeded the availability of relevant professional skills has led to a massive deterioration in the quality of projects and the effectiveness of their implementation. Superimposed on these factors was the deterioration in the international economic climate which made it even more difficult to manage the public finances and the foreign exchange budgets, thereby compounding the problems of project execution and causing capacity utilisation to decline drastically.

FUTURE OUTLOOK

The economic prospects of Eastern and Southern African countries will turn on the following:

- trends in world trade, particularly those affecting primary commodities which dominate their present exports;
- demographic factors;
- evolution in their policies and institutions;
- policies of donors and creditors who play an important role in Africa.

The trade outlook is not favourable. Primary commodities which today dominate exports (copper, coffee, cotton, sugar, tobacco and tea) are not expected to be in high demand, even if we make relatively optimistic assumptions regarding world economic recovery. Lying behind this assessment are a number of structural and technological factors which are unlikely to change very much. Copper continues to be displaced by other metals and this process is expected to continue.[8] The demand for coffee and tea in high-income countries is saturated.[9] Substitution by synthetics has affected the cotton market adversely. Sugar imports have been hit by high protectionist policies of rich countries. The health hazard has already affected demand for tobacco. The projected increase in world exports between 1980 and 1995 is likely to be as low as 1.7 per cent per annum for cotton and in no major African export commodity is growth likely to exceed 3.0 per cent per annum.[10] International prices for these commodities are likely to rise in nominal terms and in some cases quite sharply. However, taking account of expected increases in import prices, the terms of trade of these countries is likely to remain significantly worse than the average level experienced in the 1970s.

The demographic factors are also not likely to be favourable. The rate of natural increase of the population in Sub-Saharan Africa has accelerated from 2.1 per cent per annum during 1950–5 to 2.9 per cent per annum in 1975–80. The latter is the highest rate in any major region of the world.[11] Despite significant progress in living standards, a substantial fall in mortality, impressive expansion in education and a measure of urbanisation during the 1960s and 1970s, fertility rates remain extraordinarily high.[12]

Should these fertility levels persist, the growth rate of population could rise further to 3.4 per cent per annum in 1980–2000 and to almost 4.0 per cent in 2000–2020. Rapidly growing population numbers are likely to accentuate the food deficit, magnify the budgetary problem of financing basic-needs services and complicate the employment issue, unless technological and organisational progress takes place at break-neck speed.

NEAR-TERM STRATEGY

In preparing for the future, African governments need to draw a distinction between near-term and long-run strategies. Near-term, in this context, is the period over which:

- severe financial imbalances are eliminated, for example, arrears in foreign payments are wiped out and the current account deficit as a proportion of GDP is reduced to a level which can be financed by normal capital inflow;
- the economy recovers, structural adjustments are made and the normal pace of development is resumed.

Given the initial conditions today, the near-term may stretch over many years, perhaps half a decade, perhaps much more. In thinking about the speed with which African countries can adjust to the formidable difficulties they face we should keep in mind the following considerations:

- The unfavourable prospects for major African primary exports and for the terms of trade. The search for new export products must start now in earnest, but experience shows that it takes research, investment and considerable time to diversify the structure of exports.
- The heavy dependence of most African economies for imported capital goods, fuel, spare parts, fertiliser and other intermediate inputs. It is obvious that such imports are required not only for new investments but also for the rehabilitation of existing production capacity and for sustaining present production and exports.
- The newness and fragility of modern economic institutions and the fact that there is a pervasive shortage of experience and skills to design and implement new economic policies.

Under these circumstances, attempts to stabilise the economy and to restore financial balance in short order may not succeed. Demand management policies which aim at very sharp reduction in imports and budgetary outlays can have a negative impact on production and exports as well as on employment, consumption and welfare. What is required is a policy package which combines judicious and selective (rather than across the board) restraint on outlays with a set of measures aimed at eliciting a quick and strong supply response. These measures are likely to include adjustment in several key prices (exchange rates, interest rates, tariffs on imports, export subsidies, consumer subsidies, agricultural producer prices, utility rates, etc.) as well as a thorough examination of the government and foreign exchange budgets. Furthermore, it will be essential to reinforce these policies by appropriate changes in economic institutions, such as key economic ministries, agricultural marketing parastatals and delivery systems for inputs and consumer goods.

These policy changes are unlikely to be popular and institutional reform is seldom without controversy. But provided that the recovery package is well-designed, that external assistance is available in adequate amounts and that implementation is supported by the political leadership, the economy should soon get into high gear. The decline or stagnation in the volume of traditional exports can be reversed. Africa can recapture its traditional share of world markets. New export products can emerge. Growth in local food production can displace imports. Existing capacity to produce manufactured goods can be used much more fully than it is today. Investment in energy projects can help conserve use of imported petroleum, and so on.

The emphasis of near-term strategy has to be on revival of production. Longer-term goals, such as fertility reduction, poverty alleviation, self-reliance, building institutions for Africa-wide regional integration, improving the environment, etc, are all very important; but it may not be possible to pursue them all with equal vigour in the near term. The distinction I am suggesting is essentially a matter of emphasis. The need for progress in relation to these longer-run goals is ever present and whatever can be done should be done to achieve these goals even during the near-term adjustment phase. But the emphasis will have to be placed on expanding production, easing bottlenecks and obtaining the most out of scarce financial and human resources.

IMPLICATIONS FOR DONOR AND CREDITOR POLICIES

Should donors of African countries adopt a similar distinction between near-term and long-term assistance strategies? For whatever reasons, most donors have emphasised and even today continue to finance new projects. Some donors attach special priority to projects which directly alleviate poverty through primary education, health and family planning services, small-farm development and promotion of small enterprises.

What would a shift to a near-term assistance strategy imply? In the first place, it would imply a willingness to extend a much larger share of assistance in quick-disbursing non-project form, provided there is reasonable assurance that such aid can be channelled into priority uses. The rationale for non-project aid is linked, in the first place, to the current situation. Capacity utilisation, both in the public and private sectors, has fallen to very low levels and a major cause is the stringency of foreign exchange and budget funds. Under these circumstances, the pay-off from non-project assistance can be substantially bigger in size and quicker in time than that from new projects which take five to seven years to complete. Also, there are many countries in which the number of projects under execution is rather large and these projects seem to be competing for scarce local resources, for example, high-level managerial and administrative know-how. External technical assistance has filled some of these gaps in skills but the process of obtaining such assistance is far from smooth and the tolerance of governments for expatriates is limited. A period of consolidation of investment may be highly desirable in a number of cases; it should help in speeding up the pace of implementation of ongoing investments and in reducing the aid pipeline.

Among those who negotiate aid there is less than full understanding of what a specific transaction means for the recipient economy. There is a tendency to believe that projects financed by ODA are entirely a free good and that it is always in the interest of the recipient government to accept such bounty. This is not the full story, however. It is seldom that foreign financing covers the whole of the capital cost of a project and frequently there are explicit and hidden contributions required from the recipient government's budget. Furthermore, the utilisation of capacity created by new projects requires recurrent outlays, imported inputs and management attention. While these associated costs may be covered by external assistance for a time, they will have to be supported by local resources once the project period is over. For all these reasons, it would add greatly to the flexibility of recipient governments if they knew that aid was fungible and could be used *either* for starting new projects *or* for securing better utilisation of present capacity. Such an understanding would very much reduce the temptation on the part of aid recipients to start new projects in circumstances when absorptive capacity is already strained.

Second, a near-term assistance strategy would imply a much larger emphasis on projects which yield quick benefits to the recipient economy as opposed to those which involve major departures such as the establishment of new institutions or the testing of new technical packages. The latter can only be expected to fructify over an extended time-period. There is a sense in which projects incorporating major departures are more important for the development process than those which yield benefits quickly by replicating successful experiences well within the technological and institutional frontiers of society. If the economic and financial situation is urgent, however, quick-yielding investments can play a tactical role in triggering-off recovery and adjustment and thereby facilitate a resumption of the development momentum.

For example, the Sudan government regretfully concluded that it would be wise, in the present context, to concentrate agricultural investments on irrigated schemes along the Nile and adopt a much more circumspect position regarding the initiation of new projects for rural development in other parts of the country involving traditional communities and agro-ecological zones for which technical packages had not yet been fully tested. Such a reorientation may be regarded by some as a devaluation of the equity objective since the population in the irrigated areas tends on balance to be relatively prosperous, compared with that in the rest of the country. This interpretation, however, is a superficial one. The equity goal has to be pursued through a variety of instruments of which the design of projects is only one. In the circumstances of the Sudan today it makes good sense to pursue equity through fiscal instruments, that is, by full cost-recovery from and progressive taxation of the direct beneficiaries of irrigation investments. Such an approach would reduce deficits of parastatal bodies, raise tax revenues and allow the Government to prepare for the stage when it can take measures to assist poverty groups directly.

Third, a near-term strategy implies much closer collaboration than has existed up to now between providers of ODA and other agencies of DAC and OPEC member governments who have responsibility for managing export of suppliers' credit or guaranteeing loans from private banks. Several African countries borrowed excessively and indiscriminately on commercial terms during the 1970s and servicing this debt imposes a heavy burden on their balance of payments today and will continue to do so for some time. The treatment of contractual obligations (That is, the extent to which creditors insist that these claims be paid when due as against agreement to postpone or refinance) has become a central issue in the relationship of these countries to their overseas partners. The present practice of separating aid- and debt-decisions in these cases may prove to be counter-productive; it can jeopardise a promising attempt on the part of a debtor government to put through a viable policy-reform package. It is in the interest of creditors, as also of aid-givers, that economic and financial health be restored to economies of borrower countries. This requires a new approach and a new orientation on the part of aid-givers and creditors.

To recapitulate, many African countries and particularly low-income ones face extremely difficult conditions and no relief is in sight. In these circumstances, foreign partners (donors and creditors) will wish to support African governments who show courage in facing up to their problems by:

- expanding concessional assistance;
- providing a larger part of assistance in quick-disbursing form and making clear to recipient governments that aid is fungible as between financing new projects or inputs for completed investments;
- emphasising the starting of quick-yielding projects and postponing those which will take a long time to complete; and
- postponing the burden of heavy debt-service so that borrower economies are not starved of foreign exchange while they are carrying out a programme of policy reform.

NOTES

1. See Rashid Faruqee and Ravi Gulhati 'Rapid Population Growth in Sub-Saharan Africa' (Washington: World Bank, 1983) Staff Working Paper No. 559.
2. See Ravi Gulhati and Uday Sekhar 'Industrial Strategy for Late Starters: The Experience of Kenya, Tanzania and Zambia', *World Development* 10(11) November 1982.
3. See C. A. Aguirre *et al*, 'Taxation in Sub-Saharan Africa' (Washington: IMF, 1981) Occasional Paper No. 8.
4. See *IMF Government Finance Statistics Yearbook, 1982* (Washington: 1982).
5. See Ravi Gulhati and Gautam Datta, 'Capital Accumulation in Eastern and Southern Africa: A Decade of Setbacks' (Washington: World Bank, 1983) Staff Working Paper No. 562.
6. Ibid.
7. Ibid.
8. See W. Gluschke *et al, Copper: The Next Fifteen Years* (New York: United Nations, 1979).
9. See S. Singh 'Sub-Saharan Agriculture: Synthesis and Trade Prospects' (Washington: World Bank, 1983) Staff Working Paper No. 608.
10. See E. Grilli (ed.), 'The Outlook for Primary Commodities' (Washington: World Bank, 1982) Staff Commodity Working Paper No. 9.
11. *UN World Population Trends and Prospects by Country, 1950–2000: Summary Report of the 1978 Assessment* (New York: UN Department of Economic and Social Affairs, August 1979) ST/ESA/SER.R/33.
12. See Faruqee and Gulhati, 'Rapid Population Growth in Sub-Saharan Africa'.

4 Northern and Western Africa: Past Trends and Future Prospects

I. WILLIAM ZARTMAN

This chapter is an attempt to establish a likely baseline for understanding events in North and West Africa – the twenty-three or twenty-four mainland countries west of and including Libya, Chad, CAR and Congo (that is, those not treated in the preceding chapter) through the 1980s. It contains two types of forecasts – a projection of those situations or elements which are likely to remain the same into the coming decade, and an identification of other elements which are likely to change and head off in other directions. Continuation and mutation are the ingredients of this baseline; and continuation can contain both 'straightline projections' and the ups and downs of identifiable cycles.[1]

Such forecasts unabashedly exclude surprises. This is a point that critics of forecasting misunderstand. Surprises would not be surprises if they were foreseeable, and they would not be surprises if there were no baseline of normal realistic expectations against which to measure them. Baselines are like a map of a winding road: they show the foreseeable changes and dangers, but they do not foretell an accident or predict when the car will fall off into the abyss. They can even tell of the possibilities and conditions of accident and falling off, but not if or when these will occur. If they do occur, the trip will be different from what is expected, but the traveller will not include an accident in the plans for his trip.

By the same token, surprises are not mutations, so that forecasts do not exclude changes. As the man walking the plank knows, continuity alone is a poor basis for prediction. Some changes are clearly to be expected. Not to expect foreseeable mutations is to walk the plank blindfolded. The following forecasts are therefore surprise-free, as they must be, but not change-free.

RESOURCES AND REGIMES

A discussion of future prospects necessarily begins with resources. At present per capita growth rates, with oil-finds counted in, North and West African states divide sharply into two categories. Underdeveloping states with a per capita gross national product (GNP) between $100 and $300 (constant 1977 dollars) have shown little change over the entire decade of the 1970s, little change in the previous decade, and little prospect for improvement in the decade of the 1980s and beyond to the end of the century (see Table 4.1).[2]

TABLE 4.1 *GNP of regions' underdeveloping states*

	1969	*1974*	*1979*	*1984*	*1989*	*1994*
Senegal	341	341	302	300	340	400
Togo	265	284	270	304	317	350
Mauritania	278	321	279	280	280	280
Niger	190	152	185	212	240	280
Gambia	173	188	195	207	220	part of Sene–Gambia
Benin	171	163	191	202	213	250
Sierra Leone	197	212	199	200	201	250
CAR	186	189	196	201	207	220
Guinea Bissau			147	130	125	130
Guinea	180	186	130	140	170	230
Chad	134	118	124	118	113	130
Upper Volta	106	101	95	100	100	100
Mali	92	90	106	113	121	130

SOURCE Figures from the World Bank; projections by the author.

Some oil finds in Togo, Benin and perhaps even Senegal, a possible rise in the prices of phosphates for Togo and uranium for Niger, and a return of greater coherence in governmental decision-making in Chad and CAR or even in the less outstanding cases of Mauritania, Benin, Sierra Leone, Mali and Guinea are all possible improvements that are not likely to change the nature of the picture in this century, any more than is the likelihood of rain in the Sahel in the decade after 1985, welcome as all these eventualities may be as a protection against even worse futures.

On the other end of the spectrum, developing states with a per capita GNP in constant 1977 dollars between $300 and $900 in 1970 rose above $500 in 1980 heading toward $600 to $1400 by 1990, with the two exceptional cases of Gabon and Libya even further out of range of this group (see Table 4.2). Growth in all cases shows sound prospects of continuing; new oil in Cameroon, Ivory Coast, the Congo provides new fuel for growth, as it did in Nigeria in the previous decade, and even possible future political instability in Morocco may have no more dampening effect on growth than did past instability in Liberia and Nigeria.

TABLE 4.2 *GNP of regions' developing states*

	1969	*1974*	*1979*	*1984*	*1989*	*1994*
Cameroon	292	326	400	455	520	600
Liberia	390	450	475	520	570	600
Congo	470	517*	502	550	600	650
Nigeria	355	525	575	700	820	900
Morocco	415	475	575	675	750	850
Ivory Coast	695	735	845	935	1025	1100
Tunisia	505	730	865	1065	1275	1400
Algeria	912	1040	1160	1220	1450	1500
Gabon	1770	2800	2760	3110	3350	3500
Libya	8365	4900	6490	7500		

*1973

In addition to Libya, Ghana has shown very erratic growth patterns since independence but without the assurance of a generally high level found in the North African state. Rising from nearly $400 at the end of the 1960s to a level of $550 through the mid-1970s, Ghana dropped below $300 by the end of the decade and will stay down for most of the 1980s, if not longer. In contrast, what is striking for the region is that in both the underdeveloping and the developing groups the direction and even the rate of the trends are relatively constant.

There is a fairly positive correlation between these two categories of economic growth and respective groups of social conditions as measured by the Physical Quality of Life Index (PQLI), although available PQLI figures are not very sensitive to short-run change. Underdeveloping countries registered a PQLI between 14 and 27, except for Sierra Leone which scored 31; developing countries registered a PQLI between 37 and 51, except for a cluster around 28–31 (Nigeria, Cameroon, Ivory Coast) and a real exception scoring 23 (Gabon). It is not clear what kind of political behaviour or other types of evolution are indicated by various PQLI levels (see Chapter 10).

A more useful figure would be some indication of income distribution, but none is available. The data for a Gini index of income distribution North and West African countries are not obtainable (indeed, population figures are not reliable and GNP figures are an indicative convention rather than an accurate reality, it must be remembered). At best, one can look to some political action toward levelling an offensively unequal distribution in countries such as Gabon and Ivory Coast, directed either against nationals or against the French expatriates, at some time in the future based on a qualitative appreciation of inequalities, but without much precision about time or threshold. Even in these cases, more than inequality is needed for rebellion to take place, and at least in Ivory Coast there is likely to be some government action toward redistribution and reduction of the foreign presence in the aftermath of presidential succession before a public reaction takes things into its own hands. Even in the absence of precise indicators, it can be stated with assurance that Northern and Western African societies are not ripe for revolution during this century.[3] The region has already seen one of the very few revolutions in Africa – in Algeria – and that was the product of a colonisation of unusual magnitude. Purely indigenous revolutions, of which the Ethiopian case is the only one on the continent, require an older established socio-political system than exists anywhere else in Africa.

However, short of revolution and even in the absence of multiple indicators, very different politico-economic cycles can be discerned for the two groups of economies. Developing states are subject to growth cycles, relating to growth, distribution and absorption, but their place in the cycle varies between North and West Africa. North African states passed through the crest of the growth cycle in the 1970s and entered into the distribution and absorption phases at the end of the decade. Algeria under Benjedid (elected president in 1979), Tunisia after the 1978 riots, Morocco after the 1981 riots, even Libya under the 1978 plans of socialist austerity were all countries which had entered into a distributionist phase of politics. If distributionist pressures are quickly met, the country can slip into an absorptionist phase throughout the 1980s, until new pressure rises for greater growth. But if the original pressures are not met in the early 1980s, they will rise to disrupt the political systems involved.

Each country stands at this threshold: in Libya, the regime of Mu'ammar Qadhdhafi needs to meet the grumblings of its middle class claiming their benefits from the oil economy, either by even more severe repression or by greater middle-class association with the regime. In Algeria, the same grumblings were adopted by the National Liberation Front (FLN) party congress in 1980 under the slogan of 'Toward a Better Life' but tangible results must follow or the grumblings may swell behind new military leaders. In Morocco, the Saharan War needs to be ended on popularly acceptable terms or the economic distribution and national integrity issues will coincide to bring down the monarchy. In Tunisia, the distributional issue came at a time when the final steps in successionist politics were being worked out, and, wisely, were accompanied by an opening of the political scene to multi-partyism in the 1981 elections. Thus the challenges in each country are so clear that a political system could scarcely avoid meeting them responsively, although nothing is guaranteed. The most disruptive challenge is in Morocco, the greatest signs of responsiveness in Tunisia.

In West Africa, developing states are near the end of their growth cycle, although the oil-finds may have prolonged the phase for some states. Growth in Congo, Gabon, Ivory Coast, Nigeria and Liberia has slowed down at the turn of the decade and the states are close to the distributionist stage. In a number of states, this change corresponds with a political succession, at the end of the 1970s (Nigeria, Cameroon, Liberia) or – foreseeable in the 1980s (Ivory Coast). The Liberian coup should be seen as a warning that succession can be violently redistributive if the system is not responsive to distributional issues. Whether these states will take the warning seriously or not is a matter of surprises, but there is a good likelihood of a smooth transition into distributional politics.

The underdeveloping states follow different cycles more difficult to identify. One pattern – perhaps linear rather than cyclical – would be a succession of groups among the eligible élite replacing each other at regular intervals through 'succession coups' to enjoy the benefits of office for a while until replaced by the next group – politics of poverty on the earlier Latin American or Syrian pattern. However in these non-African examples, growth finally took place and new types of politics resulted; such a perspective is not now visible for the poorer West African states, and in any case is not likely in this century. Another pattern is also a series of coups at several years' interval but as problem-solvers' rather than pork-barrel coups; the major difference is something resembling ideology, which distinguishes one group from another in trying its hand at governing under conditions of poverty. CAR in the 1970s can be called a shift from one pattern to the other; Upper Volta a case of the second (problem-solvers), Niger and Mali a case of the first (pork-barrel). The third pattern is a stable government which has so worn down expectations that there are no competing groups to challenge it either in the name of benefits nor of efficiency. Many West African states are in this category. In specific terms this means that into the 1980s and probably the 1990s, West African states which have had their military coups may well have more, or may enjoy their stagnation in stability. Among the fourteen states on this list, the exceptional political heritage of pluralism in Senegal and authoritarianism in Guinea should be noted, since both political systems are likely to provide a basis of stability that overcomes the determinism of the economic conditions, Senegal's promise in this direction being greater than Guinea's.

In both groups of states, ruling élites are looking for a social base. At some point in the future, the *evolue* sector will become large enough to split into competing components, not always along socio-economic lines. Such a split may well be ethnic, as has already occurred in Guinea Bissau and Sierra Leone, although the result is not a social basis for a policy majority unless social group and ethnicity are coincident, not a healthy situation. Indeed, a real social basis to policy only comes with the pluralism and division of labour produced by development and probably only when such divisions find expression in competing political groups. Tunisia's budding multi-partyism provides such an opportunity, as do also the multi-party systems of Morocco and Senegal and to an extent Nigeria, although in none of the three last-named states is political change with the opposition in power likely in the 1980s.

It is the rural sector which poses the biggest questions about social basis of rulers and policy. The various scenarios for a 'Green Uprising' which have been identified in theory may be written for some North and West African states in the 1990s and possibly before, but it is more likely that urban dominant politics will still be most widely characteristic by the end of the century. For the peasant mobilisation that does take place is not a rural phenomenon but rather takes the form of an urban exodus. Occasionally, special – usually military – representatives of rural society may rise to kick out the urban rascals, as has already happened in Liberia, Chad and Guinea Bissau and was attempted in Gambia, all at the turn of the decade, but their arrival in power is not likely to do much for the rural society from which they come. Oil and the peasants are the sources of the surplus out of which economic development is paid for (phosphates replacing oil in a few states) and so the rural sector is not likely to provide the social basis for the ruling élite that pursues such a policy.[4]

Thus, into the 1980s and 1990s, the nature of the dominant political organisation has already been set, although its particular shape may evolve. In the poorer states, military regimes are likely to remain military regimes, without the possibilities of institutionalisation produced by design and by death in Algeria. Military coups in a very few civilian regimes, notably Sierra Leone, will bring almost all the poor states under military juntas. In the case of Guinea it is not at all certain that the military will stay out of power at the end of Sekou Toure's rule. The one exception to the military threat among the underdeveloping states is Senegal. As already noted, where a military junta is the dominant political organisation, military coup is the dominant form of succession, occurring more or less frequently according to the different patterns already indicated.

In party states, sharply different futures can be expected throughout the rest of the century. In some states, where a single party is stable and moderately effective, functioning as a sort of Ministry for Mobilisation but nothing much more, it can be expected to remain intact and incumbent throughout the century, although it may well be captured and reorganised by successive ruling groups. Such parties are the FLN in Algeria, the Democratic Parties of Ivory Coast and Gabon, the Cameroonian National Union, and the Congolese Labour Party. In Algeria at the end of the 1970s and in Ivory Coast in the beginning of the 1980s, the party serves as the framework for the mechanisms of succession and élite maintenance as well.

Multi-partyism is the future of a number of other developing states. Only one – Tunisia – finds its multi-party system as an outgrowth of a classical single party but by the end of the 1980s there should be a healthy system of several parties in place, even if the Destourian Socialist Party remains in control of government. The only shadow on this future would be an opposition challenge so great that the incumbent PSD élites could defeat it only through the judicial and police powers of the state, leading to repression of the opposition and artificial return to a single party system. This seems unlikely. In a number of other states – Morocco, Senegal, Nigeria – functioning multi-party systems are likely to continue, their chances of hanging on directly related to the degree of economic growth. Here the only shadow lies in the possibilities of political bickering and pluralistic stalemate that would make these countries' future look like Ghana's, Nigeria's or Morocco's past. If there is not enough growth for several parties to provide fruitful debate on alternative programmes and satisfactory employ for alternating political groups, debate and competition become sterile and debilitating; if there is an independent authoritative head of the polity, as in Morocco (or Egypt), the coup against the parties will come from on high, but if not, as in most countries, it will come from the military. This eventuality was frequently discussed with regard to the future of the new Nigerian democracy but with the success of the 1983 elections the chance of a military return to power seems unlikely. However, the next elections, in 1987, pose an unusual challenge because the incumbent is ineligible to run for president and his past opponents from the Independence Generation will be too old to pose a credible challenge. The 1987 elections will be a test of a new generation as well as of the party system. Senegal is certainly the most fragile of the multi-party systems in the long run because it is the least developing state of the group; Morocco is the most fragile in the short run because of the challenge that the Saharan issue poses to the monarchy.

These organisational forms in turn translate differently into different types of participation and élite-mass relations. Participation in political activity in Africa is low and will remain low as long as greater socio-economic integration is not achieved. Party life is listless and electoral participation is weak. The return to multi-partyism in Senegal, Tunisia and Nigeria have given new life to politics, but since such changes are unlikely in other countries the chances for an increase in participation elsewhere are slim. Algeria and Morocco in the 1970s and Ivory Coast in the early 1980s opened up new possibilities of participation within their political systems by holding a series of elections and intra-party discussions on institutional reforms in the North African cases and by creating competition within the party in the latter case. The provision of several candidates for one position within a single-party state was an innovation begun (in the region) by Algeria and followed by Tunisia and Ivory Coast; it can be adopted elsewhere in single-party systems to increase political involvement and participation, but it is not a replacement for real inter-party competition.

On the other hand, in the non-party states there may be some experiments in creating new transitional institutions that are deemed more authentically African, attempting to bring villages and ethnic politics into new national forms. The most far-reaching is Niger's effort to establish a Development Society based on traditional Hausa forms that are neither party nor parliament but somewhere in between. Working out the ramifications of such a scheme will take as long as Seyni Kountche is in power. Other institutional experiments may be more orthodox, such as the constitution of Benin in 1977 and Togo and Mali in 1979. New coups will bring new constitutions.

In sum, in starting with resources and pursuing implications and evolutions into political forms and processes, the 1980s frequently began with or immediately after a political turning point in constitution-making, electoral or party forms, or other governmental institutional patterns. The aftermath of these changes can be expected to be worked out in the ensuing decade and perhaps beyond. Broadly, African states can be expected to work out the consequences of patterns and routines established in the 1960s and 1970s. Many are the conceivable events that could overthrow these patterns and routines but they are not indicated by the coming ingredients of North and West African internal politics. More changes can be expected from international relations, as will be discussed later, but first one more domestic ingredient must be examined for a final reconfirmation of domestic patterns.

FROM GENERATION TO GENERATION: POLITICS OF 'CLASSES'

North and West Africa face a period of generational stability in the 1980s, with a few exceptions, and then a period of greater instability in the 1990s. Such stability is reinforcing, for it means that exceptional changes in one country are not likely to find an echo in another, the reverse of the situation in the late 1970s when the discovery of the military coup as a way of succession met many polities' needs and swept across the region.[5]

There are some remarkable patterns of generational politics in the region, largely because of the similarity of evolutions imposed by the common 'birthday' of fifteen of the twenty-four countries in 1960. Two-thirds of the states in the region have undergone major generational changes in the late 1970s or early 1980s. This means that one of the major elements of disruptive political change and policy shifts has been eliminated for a while within states, just as a major reason for common causes and contagious movements has been removed among states. It does not mean that all policy differences or intra-generational politics have been abolished, but the limited size of political élites in the young polities of the region means that there are simply not a lot of individuals left outside the incumbent group to provide political alternatives, particularly if the economy is growing enough to permit pay offs to potential dissidents.

About half the states brought in a new middle-aged generation of the Class of 1931 (the median birth date of the cohort) – Gabon, Morocco and Mali in the late 1970s, Nigeria, Algeria, Senegal, Cameroon, CAR, and, foreseeably, Ivory Coast and Tunisia in the early 1980s. The rest brought in a new younger generation of the Class of 1945 – Nigeria briefly, Benin, Niger and Congo in the late 1970s; Mauritania, Upper Volta, Ghana, Chad and Liberia in the early 1980s. Although political attitudes between the two generations differ, they are obviously not oriented in the same directions because of age and experience alone. Still, the Class of 1945 received its secondary and higher education under independent government and under the disappointments (for the most part) of the Independence Generation in power; it is further from the former metropole than its predecessors; and surveys have shown that it holds on to hopes for a democratic justification of power. When the generation includes military leaders, they tend to look for new forms mixing democratic and authoritarian politics rather than finding satisfaction in military rule *per se*. The Class of 1931 divides into a military component which tends to regard military rule as an acceptable corrective for the inadequacies of the preceding Independence Generation, and a civilian component or Post-Independence Generation which sees its incumbency as an extension of the party regime established at the beginning. None of these generations will be old at the end of the 1980s, although by the turn of that decade it will be time for a new generational shift for the Class of 1931. In any case, by the beginning of the 1990s the time will have come for new generations to replace the incumbents in any country where the last previous shift occurred in the 1970s, since fifteen years is about the length of a generation in Africa.

There are always exceptions, both to these patterns and even to the 'fifteen-year rule'. Three states – Libya, Sierra Leone, Togo – brought in new generations with new regimes at the very end of the 1960s and they are getting old in power. In Togo and Libya, the new generations were young when they arrived in office and so have many more actuarial than political years, a situation of some strain. As a result, the regime must either produce some changes that incorporate rising aspirants and provide a functional equivalent for a generational change, or else clamp down on rising opposition and dissidence. Togo and Libya have done both Togo after the abortive coup of 1977 bringing in the new constitutional institutions and officials of 1979, and Libya after the abortive coup of 1975 repressing the opposition and reshuffling the institutions of power. None of these cosmetics is likely to satisfy generational pressures in the longer run, and the 1980s will see a need for change. This pressure causes problems for new polities with only small potential élites, since a younger generation in power pre-empts the possibilities for its own succession when it wears out. The situation is not the same in Sierra Leone, where the new generation of the late 1960s was already old and by the 1980s will be more than ready for replacement. Whether the incumbents will have tired and compromised the potential successors before the latter have had their turn at power on their own, and whether the generational shift can therefore be handled by civilians or will have to be carried out by the military are questions that analysis can pose but only history can answer.

Two other states – Ivory Coast and Guinea – have not had any marked generational change since the 1960s or earlier. Ivory Coast has finally begun preparing for succession and is counted among the states which will undergo a shift to the Class of 1931 in the early 1980s. In Guinea, succession is not yet indicated, although all other analysis would suggest that the time has come and passed. Thus both pose a phenomenon to be explained – the 'seamless' absorption of rising aspirants into power and the blatant suspension of the 'fifteen-year rule'. Interestingly, the causes of the phenomenon are as different as the categories into which the countries fall. In the case of Ivory Coast, as in Gabon and Cameroon which preceded it, absorption has been possible because of the economic growth of the country and its ability to expand employment in high positions and rewards for regional clienteles so successfully that generational discontinuities did not appear and were not able to find other – especially regional or ethnic – issues with which to rally support against the government. Such absorption has been effective in Ivory Coast, which has had the necessary resources as well as a skilful policy of regional politics and absorption, but ineffective in Cameroon, where dissidence in the Bamileke and Northern regions broke out at the end of the 1970s and where regional tensions heightened in 1982. In Guinea, the reverse policy has been successful; political control and repression have kept the small élite off balance and at the mercy of the president. Obviously, the chances of a smooth generational succession appear greater at first glance in the developing than in the underdeveloping states, but reality may be more complicated. Both Guinea and Ivory Coast and Cameroon, at the extremes of their categories, may have established durable habits for their polities.

One final interesting case should be noted: in Nigeria, there has been generational back-tracking, an unusual occurrence in any area.[6] The Class of 1945 which came to power with the Murtala Muhammed and Olusegun Obasanjo coups gave up its power coups gave up its power not just to civilians in 1979, but to civilians from a previous generation, the Class of 1931. A younger élite which has had a taste of office and then retired may be an élite vaccinated against the attractions of power and responsibility, but the vaccine may wear off. In this case, the representatives of the Class of 1945 who held power were military, hence at present occupied and set aside from their classmates; this insulation may keep them out of politics and retain their position as a striking exception. Another development that reinforces this effect is the opportunity opening up political leadership to the civilian members of the Class of 1945 in the 1987 elections. At that time, President Shehu Shagari will be ineligible to succeed himself and a new competitive scramble for positions will give new life to Nigerian party politics.

Thus, exceptional states all face generational pressures in the 1980s. Three – Ivory Coast, Cameroon, Nigeria – have already begun their transition; others may continue to be interesting exceptions to a universal pressure. But most will have to come to terms with it, with changes in the incumbent élite, while the majority of the states in the region continue to operate with the generations in power until well into the 1990s, despite less important inter-generational shifts.

CONTINENTAL CHANGES AND FOREIGN POLICY CHOICES

Many of the cyclical and evolutionary changes foreseeable in North and West Africa point to a rather stable basis of politics in the coming decade, in preparation for more marked changes in the 1990s. The inter-state picture differs sharply, although the starting point is the same. As the resource projections indicate, a number of states will increase their power-base well above the rest and will therefore be able to increase their power, in some cases, over the rest. The relation between ends and means has been a constant parameter in the understanding of international politics; increased means give rise to a growth in goals and increased ends must either find the means of their politics or reduce. By coincidence, North and West Africa contain the major powers of the continent and they are in competition among themselves for regional leadership and dominance just as they coalesce and compete for continental leadership and alliance. Morocco, Algeria, Libya and Nigeria are brought into conflict by the vast power vacuum on their borders that stretches across the Sahara and the Sahel, and the first three are rivals for predominance in their own North African region. Libya's participation in these rivalries and conflicts is intense but short-lived, for other than its tremendous oil-wealth, it does not have the basic ingredients of power and leadership.

Again, the rule of ends and means holds, even in the short run, and helps explain Libyan behaviour.

The attempts of the growing African powers to extend their influence will take a number of forms. On the continental level and beyond, these four states will be leading parties in African and Third World coalitions on various issues, sometimes on the same side (as three are in OPEC on the side of high prices, or two are in the Arab Steadfastness Front on the side of hostility against Israel or as the same two are in the Algerian–Libyan Alliance of Hassi-Hessaoud since 1975). But they may also strike out alone, as Algeria did under Boumedienne when it sought to lead the 'Group of 77' on New International Economic Order issues. Nigeria's NIEO position has been more closely tied to leadership of the African, Caribbean and Pacific associates of the European Communities in the Lome Treaties, and Morocco has had a more solitary position.

Rivalry will also take the form of struggles for spheres of influence in the zone of power vacuum and beyond, and might even break out as direct conflict between the states, either over a common border or over an interposed zone of influence.[7] Algeria has currently offered protection to Tunisia against a Libyan attack and also suggested similar arrangements for Niger and Mali, the latter against externally-based subversion, and it seeks to renew a zone-of-influence relationship over the Mauritanian and Western Saharan region. Libya seeks to extend its zone of influences throughout the Sahelian zone eastward and westward from Chad, notably into Niger, Mali and Mauritania-Sahara, the same countries as interest Algeria but from a more fragile because non-contiguous base. Morocco too crosses zones, by seeking to maintain its influence over the Saharan regions south of it, notably Mauritania and whatever territory lies between Mauritania and Morocco, but its zone does not extend eastward. Nigeria is characteristically less certain of its geographic sphere of influence; while it seeks to replace French influence in French-speaking West Africa, its notion of an actual zone of predominance over some of its more vulnerable neighbours – such as Benin, Togo, Niger and Chad – was not well-developed by the early 1980s, and it will probably take more threats and challenges from this region before a clear policy develops.

In this process of working out ranks and zones, wars are not to be excluded but OAU inhibitions and military limitations do reduce their likelihood. The Chadian problem will certainly continue during the 1980s, as conflicts over the presence and role of the Inter-African Force, the relation between the various Chadian Armed Forces and National Liberation Fronts and the government, and the conduct of elections and the composition of the government are all ingredients of possible military confrontations among Algeria, Libya and Nigeria. Libyan-based and Libyan-backed subversion of Niger and Mali could provoke the same confrontation. Morocco and Algeria have waged a semi-proxy war in the western Sahara (including in Mauritania) since 1975, with Libya joining as a major proxy supporter by the end of the decade; a settlement by referendum in the mid-1980s – the best that can be hoped for – would considerably reduce the chances of non-proxy war, although trailings of the conflict would continue for some years, and the absence of such a settlement would greatly increase the frustration of both Morocco and Algeria and with it the chances of a desperate escalation. At the beginning of the 1980s, Nigeria appeared to have no such causes that would justify a military engagement other than a possible re-escalation of the Chadian collapse, but Nigeria has so often carried a chip on its shoulder in its handling of border incidents with Cameroon and Benin that an inadvertent conflict and even conquest of neighbouring territory is not to be excluded.

There are also lesser states in the region that are increasing their regional security role, in an interesting division of labour that has important future implications. A number of states act as external policemen for neighbours who are reluctant to develop large security forces of their own, both because of their cost and because of the danger of military coups that larger unoccupied armies pose. Thus Senegal intervened regularly in Gambia in the early 1980s until a permanent 'security community' or confederation ensued (to be discussed further later) and Guinea performed the same role with the same regularity in Sierra Leone throughout the 1970s and offered its services in Liberia at the time of the Doe coup. Such security roles are played when civil disturbances (such as food and price riots) and military coups exceed national policy capabilities, and they may be of crucial importance in a country such as Sierra Leone where a difficult succession and military coup may be expected. Although they depend on the disinterested position of the intervening neighbour and its demonstrated willingness to withdraw after restoring order, interventions, as the Gambian events show clearly, can be habit-forming and can lead to changes in the relationship between intervener and intervenee. Short of being the first step toward confederation, interventions indicate the appearance of small spheres of influence. It is notable that such relations have not appeared in the former area of Equatorial Africa, where French dominance in Gabon and CAR and the strong ideological differences among the states inhibit intervention among neighbours.

Many of these relationships constitute the political underpinnings of actual changes in the constituent state units of the regions, either as boundary changes or as annexations. Strong OAU norms govern both, consecrating the boundaries inherited at the moment of independence and legitimising the colonially-inherited state. Events of the 1970s began to nibble at these norms: the Saharan affair posed questions about unions and boundaries, the Libyan claim on the Aouzou strip of Chad and the Ugandan claim on the Kagera salient raised new criteria for boundaries, and the Libyan merger with Chad again posed the problem of unifications. All these aroused criticism from the African community. More important has been the confederation of Sene–Gambia, announced in 1981 and consummated in 1982 with neither criticism nor referendum. Gambia has not quite disappeared in the process, but like Western Cameroon, Eritrea and Zanzibar it is destined to fade away in the long run. Guinea Bissau may be next. As these parallels indicate, however, the fading will not be total nor painless. Equatorial Guinea or at least its insular portion of Fernando Po was in danger of becoming part of Nigeria at an earlier moment but the danger is probably past. Since few other states are so small, mergers are likely to involve more consent and mutual movement and will arrive in one of three ways, in ascending order of time required: (i) as a self-protective act of an incumbent or newly incumbent élite trading state sovereignty for support for its own incumbency; (ii) as a careful movement of two states planning a paced unification together, or (iii) as the outcome of a larger sub-regional economic organisation gradually harmonising its economy and eventually its polity. Although sub-regional organisations are in place (to be discussed later) their timetables for unification stretch beyond the span of this study. Similarly, other than Sene–Gambia, no two states in the early 1980s were planning their unification and the sudden move of a regime to join another is not foreseeable ahead of time. Yet, by the facts, the latter may be the most likely, as the OAU norms against unification continue to be put to the test.

Boundaries too will be put to the test. One way will be with incidents that call for a riposte and lead to a readjustment, either reaffirming or rectifying the current delimitation. The greatest chance for such incidents is on the territorial sea, where new oil-finds along the West African coast will pose conflicts where lines were never very clear. Since a concave coast, with converging boundary lines, is most conflict-prone, the prototype conflicts have already arisen between Nigeria and Cameroon and between Libya and Tunisia in the late 1970s and early 1980s, but other oil finds have appeared since then, with conflict-potential both west and south of Nigeria. These conflicts do not give rise to the same type of boundary changes as land disputes, however, since sea boundaries only involve oil rigs, not people.

In the early 1980s, there were already disputed boundaries between Libya and Chad, Libya and Niger, Libya and Algeria, Morocco–Mauritania–Algeria, and Upper Volta and Mali, and incidents over a boundary line where no dispute was supposed to have existed took place on the Nigerian boundaries with Benin and Cameroon. As this list shows, some boundary problems are old sores that will take years to heal over, particularly since new events and minor incidents are continually reopening them, but many others are completely new wounds where no doubt had been thought to exist on the boundary, and where the motor cause lies in bilateral relations, not in boundary uncertainties. It is therefore not productive to try to predict which boundaries will cause problems in the coming decades: any of them can, and relations among the bounded states are frequently fluid enough to give rise to a boundary dispute.

As a result of these considerations, it is possible to put boundary, intervention, unification and influence problems into some sort of perspective. Boundary disputes can arise anywhere to trouble uncertain relations between states already suspicious of each other, and can escalate to the point where boundary rectifications or reaffirmations are the result. Only bully regimes, such as Uganda's Amin or Libya's Qadhdhafi, are likely to carry such problems further, to the point of claiming sizeable pieces of neighbouring territory, and (in 1984) no other bullies but Qadhdhafi are around for the moment. But for other growing states, new means of dominance and aggrandisement are available that go beyond boundary disputes. The possibility of intervention to help a beleaguered neighbouring regime, the ability to provide advisors, assistance and security guarantees over a sphere of influence, and even the occasion to enter into a self-intensifying confederation are all scenarios for the 1980s and 1990s, particularly in West Africa but also with players from North Africa as well.

The possibilities of reaction as well as action must also be considered, for, as seen, African states' support of OAU norms has been as much of a restraint on African states as has been the low level of means to act. The most common form of reaction is the balance-of-power alliance against the rising power, as exemplified (with a little help from some non-African states) by the African meetings and countermeasures against Libya in Chad in the early 1980s. No one is likely to coalesce to save Gambia, which is just as well, nor would a coming-together of Guinea, Liberia and Sierra Leone provoke much reaction. A strong move by Algeria, Morocco,

Libya, or Nigeria against a neighbour, or against each other could lead to African states taking sides, particularly if an ideological dimension were involved or if the conflict were part of one of the states' drive for continental leadership. Such possibilities are quite likely in the coming decades, particularly if domestic politics enters a distributionist period. They may be even more likely at the end of the 1980s and into the 1990s when new generational shifts appear. These coalitions and alliances, however, are likely to exist within the OAU and not grow in solidarity, organisation and importance to the point where they challenge the organisation itself as a framework for Africa's concert system of politics.

Short of the continent, however, there is an organisation with some serious decisions to make and conflicts to contain and this is West Africa's Economic Community (ECOWAS).[8] In general, one may expect sub-regional interaction to intensify in Africa in the future, and ECOWAS is merely one of the examples of this intensification. Its growth is mapped out for the future in its economic integration plans; deadlines have not been respected to date, but they cannot continue to be postponed if the Community is to exist as planned. The more it integrates, the more it creates tensions among members and demands changes in their orientations. Two types of conflict are foreseeable within ECOWAS, which, if overcome, will create a strong organisation of co-operation by the end of the century.

One is the conflict inherent in the relation between the large economy of Nigeria and the rest. Nigeria has a market, in population terms, half as large again as the rest of ECOWAS combined, and a GNP twice as large as the rest of the ECOWAS members, even though its GNP per capita is by no means the highest. Even though the stakes and details are economic, the tactics can be classically political: smallest states can put themselves under the protection of the giant or group along with a middle-sized state against the giant; middle-sized states can try to raise themselves to the level of a lieutenant of the giant or to gather the smallest states around it. Thus, Togo worked with Nigeria to foster the creation of the Community, Ivory Coast and Ghana joined in the effort to bring in the remaining states. Once these dynamics of creation were worked out, the discussions on the mechanics of integration began and will continue along the same lines.

The other conflict is between ECOWAS' efforts at self-sufficiency and integration and the counter-attractions of external ties and integration, notably in the franc zone. These competing ties are formalised in two organisations, the West African Monetary Union (UMOA) of Senegal, Mali, Ivory Coast, Upper Volta, Niger, Dahomey and Togo, and the West African Economic Community (CEAO) of Senegal, Mali, Mauritania,

Ivory Coast, Upper Volta, and Niger. Currently, the latter competes with ECOWAS for funding and development projects, although the result is probably more parallel complementarity than actual competition. At some point, CEAO will become either superfluous or a real competitor for efforts and allegiance; in the early 1980s, for example, both had newly-created defence agreements, the smaller of which (CEAO) was doubtless already superfluous if the larger had any validity. Even more of a conflict will arise toward the end of the 1980s or the 1990s from the efforts to create an ECOWAS economic union against the franc zone Monetary Union (UMOA). The two cannot coexist, and how willing franc zone states will be to leave the fold for reliance on the Nigeria *naira* or how willing France will be to loosen an important strand in the African role are important questions to be fought out. If much of the answer depends on the vigour of the Economic Community, the rest depends on the political will of the members and their outside ally. There is no way to predict this outcome; one can only foresee the conflict and its ingredients.

GLOBAL CONDITIONS AND REGIONAL RESPONSES

Attempts to understand the parameters of future developments in North and West Africa in this survey have thus far concentrated on the region itself, in the belief that events in Africa are primarily self-determined. This is more than an analytical assumption, it is also a factual observation and a philosophical or epistemological position. The time when events in Africa were primarily determined abroad is past and with its passing observers' mentalities and analytical positions have (or should have) changed. Africans are independent, operating in an interdependent world, and to think that they cannot make their own decisions about their own destinies is neo-colonialist analysis. To be sure, Africa is not a planet: events from the other islands of the world impinge on it and these outside events are not determined by Africa. But Africans determine the way in which they will react to these events, and they provide events of their own to which outsiders decide their own reactions. If Africans' range of choices in a particular reaction is sometimes limited, it should be remembered that outsiders' range of choices is also often limited in reacting to African events. This survey cannot extend to a forecast of external events that are likely to impinge on Africa in the rest of the century, but it can identify two sets of external relations and identify likely ranges and directions of choice.

The first concerns the French commitment, a moral obligation and politico-economic opportunity which France perceives toward North and West Africa (and not toward most of South and East Africa).[9] This commitment covers economic support, including aid and investment, cultural presence, and politico-military intervention. No other Western state bears the same sort of commitment, so that it makes sense to single out France for special examination. There is no likely diminution of French feelings of engagement toward Africa. The beginning of the 1980s saw the second most important shift in French politics since World War Two, and yet the strength and direction of French operations in Africa remained unchanged.

The Gaullist legacy in French politics is proving to be as powerful as the Napoleonic tradition, and an important element in Gaullism is the use of African states as a French zone of influence, a source of French support, and an area of French cultural and economic presence. All this requires an equal commitment from the French side for support for its Africans. However, as African needs and opportunities grow, this commitment will require a little help from France's friends in order to remain credible, and so French interest in Africa will oblige France to bring in its Western allies in support of its own concerns, both economic, political and security. While recognising this need, France will also continue to react against it, its hesitations undermining the reliability of its commitment. France's primary area of concern is the 'active zone' from Senegal–Mauritania to Zaire, where its cultural, economic, political and security interests are strongest. Should these interests weaken or the sense of commitment falter, inter-African conflict would probably increase in the absence of an effective damper. No one else can pick up France's role: Nigeria will not be ready during the 1980s, an Inter-African Force of the OAU or of the competing West African regional organisations (CEAO and ECOWAS) is not capable of an organised and decisive action, and Libya's military power would find no effective counter if France does not maintain its role of military backstop to African norms.

The other theme of external relations concerns Africa in the Cold War. The first two decades in independence were characterised by remarkably little cold war conflict in Africa. In part, this was because, ever since the defining incident of the Congo affair in the early 1960s, Africa was recognised to be a non-aligned part of the West, its conflicts outside direct East–West involvement and its political system free to take their own forms independent of Eastern or Western models. In part, the absence of cold war conflict was testimony to the force of a cold war convention that banned direct East–West confrontation; whoever was there first won the hand, it being understood that the West was there first until the Soviet Union turned the table in a few places in the late 1970s. The question for the future is therefore whether new targets of opportunity for the Soviet Union such as the Ethiopian revolution and the Angolan liberation will arise to provoke an American reaction in North and West Africa.

There is no doubt that recognisable revolutions are not for this century in the area, just as certainly as wars of national liberation against colonial rulers are a thing of the past. But this does not prevent wars of national liberation to be undertaken against African governments by movements fighting for a 'second independence' or redistributionist regimes coming to power through coups and then calling on Soviet assistance. Polisario and Frolinat were examples of the former in the late 1970s and early 1980s, and Sergeant Doe and Captain Sankara moved in the latter direction until the United States and France caught them in time. Such possibilities are not to be excluded, leading to a kind of Cuban missile crisis in Western Sahara, Guinea, Sierra Leone, Togo, Benin, or Congo (since 1981 the only North or West African state with a friendship treaty with the Soviet Union).[10] Alternatively, a Syrian or even Afghan type of event in Libya, leading to direct Soviet intervention and even replacement of Qadhdhafi, is conceivable.

Whatever the Western tolerance for a radical African regime – and such tolerance has been great in the past – Soviet presence behind such a regime in a region as close to NATO as North and West Africa would almost certainly draw a Western (French and American) reaction and a cold war confrontation. To evaluate the chances of such an eventuality is obviously more difficult than identifying the scenario itself, since much depends on the direction of politics within the Kremlin. But the change in global relations that such an eventuality represents is so great – as great as the Angolan or Ethiopian events – that it can be judged unlikely, even if not impossible. Angola and Ethiopia were unique events, not repetitions, and a new Cuban missile crisis (or Guinean naval crisis) would also be unique. Much more likely is the continuation of Africa's struggle with limited means against its own conditions of underdevelopment at home and neglect by the outside world.

NOTES

1. Out of a growing and not always helpful literature, some useful references include Oskar Morgenstern, Klaus Knoor and Klaus Heiss,

Long Term Projections of Power: Political, Economic and Military Forecasting (Cambridge: Ballinger, 1973) and Stephen J. Korbrin, *Managing Political Risk Assessment: Strategic Response to Environmental Change* (Berkeley: University of California Press, 1982).
2. Figures in the tables and the text on Gross National Product (GNP) are from the World Bank; projections are by the author.
3. See Richard Sandbrook, *The Politics of Basic Needs: Urban Aspects of Assaulting Poverty in Africa* (Toronto: University of Toronto Press, 1982).
4. See Keith Hart, *The Political Economy of West African Agriculture* (New York: Cambridge, 1983) and I. William Zartman and Christopher Delgado (eds), *The Political Economy of Ivory Coast* (New York: Praeger, 1984).
5. See Colin Legum *et al.*, *Africa in the 1980s* (New York: McGraw-Hill, 1979), I. William Zartman (ed.), *The Political Economy of Nigeria* (New York: Praeger, 1983), Naomi Chazan, *The Anatomy of Ghanaian Politics: Managing Political Recession, 1969–1982* (Boulder: Westview, 1983), and Yves Faure and J. F. Medard (eds), *Etat et bourgeoisie en Cote d'Ivoire* (Paris: Karthala, 1982).
6. See Zartman (ed.) *The Political Economy of Nigeria*. This chapter was written before the Buhari coup on the last day of 1983.
7. See Yassin El-Ayouty and I. William Zartman (eds), *The Organization of African Unity after Twenty Years* (New York: Praeger, 1984).
8. Peter Robson, *Integration, Development and Equity: Economic Integration in West Africa* (London: George Allen & Unwin, 1983) and Achi Atsain, 'West African Economic Groupings', in Zartman and Delgado (eds), *The Political Economy of Ivory Coast*.
9. See Bruce Arlinghaus (ed.), *African Security Issues* (Boulder: Westview, 1984).
10. Libya and USSR agreed 'in principle' to sign a Friendship Treaty but have not yet done so; (*Le Monde*, 22 March 1983).

5 Regional Trends and South Africa's Future

ROGER SOUTHALL

More attention has been devoted in the past to the analysis of the future of southern Africa than to that of any other region on the continent. The region's mineral and industrial wealth, the complex *mèlange* of races and cultures, the long history of co-operation and conflict between settlers and indigenes, and the extent of Western involvement in capital formation and investment in the diverse states have all played their part in granting southern Africa this prominence in debate about Africa's future. But in particular, the slower progress of the different countries of Southern Africa towards decolonisation and/or 'majority rule' as compared with virtually the whole of the rest of the continent has centred analysis upon the issues raised by the longevity of white minority rule; in other words, what are the prospects for regional stability or change, reform or revolution? To what extent is settler-rule dependent upon or independent of support from the capitalist west? What would be the global and strategic consequences of a fundamental change in class and race relations throughout the region? And so on.

Because South Africa has emerged, historically, as the hegemonic power, and because, too, of its geographic isolation from black Africa until recent times, analysis of regional change initially centred upon the prospects for development and liberation in the surrounding or 'buffer' territories. But the rapid pace of events during the last few years – the collapse of Portuguese rule in Angola and Mozambique, the manifest rise of black resistance in South Africa itself, the militant struggle being waged for the liberation of Namibia and, most recently and symbolically, the transition to 'majority rule' in Zimbabwe – has ensured that detailed consideration of the future prospects for the final liberation of the people of South Africa from apartheid rule has now been placed high upon the historical agenda.

The intent in this chapter is to provide a somewhat speculative review of South Africa's options, not merely to elucidate the potentialities of these diverse alternatives, but in particular to relate them to the broader regional context, for fundamental restructuring of the 'core' is widely recognised as having liberating possibilities for the 'periphery'. Such an immodest topic can hardly be adequately completed within the space of a few pages, so the sweep of the discussion that follows is based on analysis of some very general identifiable trends. Certainly, there is no rash attempt here to spell out the likely specifics of future change nor to proffer any particular timetable of events; on the other hand, the scope of the subject suggests that excessive caution would be misplaced, if only because a major purpose of the present exercise is to provoke further discussion. With this in mind, therefore, possible futures for South Africa will be located within the context of four broad probable tendencies within the region. These are: (i) increasing militarisation; (ii) increasing political confrontation between South Africa and neighbouring states, (iii) the increasing economic disengagement of black from white Africa and (iv) the increasing internationalisation of conflict within southern Africa.

PRELUDE TO LIBERATION? TRENDS WITHIN THE REGION

The Portuguese coup of 1974 and the dramatic events that it engendered were widely acknowledged as breaking the logjam in southern Africa. Whereas to many it had previously appeared that white power in southern Africa was secure, the decolonisation of Angola and Mozambique now clearly undermined the position of the white minority regimes in Rhodesia, Namibia and South Africa. Subsequently, the accession to independence of Zimbabwe under the most radical option that was available plunged the apartheid regime into a crisis involving, ***inter alia***, a dissipation of confidence amongst whites and the fissure of the ruling National Party, hesitant government-led attempts to stabilise the system of racial domination by reform from within and an inability to pursue a coherent policy towards the future of Namibia. It is the continuation of this crisis to the present day which has propelled South Africa towards a higher level of confrontation with neighbouring African states. The brief examination that follows will suggest that these present developments point to the direction that conflict will take regionally.

The Militarisation of the Region

One of the major developments in recent years has been the development of armed struggle by the liberation movements (most notably the African National Congress) against the apartheid regime. This growing offensive is a consequence of two main factors. First, the collapse of South Africa's protective *cordon sanitaire* of white-ruled states which has enabled the liberation movements to conduct their armed operations (with or without the permission of host governments) from the sanctuary of neighbouring territories. Second, the flow of black youths out of South Africa after the 1976 Soweto uprising has provided a continuing supply of recruits for the liberation movements. Consequently, since 1977, South Africa has been confronted by a marked upward trend in guerrilla activity which is today characterised by a far greater efficiency than the sabotage campaign conducted by the ANC or PAC in the early 1960s.

According to one source, the recent development of armed resistance has passed through distinct phases. The *first* arose out of the events of 1976 and the confrontations of the Soweto youth with the state. Initially resorting to improvised weapons to protect themselves against armed assault by the police, the students responded by attacks upon the symbols of authority and later upon police, vehicles and industrial and rural targets. The *second* phase, beginning in late 1976, was characterised by more organised forms of attack and sabotage, with individuals acquiring explosives and groups being formed to conduct specific acts of armed struggle. Illustrative of this stage were the acts of sabotage, such as a petrol-bomb attack on the Jabulani police station in Soweto conducted by the so-called 'Suicide Squad' of the Soweto Students Representative Council, there probably being some link with the ANC, with the latter providing elementary training in guerrilla warfare and possibly also some explosives. Finally, the *third* phase, characterised by deliberate confrontation by insurgents with the security forces was inaugurated with an attack by three ANC guerrillas against the Moroka police station in Soweto in May 1979, being followed thereafter by a series of such assaults, including the successful sabotage of the Sasolburg and Secunda oil refineries in June 1980 and the August 1981 rocket attack upon the major Voortrekkerhoogte military base outside Pretoria.[1]

The significance of this higher level of insurgency lies not in any immediate threat to white rule and state security, but in its longer-term implications. Together with the scores of trials involving ANC guerrillas in recent years, the attacks on SASOL, the several raids on police stations, the assassinations of state witnesses, black policemen and security agents, all testify to the ANC's growing military campaign. Furthermore, while the increasing scale of the ANC's guerrilla operations is bound to impress the black population, the apparent policy of generally restricting attacks to strategic rather than civilian targets enables the movement to enhance its international as well as its domestic acceptability. However, successful as some of its military operations have been, the ANC has not yet been able to mount a sustained campaign of insurgency, even if the scattered actions of the insurgents make considerable demands on the security forces; and whilst there is ample evidence of the ANC's developing capacity to wage a campaign of urban sabotage, the regime's strategists also warn of the dangers of the Bantustans becoming guerrilla sanctuaries.[2]

Hitherto, the ANC's guerrilla campaign has been constrained by the limitations imposed by the governments of countries neighbouring South Africa. Whilst Malawi continues to refuse to have any links with the external movements (and maintains its political and diplomatic links with South Africa) the BLS states (Botswana, Lesotho and Swaziland) – which are all acutely dependent upon South Africa – are adamant in denying the use of their territories for guerrilla operations, even though they are prepared to offer sanctuary to South African refugees and political exiles. Mozambique – with whose government the ANC enjoys close relations – allows guerrilla cadres to use its space for transit to South Africa, but not to maintain training or military camps on its soil, whilst the Zimbabwe Government allows the Congress a political presence with promise of practical support but denies it use of its territory for establishing guerrilla bases on the grounds that this would invite South African military aggression. (Beyond the immediate front line, the ANC has camps in Tanzania and Angola, and maintains friendly ties with Zambia.) Yet despite the fact that South Africa's neighbours are understandably nervous about harbouring too large or open an insurgent presence, it is probable that, as time wears on, ANC guerrillas will make increasing use of their territories as sanctuaries (with or without official assent) and that, come what may, these states will be drawn into the maelstrom of escalating armed conflict.[3] Cross-border raids by South Africa upon ANC refugee and guerrilla camps will necessitate a marked increase in military expenditure and defensive preparedness, this in turn diverting funds and effort from the development process, heightening instability and leading to the increased prominence of the military in political life.

The South African response to the rising tide of armed struggle has been fourfold. First, it has undertaken a mobilisation of its armed forces and an expansion of its military capacity. Thus military expenditure in

South Africa has soared from R707m. in 1974 to around R3000m. in 1981–2, whilst defence expenditure since 1970 has risen 15 per cent per annum and in 1980 represented over 14 per cent of the total budget.[4] Meanwhile, the size of the defence force has increased correspondingly. Official figures are not released, but according to available information, total armed forces increased from 63 250 (including 45 250 conscripts) in July 1979 to 86 050 (including 66 250 conscripts) in 1980. Additional to these are some 100 000 Army, 10 000 Navy and 25 000 Air Force reservists, as well as some 110 000 Commandos (civilian members of local guard units), 35 000 police and 20 000 police reserves, while recent developments have also included the formation of ethnically based black units within the Republic, Namibia and the 'independent' Bantustans.[5]

Associated with this mobilisation of military manpower is a closer relationship between the government and private sector in the military–industrial complex. South Africa's own arms industry has been long-established (so that now the country produces about 80 per cent of all its weapons with some thousand companies holding contracts or sub-contracts from the Armaments Board) but since 1976 (and the 1977 UN Mandatory Arms Embargo) there has been an increased emphasis on an import substitution programme both in weapons and in other strategic areas (such as fuel production and storage). Finally, the most ominous aspect of the apartheid regime's military build-up is its (not admitted but not denied) development of nuclear weapon capability.[6] Pretoria's refusal to sign the Non-Proliferation Treaty has led to growing international concern, and has prompted Nigeria to express interest in developing its own bomb if South Africa turns out to have one.[7]

The third aspect of the South African military response has been an aggressive campaign of destabilisation designed to heighten the costs to regional governments of giving support to the ANC. This was most vividly illustrated by a raid across the Mozambican border in January 1981 upon an alleged ANC headquarters at Matolo (a suburb of Maputo) in which about a dozen Congress members were captured or killed, and a similar assault upon Maseru in December 1982, when some thirty ANC guerrillas (which the Lesotho Government subsequently indicated were all legitimate refugees or visitors to the country) along with some dozen unfortunate Basotho civilians. Meanwhile, South Africa also gives military and logistical support to the Mozambique National Resistance Movement, an anti-Frelimo force which was previously supported by the white regime in Rhodesia. Estimated as numbering between 2000 and 4000 activists at any one time, the MRM has been responsible since 1980 for extensive sabotage (such as the blowing up of the Pungue River bridge and the vital oil-pipeline from Beira to Mtare which, closed since sanctions were applied to rebel Rhodesia in 1966, would – if left unmolested – curtail Zimbabwe's total dependence upon South Africa for fuel. Meanwhile, the Zimbabwe Government has persistently accused South Africa of being engaged in recruiting Zimbabweans with a view to the future destabilisation of Zimbabwe. Apart from the well-known incorporation of former Selous Scouts and other Rhodesian whites into the South African Defence Force, Pretoria is also known to have recruited up to 5000 Shona-speaking soldiers (many of them former members of Bishop Muzorewa's auxiliary forces) and to be training them in the northern Transvaal. Further, while it would seem that the collapse of the accord between the ZANU and ZAPU wings of the Zimbabwean government reflects indigenous conflict, there is little doubt that South Africa has been fuelling the flames, notably by supporting rebel activities (such as the destruction on the ground of fully one-quarter of the Zimbabwean Air Force in July 1982) carried out by former white Rhodesians. In addition, numerous acts of cross-border violence perpetrated against South African refugees, together with such incidents as bomb explosions, have also been recorded in Botswana, Lesotho and Swaziland, whilst Zambia has complained of armed attacks by South Africa across the Caprivi Strip.[8]

Qualitatively different from the destabilisation strategy (because of its greater scale and different objectives) is the fourth factor, that is, the extent of South Africa's current military operations in Angola. During 1981, the Angolan authorities recorded a total of 2045 military attacks by South Africa. These were composed of 95 ground operations; 74 'concentrations of men and materials' (*sic*); 1651 reconnaissance flights; 161 bombing raids and strafing attacks; and 64 landings of heliported troops.[9] Designed in this case to counter the long-running insurgency campaign waged by SWAPO, the South African operations are closely linked to the government's broader political objectives in Namibia.

Since the civil war in 1975–6, the Angolan army has been gradually built up from an improvised guerrilla force into a conventional army using sophisticated equipment on the assumption that the country's front-line position would sooner or later bring it into direct confrontation with South Africa. Importantly, this defensive build-up has included the installation of Soviet-supplied missiles around key towns and some of the more important SWAPO bases in a bid to curtail South African control of southern Angolan air-space. It was in large measure to confront this developing Angolan defensive capability that the SADF launched Operation Protea in August 1981. A major incursion involving a force of up to 11 000 men on the ground with extensive air support, the eight-day invasion involved a major engagement with the Angolan army (South Africa claiming to have killed as many as 1000 Angolan soldiers and SWAPO guerrillas).[10] Combined with their extensive backing given to the still active UNITA movement of Jonas Savimbi in southern Angola, the South African objective appears to be the destruction of SWAPO's fighting capabilities as the prelude to a Pretoria-designed political settlement in Namibia forged with or without international approval.

The cycle of violence and counter-violence into which southern Africa has now been plunged by the intransigence of the apartheid regime will inevitably spiral upwards. Indeed, the prospect at the moment is one of an intractable war whose likely outcome will be ambiguous. But before elaborating upon this prospective ambiguity it is necessary to turn to analysis of other long-term trends.

Growing Political Confrontation

Detailed analyses of the political and diplomatic networks in southern Africa, as well as of the economic and transport relationships between South Africa (as the core state) and other (variously dependent) national entities within the region, stress that there is necessarily accommodation as well as confrontation between the apartheid Republic and surrounding African states.[11] Indeed, it was upon the basis of common ground existing between Pretoria and the Front Line States (particularly Zambia) in bringing about an end to the Rhodesian conflict that the entire *dètente* exercise was premissed. Now that Zambabwe has been prised free from minority rule (see next chapter), however, the indications are that South Africa and her neighbours are set on an opposing course which will escalate political confrontation at the expense of pragmatic mutual accommodation.

In the first place, the militarisation of the region is itself a major precipitant of a higher level of tension. In particular, continuing South African occupation of Namibia provides a basis for extensive diplomatic co-operation between the Front Line States (FLS). For so long as South African forces attempt to pound SWAPO into submission, to sustain UNITA subversion of the MPLA government in Luanda and to engage Angolan forces freely in aggressive forays far beyond the border, awareness of the need for a defensive bond, perhaps extending beyond diplomatic and political to explicit military co-operation, will foster the developing linkages between neighbouring black regimes. Furthermore, refusal by South Africa to accept terms for an internationally approved settlement in Namibia will only strengthen the resolve of the FLS to isolate South Africa, leading to increased pressure at the UN for the implementation of sanctions. Whereas, since 1978, Pretoria has stalled successive efforts by the Contact Group of five Western nations (US, Britain, West Germany, France and Canada) to forge agreement between South Africa, SWAPO and the FLS, continued sabotage of international negotiations, and any attempt to promote an 'internal' settlement (by building up so-called 'moderate' domestic forces) will further polarise regional relations and serve only to convince African states of the necessity for greater force in confronting South African intransigence.[12]

The basis for greater political co-operation amongst African states has already been laid with the formation of SADCC (the Southern African Development Co-ordination Conference) a regional grouping which includes all the internationally-recognised black-ruled states of Southern Africa, namely, Angola, Botswana, Lesotho, Malawi, Mozambique, Swaziland, Tanzania, Zambia and Zimbabwe. Although designed primarily to promote economic liberation through co-ordinated development initiatives, SADCC is likely also to forge political solidarity between regional states of diverse ideological perspectives united by their common opposition to apartheid. Originating in an anticipation of Zimbabwean independence and a desire for a more comprehensive organisation promoting regional conflict resolution and economic development amongst the Front Line States, there was a recognitition of the need to draw in the three non-participant states (Lesotho, Malawi and Swaziland) and loosen the ties which their conservative leaderships maintained with Pretoria. Whilst membership of an internationally-recognised independent Namibia would do much to underwrite its strategic and economic significance, SADCC's likely close relations with the South African liberation movements will increase its distance from Pretoria, which already views it as subversive of its own 'Constellation of Southern African States' initiative. Thus although SADCC faces formidable obstacles in its attempt to ensure that internal dissension flowing from diverse national interests does not preclude or delay attainment of its most crucial objectives, a common awareness among member states of the complexities of dependence, a willingness to tolerate aparently contradictory policies arising therefrom, and a growing consciousness of the aggressive nature of South African hegemony all contribute to the prospect of a developing regional solidarity.[13]

All this is not to say that the liberation struggle will henceforth be graced by unanimity of action and purpose by the SADCC nine. Countries as far apart in their foreign policies, ideologies and development strategies as Malawi and neighbouring Mozambique are unlikely to reach agreement over a wide spectrum of issues; and, notwithstanding a growing understanding of the common problems which they share stemming from their dependency and underdevelopment, their leaderships will at times adopt divergent, even opposing, policies in response to their own particular needs. In addition, there will be occasions when African governments make deals with Pretoria which will be thoroughly dictated by political expediency, and which will be plainly counterproductive to the liberation process. But overall, as South African regional hegemony, so convincing just a decade ago, becomes ever less daunting now that the minority regime has lost its protective buffer and is being perceptibly weakened by mounting black political consciousness, developing labour militancy, ANC military penetration and acute white uncertainty, black African states within the region are likely to be drawn together by a growing conviction that time is running out for the apartheid regime. If, as is likely, support and recognition of the ANC as the legitimate successor to white power grow in proportion (not only from a commitment to the liberation struggle *per se* but as a result of a deft sense of historical timing which suggests the wisdom of aligning with the perceived future victors) then South Africa will be locked into a political isolation from which no outward-looking African policy will be able to bring long-lasting relief.

Economic Disengagement from South Africa

The extent to which neighbouring African states are economically subordinate to South Africa has been elaborated in a host of works.[14] Suffice to note here that, historically, while they have been drawn into a condition of dependence (to a lesser or greater extent) as suppliers of migrant labour to South Africa's mines, farms and industries, the economies of the surrounding territories have also been structured by such factors as South Africa's centrality in the regional communications network and their reliance upon an adequate flow of capital and consumer goods, investment, technology and fuel (especially oil) from the apartheid republic. Even so, despite the enormity and complexity of the development problems which they face, there are a number of indications which suggest that, although the white republic's black neighbours will by no means be able to disentangle themselves from the web of dependence in which they are enmeshed, there will probably be something of a trend towards economic disengagement from South Africa.

A move towards disengagement is, first and foremost, an act of deliberate policy. Thus SADCC's objectives – the reduction of regional dependence upon South Africa, the promotion of regional integration, and the mobilisation of resources for development, all involving a higher level of international co-operation – indicate a political commitment to 'economic liberation'. SADCC is perhaps remarkable for its deliberately modest, pragmatic goals. Accepting that the nine member states are committed to diverse political–economic paths and ideologies, the emphasis is upon co-ordination of concrete joint programmes (on a bilateral or multilateral basis) which are of common interest to all participants. Initial priority is therefore being given to (i) restoring and upgrading the transportation and communication networks (Zimbabwean independence having been crucial to the viability of SADCC in that its roads, railways and borders with three FLS together with its relatively diversified economy, plug an otherwise gaping hole) and (ii) increasing food security, 'involving improved storage, increased production, joint approaches to food-aid and importing, and emergency food transfers between member states.'[15] Thus 'development co-ordination, in this context, involves not the assertion of alternative priorities (which might be divisive) but consolidation of linkages across national boundaries'; and because the approach is geared towards meeting basic needs, 'governments can agree on their security in spite of underlying ideological differences or disagreements on details of implementation'.[16]

Sobered by the unhappy experiences of previous integrative efforts in East and Southern Africa, there is a determination to ensure that SADCC can walk before it attempts to run. Indeed, although SADCC is viewed as part of the broader liberation process, its present objective is to co-ordinate regional economic activities for development rather than to implement an economic offensive against South Africa. Liberation is accepted as an ultimate goal, but the gradual alteration of functional economic patterns is seen as a prior step towards that longer-term end. Necessarily, however, SADCC also involves preparation for the likely response of South Africa (probably involving cutting off food supplies, transport and key imports) to the imposition of sanctions, recognition being granted to the fact that although South Africa is clearly capable of destroying virtually any key facility within the region (such as the Beira–Mtare pipeline), too overt aggression would alienate international sympathy and involve corresponding costs.

Yet too much should not be expected of SADCC. Clearly, a fundamental re-structuring of regional relations is beyond its foreseeable scope. However, its importance lies in the fact that, because all member states recognise the immense threat posed by an aggressively defensive South Africa, SADCC is likely to develop as a factor of regional importance, and one which will chip away at the foundations of South African hegemony.

There are other factors which are likely to be important in weakening the links between South Africa and her neighbours. Firstly, the proportion of South African exports going to the rest of Africa is declining. With post-war expansion of the manufacturing sector in South Africa being premissed upon the promotion of exports, Pretoria's 'outward-looking' foreign policy in the 1960s and early 1970s was in significant measure directed at expanding the continental African market to compensate for the Republic's lack of competitiveness with other industrial countries and long distance from other markets. Notwithstanding an OAU boycott on trade with South Africa, the outward thrust initially prospered, not only as the white Republic expanded its role as the major supplier of capital and consumer goods to neighbouring states (this being enhanced rather than diminished by the post-UDI imposition of sanctions upon Rhodesia, an alternative producer) but also by a successful connection with a number of francophone states. Thus between 1966 and 1976, South African exports to other parts of Africa rose by R256m. to R453m. an increase of 130 per cent; imports rose by R181m. to R310m. an increase of 141 per cent, giving a healthy balance of trade surplus in South Africa's favour. Yet despite this growth in the absolute levels of trade, the outward thrust was soon to encounter serious obstacles, so that while 19 per cent of South African exports went to Africa in 1964 holding constant until 1971 (18.6 per cent) the proportion dropped thereafter to 10 per cent by 1980. This was because (i) despite the fact that South Africa today claims to deal directly or indirectly with some 47 of Africa's 51 independent states, much of this trade is conducted by the 'back door'. In other words, apartheid continues to form a major obstacle to the full and open exploitation of the African market, and (ii) South Africa's exclusion from special access rights to the EEC (which she might have received had she been able to retain her Commonwealth membership) hampers her export drive into Africa, as many African states are now re-emphasising their trading relations with Europe under the Lome Convention.

At the present time (1984), the bulk of South Africa's trade is accounted for by the southern African periphery, especially Zimbabwe, but also the three BLS states, Mozambique, Zambia, Zaire and Mauritius.

Paradoxically, however, this regional strength could well turn out a weakness, for if – as indicated above – disengagement initiatives undertaken by SADCC states, either together or singly, were to meet with any extent of success, then their impact upon South Africa would be likely to be disproportionate.[17]

There is another link with regional states that South Africa herself is weakening. Since the early 1970s, a complex of reasons (notably the rise in the price of gold facilitating the payment of wages that are more competitive with the previously higher-paying industrial sector, a growing surplus of domestic black labour and the uncertainties of dependence upon foreign suppliers) has led to a shift by the mines away from the utilisation of foreign labour towards the increased recruitment of workers from within the borders of the Republic itself; hence the South African component of the gold-mines rose from some 22 per cent in 1974 to approximately 50 per cent in 1977, with the trend continuing. Although this necessarily posits a critical situation for the labour-supplying territories (especially such highly dependent entities as Botswana and Lesotho) it further polarises the region economically, for countries receiving reduced migrant remittances will be proportionately less able to absorb South African exports. More significant over the long term, however, is that countries such as Mozambique and Zimbabwe (upon which the axe has fallen particularly hard) will have had the necessity of disengagement, and the provision of alternative employment opportunities, thrust upon them. Both their direct dependence and South Africa's leverage will have been reduced.[18]

Finally, there is one last factor which, over the long term, could prove important: South Africa is short of the power on which her industrial expansion is in large measure predicated, and has consequently found it necessary to draw these from sources such as the Ruacana Dam in Angola, the Cabora Bassa dam in Mozambique, and (in time to come) the Malibamatso Hydro-electric scheme in Lesotho (for which negotiations are being conducted at the present time). Thus although there is no doubt that the Republic will remain the region's overwhelmingly dominant economic power, control over the supply of a major portion of its power and resource requirements could constitute an important counter-balance for South Africa's neighbours. Combining with the various problems – such as the growing militancy of black labour, skill shortages and the (unproductive) manpower demands made by the extensive military call up – which will increasingly beset the apartheid economy, a shift by South Africa to dependence upon resources supplied by African countries which are disengaging in other spheres could significantly weaken the white regime's ability to survive over the longer term.

The Increasing Internationalisation of Conflict

As regional conflict intensifies, it is likely that Southern Africa will become the focus of a far higher level of international involvement than obtains at the present. This follows, not only because of the massive extent of Western investment in South Africa, but also because the region's future is viewed in global terms. From this perspective (which is certainly dominant within the Reagan Administration) the world correlation of forces has shifted significantly in recent years in favour of the Soviet Union, which is perceived as an aggressively expanding power.

One aspect of this changing global balance has been the increased Soviet involvement in Africa, most notably by its support for the MPLA in 1975 and from 1978 by its active military commitment on the side of Ethiopia against Somalia. Indeed, a Soviet strategic presence in the Horn is seen as critically enhancing the USSR's capability to intervene in Southern Africa, for it provides a critical link in providing a secure air corridor to South Africa with intermediate fuelling and service stations and dependable allies (such as Mozambique) on the way. In addition, it is suggested that not only is Western strength visibly paling beside Moscow's growing capability, but nearly every 'industrial democracy' is becoming more dependent upon distant, easily subverted Third World nations for their energy and mineral imports, so that with Zimbabwe (and soon, perhaps, Namibia) removed as buffers to direct intervention, South Africa will become a logical target for Soviet expansionism.[19]

The particular importance of South Africa is stressed because present Soviet strategy is perceived as having moved towards denying resources to the West. The Soviets' aim, argue Gann and Duignan, is ultimately to restrict access to the Republic's resources to the NATO powers:

> The loss to the Western World of Southern Africa's minerals, port facilities, and similar resources, would be serious enough in itself; but were these riches to be added to the Soviet sphere, the USSR would obtain a staggering addition to its economic power.
>
> By some quirk of nature, the Soviet Union and South Africa are major sources of several vital materials. Together they produce more than 90 per cent of the world's platinum, 60 per cent of the world's gem diamonds, about 80 per cent of the world's gold, and sizeable

> percentages of global supplies of asbestos, uranium, fluospar, and other materials. Soviet control over the Cape route would also enable the Kremlin to pressure NATO and OPEC . . . states by a Soviet threat to hamper or interrupt maritime traffic.[20]

If until recently the prospect of a communist confrontation with South Africa would have been regarded as fantasy, this is no longer so. Certain US analysts now stress that Soviet–Cuban intervention must be regarded as a distinct possibility in the 1980s – although this depends upon a complex of factors including the availability to the USSR of land and sea bases adjacent to the Republic, the capability of the Cubans to launch a major offensive in support of guerrillas, the political will of the West to intervene against any Soviet engagement, and the size and quality of the South African military forces.

The worst possible case from (white) South Africa's perspective is seen as a large-scale invasion and seizure of important mineral-producing areas by Russian (or proxy) naval, air and army units. If this is still seen as the most unlikely contingency, it is none the less significant that its possibility is being seriously discussed.[21] It is from this viewpoint that, whether it is officially approved or not, South African nuclear potential is perceived as representing a major deterrent which would raise the costs and risks of direct Soviet intervention.

A more probable scenario (so it is argued) is that the Soviet Union will attempt to realise its objectives during the 1980s without launching any such risky invasion. Instead, its strategy is more likely to hinge upon support for the ANC in its guerrilla operations, combined with pressure for the implementation of a blockade in South Africa in fulfilment of UN aid and trade embargoes against the Republic. With potential for bases in an independent Namibia, Zimbabwe and Mozambique in the 1980s, Cuban proxies could be utilised to organise black revolutionaries for incursions into South Africa, supported in their efforts by Soviet military backing. Such a prospect, argue US strategic observers, can no longer be ruled out, and if, hitherto, Soviet expansionism has been enabled to make progress through a paralysis of political will on the part of the West, it is now necessary for the capitalist powers to give notice of their firm intent to defend their legitimate sphere of influence. Even if the more hysterical analyses of Soviet expansionism are discounted, and it is suggested that the Soviet interest is merely to exploit the West's growing embarrassment over apartheid and thereby to increase the USSR's prestige, it is still suggested by strategists that the crucial factor facilitating Soviet expansion is a Western weakness which calls for an active reassessment of priorities in southern Africa. Thus it is that there can be little doubt that the rest of the 1980s will see a more aggressive stance towards Soviet expansionism in the southern hemisphere, even if, simultaneously, US foreign policy were to be seriously directed at pressing Pretoria to enact more vigorous domestic reform.[22]

At this point, it is perhaps apposite to note that one of the striking features of the present political scene is that many 'leftist' perceptions of the Soviet role in southern Africa do not differ very markedly from those of Western strategists. As Callanicos and Rogers opined of the Soviet engagement in the Angolan War in 1975: 'Neither the Russians nor the Cubans supported the MPLA out of pure altruism. The Moscow bureaucracy had a great deal to gain from the collapse of the existing regimes in the region, if only because of the blow that this would represent to western economic and strategic interests.'[23] Similarly, Jitendra Mohan has argued that 'there is an uncanny parallelism in the ways of the superpowers in Africa, as well as the subtle differences of approach, style and technique reflecting their somewhat different circumstances and priorities.'[24]

At one level, of course, there is almost a conspiracy of silence on the left concerning the contemporary Soviet role in Africa because (presumably) it is felt improper to address the motives of those who arm and otherwise give material support to the various liberation movements. But as Mohan further argues, whereas US policy emphasises the primacy of peaceful change, the Soviet preference would seem to lie with a militarist solution:

> This militarism is, indeed, the masterkey to understanding the whole underlying strategy behind the Soviet offensive, not only in Africa but in the Third World in general, and it should be clearly distinguished from its polar opposite, a protracted people's war type of political-military strategy, stressing mass mobilization and self-reliance in struggle . . . the offensive on which the Soviet Union is currently engaged in Africa is neither primarily ideological nor economic. It refers, quite simply, to Moscow's systematic use of its very considerable military resources both to alter the strategic balance of power between itself and the US in its own favour and to bring more and more of the African and third world countries under its own influence and control.[25]

What Mohan is objecting to is not political and military support to the African liberation movements (which is wholly proper up to a point) but the 'outright, large-scale military intervention of the type carried out by the Soviets and Cubans in Angola'. For whatever the justification at the time, the Soviet–Cuban partnership is in his view primarily designed to secure a strategically favourable outcome in Southern Africa relative to US interests. In so doing, it is prepared to exploit divisions within the liberation movements, to favour some at the expense of others, and hence may be seen to be 'actively preparing for and encouraging civil war in Southern Africa . . . as a means of improving its strategic position *vis à vis* the US, as well as maintaining its privileged position as a ready supplier of weapons and men for use, not against racists and imperialists, but against Africans.'[26] Hence although there is no inherent reason to suppose that the ANC and regional governments are unaware of the dangers of being embraced by the Russian bear, the main danger would seem to be, in the words of the adage, that when two elephants fight, the grass beneath gets crushed. In other words, as the conflict in Southern Africa becomes increasingly internationalised – as appears inevitable – the interests of those actually fighting the liberation struggle may well be subordinated to the strategic interests and aims of the rival imperialist powers.

SOUTH AFRICA'S OPTIONS

The preceding discussion of regional trends has been based on the assumption that, because South Africa is the regionally hegemonic power, genuine development for the region's liberated territories is largely dependent, in the long run, upon the overthrow of white supremacy in the apartheid republic. The future of South Africa is thus seen as shaping the developmental possibilities for the entire region, and it is therefore to a brief examination of the Republic's political–economic alternatives that the chapter will now turn. Following other reviewers,[27] these alternatives may be grouped into three broad (but not wholly mutually exclusive) categories, namely (i) ethnic exclusivist, (ii) reformist and (iii) revolutionary. Each of these will now be briefly discussed in turn.

Ethnic Exclusivist Options

The ideological expression of segregationist and apartheid strategy reached its highest form in the Verwoerdian notion of a South African commonwealth of ethnic member states whereby the Republic would be carved up into a white heartland and a set of 'independent' (but dependent) black states. Perhaps linking up with surrounding territories such as Botswana, Lesotho and Swaziland in a sphere of 'co-prosperity', this arrangement (under which all Africans would be linked politically as citizens to a particular 'homeland' by virtue of ethnicity) would thus operate to endorse internationally the existent domestic unequal distribution of power and privilege between white and black, and would exclude Africans from participation in the political economy of the white heartland except in so far as their labour would contribute to its wealth.

This apartheid strategy, brought about by the segregationist emphasis upon white supremacy whose rationale was promoted as the incompatability of diverse national and racial groups within one polity, was largely aimed at fragmenting the perceived threat represented by the demographic black majority. Dismissed variously as Utopian, impractical, racist and abhorrent by its critics, the Verwoerdian notion none the less continued to guide South African government policy well into the Vorster era, even though apprehension concerning the likely consequences of harbouring 'independent' black states within the Republic's borders was in no small measure responsible for delaying its substantive implementation until the Portuguese collapse spurred the government into devolving legal 'sovereignty' upon first Transkei in 1976, and then Bophuthatswana (1977), Venda (1979) and Ciskei (1981). By this time, however, although such devolution was deemed, in some quarters, to be irreversible, changes within the region were taking place so fast that official ideology became more and more subject to pragmatic adaptation and alteration. Whilst the mechanics, motivation and momentum of this process are complex and controversial (going well beyond the confines of the present chapter), it is of considerable contemporary and future significance that so-called '*Verligte*' (enlightened) Nationalists, as well as Opposition spokesmen, are now joining conservative and liberal external commentators in assessing the prospects and possibilities for constitutional engineering in terms of 'power-sharing', federalism, partition and consociationalism, devices whose explicit focus is to promote a new, 'more just' political order whereby one 'race group' could not dominate another.[28]

Limitations of space prevent any detailed analysis of the probabilities and possibilities of these diverse options. However, it is worth noting that the discussion of these particular alternatives is conducted on at least two levels. First, the credibility of the justice and practicality of such ventures is undermined by the realisation that they are, in considerable measure, expressly designed to block majoritarian rule in South Africa and would thus function to prevent a radical redistribution of wealth and power. For instance, postulated reform of the existent polity into a confederation of black states ('independent' or otherwise) and a white core (wherein the Coloured and Indian minorities – or elements within them – might be co-opted within a power-sharing framework) is best regarded in this light, for even if an overarching authority and common citizenship were to take such a dispensation beyond the existent apartheid framework, the constituent units of government would still be founded upon some adjusted ***racial*** definition of citizenship and residential rights which would clearly be unacceptable to the racial majority which was excluded from political participation in the central core. Consequently, whatever the clothing in which 'power-sharing' between the diverse 'racial groups' might be dressed up, the denial of fundamental equality to blacks would, by definition, prevent the emergence of a consensual democracy.

More concretely, however, it is arguable that given the polarisation of racial and class conflict that has taken place over the last decade and the concomitant process of radicalisation which has raised the liberation struggle to a higher level, the best chances for such political arrangements have long since disappeared. Thus, although the proponents of 'ethnic' federation, partition or consociation argue that their solutions are designed precisely to bring an end to such violent conflict, it is worthy of note that their discussions are generally couched in rarified, academic terms which are far distant from the future context of an apartheid political economy placed under intense stress from the effects of guerrilla activity, regional confrontation, trade union activism, black militancy and very possibly too, global confrontation. In essence, ethnically exclusivist options are generally the white man's proposals for countering and diluting the efficacy of the black man's struggles. They are also ultimately based upon the assumption that South African whites will retain the capacity to shape their own future without undue reference to countervailing forces in the form of the UN, OAU, FLS, ANC and, most crucially, the black majority.

However, precisely because South Africa's rulers are gradually losing the political initiative (as indicated by the regional trends elaborated above) they will not be able to dictate their own favoured 'compromise' solution (even though it may entail considerable concessions). If it may be assumed that the assault upon the state will not cease until certain minimal conditions acceptable to the opposing parties in the South African conflict are met, then it may be further assumed that any 'solutions' based upon race or ethnicity will prove unviable precisely because they will be closely identified with the present basis of apartheid.

Thus when (and, we may add, not if) the time comes for genuine negotiation between the major parties concerned (and this will necessarily include external actors – notably the ANC – with whom Pretoria at present (1984) disdains to treat), the probability (bordering upon certainty) is that this will be carried out within a reformist or revolutionary, but *not* an ethnically exclusivist framework.

Reformism

The reformist option is usually described as a 'liberal' strategy. Paradoxically, however, observers have long noted that South Africa has virtually extinguished its liberal tradition, whilst within the dominant white supremacist ethos, the term 'liberal' had degenerated into an abusive epithet. Consequently, the reformist perspective is in practice espoused as much, if not more, by conservative interests. In particular, it can be argued that, especially since the collapse of Portuguese colonialism in 1974, the Western powers have sought to counter the rising tide of liberation in southern Africa by a frankly counter-revolutionary and neo-colonial strategy which seeks, however timidly or ineffectively, to propel Pretoria into 'reform' whose purpose is clearly to undercut revolutionary prospects.

The main tenets of the reformist argument are well known.[29] In drastic précis, it is generally proposed that the contradictions between an irrational racial order and a modern industrial economy will be overcome, in the long term, by the logic of capitalist rationality. Crude argument that democratisation is the inevitable companion of industrialisation has been abandoned;[30] and similarly, the liberal has generally conceded to the Marxist viewpoint that, under apartheid, racism has served to promote, rather than inhibit, capital accumulation and development. None the less, it is maintained that such factors as the shortage of skilled white labour, the development of black trade unionism and the expansion of black consumer power (which is limited but not insignificant) will increase black salience within the political economy. Taken together with such factors as international pressure, 'constructive engagement' by transnational firms which commonly breach the colour bar in labour relations and, increasingly, fissures within the ruling bloc in response to internal and external stress, such domestic factors are likely to culminate in the dominant white elements accommodating to black interests and eventually engaging in negotiation and compromise with genuine (not collaborative) black leaders in a bid for a lasting political settlement.

The most sophisticated exponent of this viewpoint is Heribert Adam, who has long argued that apartheid has operated to stabilise racial dominance and to hamper revolutionary change in a polarised situation where it might otherwise seem most theoretically likely. In short, with a thesis that has gained quite wide acceptance, he has sought to counter the notion of white irrationality and perversity by suggesting that the National Party has constructed a 'pragmatic racial oligarchy' which is able to adjust and respond to the various challenges that the apartheid system has encountered.[31]

It has been objected by one critic that Adam's analysis is situational. That is, whilst it may have been appropriate to the 1960s when the South African Government successfully maintained tight political and police control and was less threatened by internal opposition and international pressure, it less convincingly explains the period following the Durban strikes of 1973, the Portuguese coup and, thereafter, the Soweto uprising. In other words, it is argued that far from responding to these diverse events pragmatically and rationally, the regime's reactions (the invasion of Angola, the massive retaliation against black protest etc.) marked a growing inflexibility and dogmatism in face of stress.[32]

In response to such criticism, Adam has recently focused upon 'Recent Policy Shifts of the South African State.'[33] Basically, he argues that the ruling class in South Africa is at present (1984) in a state of ideological confusion which has facilitated new alliances and orientations:

> The recent policy shifts of the South African state range from labour legislation to investigations about constitutional alternatives, influx control, Bantustan consolidation, and security laws, as well as a restructuring of the administration itself. To be sure, the revisions do not signal in any way an abdication of white privilege. On the contrary, they aim at lubricating a cumbersome, wasteful machinery for smoother control. But at the same time, they indicate the perceived need to seek new alliances and to reconsider past practices.[34]

The most significant shift, Adam argues, lies in the rapprochement between the state and big business, with the two fractions of the bourgeoisie linking together to forge a new era of corporate growth which involves the co-optation of an urban African middle class, and more importantly, the abandonment of outdated labour legislation. Thus recent policy changes have revised the system of influx control linking the flow of black labour to job openings and housing provisions whilst it has also sought to control black-worker militancy by allowing for the recognition and registration of black trade unions. If, on the one hand, this strategy has undermined the privileges of white workers, it has, on the other, provided for the emergence of an urban black 'labour aristocracy' *vis-à-vis* less secure migrants.

Adam perceives these various economic trends as leading to the 'Americanisation' of South Africa, with class stratification gradually replacing a dysfunctional racial order. However, he qualifies his argument by noting that hitherto the apartheid regime has not yet found an acceptable formula for the political incorporation of the majority 'The longer the South African state delays political deracialisation and masks mere consultation as negotiation, the more this politicises the excluded in search of alternatives.'[35] In other words, the thrust of his analysis is to suggest that the reformist option will fail to achieve stability unless the government seeks to make genuinely representative black leaders part of the deal. In practical terms, he implies, this must involve negotiation with the militant activists of the ANC. If this is at present regarded as wholly unacceptable, the future prospects are not so immutable – but with an important qualification:

> As far as the activists are historically associated with a socialist transformation of South African society, accommodation or even negotiation is out of the question from the perspective of both sides. However, South African capital could easily come to terms with African nationalism as such, as it has in the rest of Africa . . . In other words, black political power is conceivable and even considered legitimate, as long as it leaves the existing economic order basically intact.[36]

It is with this provocative thought in mind that I will now progress to a consideration of the revolutionary alternative before returning to discussion of Adam's thesis in the conclusion.

The Revolutionary Alternative

The revolutionary perspective on South Africa is a well-established one. Broadly, it argues that white intransigence under apartheid has blocked all paths to non-violent accommodation of opposing racial and class interests, and that as a consequence the exploited majority have no other way forward than by militant (including armed) struggle. Systematic oppression in South Africa has therefore led to a situation which cannot be resolved other than by violent conflict between the white state and the countervailing forces of liberation.

The revolutionary perspective is, in large measure, based upon a notion of settler colonialism which suggests that the capacity for independent capitalist growth which settler-colonies exhibit brings forth new social classes among the indigenous population which develop a particularly dynamic potential for revolutionary class action. Precisely because economic exploitation of the indigenous majority is secured by *political* domination, settler regimes exhibit a political rigidity that propels the subordinated classes towards popular armed struggle, causing ultimately a reassessment of metropolitan interests and, on this basis, bringing about the overthrow of the settler-state. Hence the international legality of its political independence notwithstanding, South Africa – where advanced industrialisation (aided and abetted by the Western connection) has summoned up the largest black proletariat on the continent – today presents a great latent threat to imperialism. Consequently, whilst the exact form in which revolutionary class action will be sustained cannot yet be seen, 'it seems reasonable to believe that even the power of the South African settler state – its capacity for far-reaching pragmatic manoeuvre, as Heribert Adam would have it – is finite.'[37]

Under the impact of this line of argument, there is a dangerous tendency for radicals to assume the 'inevitability' of a revolutionary triumph of the popular forces. Thus Jitendra Mohan has written not so long ago (albeit in a deliberately polemical piece) that South Africa is a 'paper tiger' whose days 'are surely numbered'.[38] On the one hand, this stems from a commonsensical, if rather mechanistic, application of domino theory. Thus the ANC:

> Those who place themselves in the path of the struggling masses shall inevitably be swept away together with their racist master whom they serve. In our region that is a lesson which has been confirmed in the recent past by the victories of Frelimo, the MPLA and the Patriotic Front alliance in Mozambique, Angola and Zimbabwe respectively. South Africa will be no exception! Indeed the very same lesson is being confirmed in Namibia today.[39]

On the other hand, the 'inevitability' thesis would seem to flow directly from the notion of settler colonialism itself, with the Soweto uprising, and the mass struggles that have followed thereafter being taken as an indication of the growth and development of revolutionary class action. Indeed, the crisis of settler colonialism is now perceived as so acute that it is widely argued within liberation circles that the struggle is now not so much for national liberation as for socialism. From this perspective, therefore, the national–democratic revolution (whereby the oppressed nation throws off the imperial yoke) and the socialist (whereby oppressed classes throw off their domination and exploitation by capital) are increasingly seen as co-terminous. This view was eloquently expressed by Ruth First not long before her brutal assassination:

> because workers are exploited as workers and also as members of nationally oppressed groups, and not even their national demands can be met without the destruction of the capitalist order . . . the struggle for national liberation . . . will at the same time be part of the struggle for socialism.[40]

What Ruth First did not argue, however, was that such a development was inevitable; rather, she emphasised that it would only come about through a process of struggle and assertion of the necessity of a socialist solution by a proletarian leadership if popular aspirations and needs were to be met. Clearly, however, this is premissed upon a realisation that no particular historical outcome is assured and that, in turn, a revolutionary struggle could indeed be subverted by a reformist alternative in the manner indicated by Adam. It is, therefore, to the further elaboration of these diverse options that I will, in conclusion, now turn.

REFORM OR REVOLUTION?

The purpose of the present chapter was to speculate on South Africa's options given certain regional trends, these being identified as increasing militarisation, political confrontation between South Africa and neighbouring African states, a steady disengagement by black Africa from the apartheid economy and the growing involvement of external powers in regional conflict. In broad terms, the prospect for South Africa over coming years would seem to be that of the much-predicted garrison state. Protected by her military might, the white Republic will experience growing political isolation within a context of declining regional hegemony and a stalling economy, buffeted not only by the external forces of liberation fighters and an increasingly militant black workforce, but also by the Western powers which will be keen both to protect their direct material stake and to counter growing Soviet influence.

This vision suggests a change in the regional and domestic balance of forces such that South Africa's whites will not be able to determine their own future over the long term. They will be unable to maintain their monopoly of power within South Africa and will inevitably have to make fundamental concessions to the forces that oppose them. Consequently, although the future of South Africa is widely perceived as falling within three broad alternative categories – ethnic exclusivist, reformist and revolutionary – it has been argued about that, for a complex of reasons, the first of these tends to reflect fissures within the ruling bloc rather than to constitute a viable alternative (although such options will undoubtedly be of significance in the intermediate future, as apartheid seeks to contain opposing pressures by adapting present structures). Accordingly, the key to South Africa's *post-apartheid* future would seem to lie within the broad area mapped out by the reformist and revolutionary paths.

Clearly, this discussion cannot be divorced from a consideration of South Africa's relation to the global economy. From this perspective, South Africa may be identified as one of a number of middle (or 'sub-imperialist') powers within the global framework whose distinctive quality is that they are nether dominant nor dependent, but 'able to dominate a particular part of the international system whilst remaining somewhat dependent at the global level'.[41] More concretely, linking up with the contemporary debate about nature of the South African state, emphasis is placed upon the autonomy of white power. Samir Amin, for instance, argues that the Republic has gone beyond the stage of peripheral capitalism, its development having been based upon the phenomenon of internal colonialism whereby industry that was built up was historically oriented not so much towards import substitution of manufactures for consumption by the African masses as for satisfaction of the demands of the settler population.[42] In South Africa, he argues, local capital has indeed merged with American, Japanese and European monopolies. However, rather than having subordinated the former, foreign capital has been forced by the political hegemony of the local bourgeoisie to establish 'an integrated auto-centred structure and not an externally-oriented structure as in the Third World'.[43] Yet precisely because (given the impoverishment of the African masses) there is a limited internal market, South African capital requires an outward policy of expansion so that, ultimately, internal colonialism becomes co-terminous with sub-imperialism.

As a result of this analysis, Amin's conclusion is stark:

> Having gone from subjection to foreign capital to alliance with it, cannot the state become stronger here and open the way to an autonomous capitalist development? Autonomous (not autarkic) capitalism, integrated into a network of inter-dependence (no longer qualitatively asymmetrical dependence) even if it is unequal interdependence.[44]

Whilst this possibility is excluded for the Third World as a whole, there are countries (Brazil, Mexico, Argentina and the like) for whom such development may be on the historical agenda. Neither is it excluded for South Africa, which is already at the advanced stage 'which leaves no other alternative but *socialism* or *barbarism*'.[45]

The point at issue here is not so much whether we accept Amin's outline of South African political economy as whether we choose to reject his warning about the possibility of barbarism and, in turn, whether or not we agree with him that non-socialist options are necessarily barbaric.

It is to the first question – whether or not revolution can be avoided – that so much Western analysis addresses itself, with conservative arguments stressing in particular the vital strategic and material importance of South Africa to the West. Linked to this latter approach, of course, ia an appreciative enumeration of the apartheid Republic's 'awesome' regional military and industrial ascendancy. 'South Africa' gloat Gann and Duignan 'is the industrial giant of the African continent . . . The Republic's military power is thus enhanced by a substantial industrial and logistic infrastructure on a scale that has been attained nowhere else in Africa.' Given its acquisition and development of nuclear technology, its possession of vast resources of raw materials, the availability of skilled manpower, its stockpile of oil and arms, its ability to pay for imports in gold and so on, its military power is now 'greater than at any other time in its history.'[46] 'Hence' argues Chester Crocker 'there is no basis for questioning the conventional superiority of the Republic in relation to any foreseeable combination of independent African states.'[47]

Given this military muscle, Western strategists generally concur with Crocker when he argues that violent upheaval in South Africa is not imminent. There is little prospect, he suggests, of any violent assault by revolutionary forces which would be capable of re-ordering basic power relationships, for the South African state is structured politically and organised militarily to withstand significant levels of unrest. In any case resistance in South Africa is hampered by continuing divisions amongst its leadership (PAC v. ANC; white v. black; internal v. external), whilst the black working class remains largely unorganised and is split along urban and rural lines. Civil disobedience, riots, and sabotage have hitherto demonstrated little capacity to make any lasting impact upon the power structure, and whilst blacks will undoubtedly increase their bargaining power through trade unions, industrial action cannot easily be turned into insurrectionary activity. Meanwhile, the existent conditions are largely unfavourable to guerrilla activity, whilst urban terrorism will alienate as many as it inspires to further acts of rebellion. In addition, the ruling group is confident, the security forces are watchful, the police force is efficient, and the army is cohesive (in no way suffering from the class and status divisions which plagued the Portuguese military). Given these various factors (and many more), it is thus inherently unlikely that revolution will come in the 1980s.

External factors – varying from pressures exerted by the OAU (seen as largely ineffective) the FLS, the West and so on will provide the background, but change in South Africa will be primarily an internal matter, although (and this is an important qualification) over the longer term, the Republic may lose its military dominance as, with Soviet aid, the neighbouring territories may well take major strides in the arms race. Yet even then a more likely prospect that African triumph would be a politico-military balance akin to the present Arab–Israeli stalemate, in which case South Africa's strength would come to rest on the less tangible aspects of white strength.[48]

Although we may clearly question the motives (and, indeed, the accuracy) of such analysis, it would be not merely naive, but rather criminally negligent for observers to dismiss the considerable viability of white power whilst black youths are consumed as cannon fodder by the apartheid military machine. It is therefore apposite to return to Adam's contribution wherein he suggests that the settler colonial analogy serves to obfuscate the unique and specific South African circumstances:

> To romanticise the final decolonisation of a stubborn rebel regime is to overlook the different problematic of changing a political minority monopoly in a sovereign, independent, powerful, industrial state. In Zimbabwe, liberation occured in a basically argicultural society with a numerically weak and relatively recent settler population, heavily dependent on outside support to achieve a military stalemate. In South Africa, a much stronger, self-confident minority controls an industrial empire whose resources and advanced manufacturing capacity have become an integral part of the world capitalist system. For the West Rhodesia was expendable, South Africa is not.[49]

In other words, Adam suggests that the South African future may well be shaped by a programme of Western-backed reform (and proposes, by implication, that a black-ruled Republic would continue as a sub-imperialist, or in Amin's terms 'barbaric' power). This is not, it must be stressed, an argument that significant change will result from the present reformist strategy being pursued by the Botha Government (for the nature of such reform is largely illusory). Rather, it is to imply (as Johnson has argued)[50] that when Pretoria is faced by some combination of guerrilla struggle backed by the USSR and internal revolt which it cannot hope to defeat (even though the strength of white power may deny the capacity of its opponents to 'win') the West will attempt to 'save' South Africa by imposing a programme of reform which deprives the settlers of political power. In other words, if it is assumed that Pretoria'a economic and military reliance upon the West will increase as conflict in southern Africa escalates, the West will gain the muscle (which it presently lacks) to cajole the apartheid regime into accepting majority rule. The time for 'power-sharing' will long have gone, and only a majoritarian solution will provide a minimum basis for settlement acceptable to the revolutionary parties. But – if the Lancaster House agreement under which Zimbabwe gained its freedom is any guide – the 'inevitable' majority rule settlement will represent a compromise of conflicting tendencies whereby political power is severely beset by a host of constraints and limitations imposed by Western capital.

Yet if, in contrast to Adam's vision, the revolution in South Africa is to be resolved in socialist terms it will only do so as a result of a proletarian-based liberation movement. In concrete terms, this means that the present internal process within the ANC which is seeing it transformed from an old-style nationalist into a proletarian revolutionary movement must continue. This means, as indicated by Saul and Gelb in a contribution which discusses the matter with lucidity, that the ANC is faced with the difficult task of promoting 'the more broadly nationalist project' with a proletarian line without thereby 'handing over the highly charged nationalist-cum-racial card to PAC remnants and/or the more demagogic wing of the Black Consciousness Movement'. Equally, however, although 'the ANC can be seen to provide the political context within which the general run of revolutionary energies in South Africa is likely to come', there is nothing predictable about the ANC's response. In short, even if it is not particularly helpful – even if it is possible – to spell out the likely circumstances under which a socialist outcome might be brought about, 'the continuing dialectic between (the ANC) and the considerable revolutionary energies at play within the society has become the single most important process at work in South Africa's political economy'.[51]

Recognition of the openness of South Africa's future (even if, as argued here, some form of majoritarian solution is clearly on the agenda) implies that, if reformism is an historical alternative, then the barbaric prospect outlined by Amin is indeed an option. Leaving aside the difficulties which would accompany any attempt at a neo-colonial accommodation by the incumbent state bourgeoisie with a black middle class,[52] it has to be frankly acknowledged that a nationalist–majoritarian solution under bourgeois hegemony could be infinitely preferable to the continuation of apartheid. In other words, when we are contemplating the continuing existence of the present form of state whose mode of repression of the majority is so extreme, we should not devalue the greater freedoms which a genuinely deracialised system could bring. In that sense, it is submitted that Amin's dichotomy between socialism *or* barbarism is, indeed, too extreme, and that it fails to acknowledge the tactical advances that could be offered by an interim 'solution'. Having said that, it may none the less be argued that were the political polarity resulting from the intensity of the struggle against apartheid to mean that a nationalist leadership was propelled along a socialist path, then the very level of industrial development that has been achieved could mean that South Africa becomes the first meaningfully socialist society on the continent; and were such a process to be linked to the development of self-reliant strategies in such potentially prosperous countries as Zimbabwe and Namibia, this could make a major contribution to alternative development strategy for the entire region and beyond. But at present, such a prospect hovers as a relatively distant goal, and the reality of the present remains to confront the apartheid regime.

NOTES

1. For a thoughtful overviewof this period, see Alex Callanicos, *Southern Africa after Zimbabwe* (London: Pluto Press, 1981).
2. International Defence and Aid Fund for Southern Africa (IDAFSA), 'Developments in South Africa since the Uprising of 1976', International Conference on Sanctions against South Africa, Paris 20–27 May 1981 (UN General Assembly, Africa Conference 107/3, 20 April 1981) 10–14.
3. Colin Legum, 'The Southern African Crisis: the failure of diplomacy and Weapons' in Colin Legum (ed.) *Africa Contemporary Record (ACR) Volume 13, 1980–81* (New York and London: Holmes and Meier, 1981) A3–A23.
4. IDAFSA, 1981, 35; South African Institute of Race Relations, (SAIRR), *A Survey of Race Relations in South Africa, 1981* (Johannesburg, 1981), 205.
5. *ACR Volume 13, 1980–81*, B805; SAIRR, *Survey, 1981*, 205–9.
6. Colin Legum, 'South Africa in the Contemporary World' in Robert M. Price and Carl G. Rosberg (eds) *The Apartheid Regime: Political Power and Racial Domination* (Berkeley: Institute of International Studies, University of California, 1980) 281–96.
7. *ACR Volume 13, 1980–81* B810.
8. *Strategic Survey 1981–82* plus relevant country entries in *ACR Volume 13, 1980–81.*
9. *Focus* (IDAFSA, London, May–June 1982) 40.

10. *Strategic Survey 1981–82.*
11. Kenneth Grundy, *Confrontation and Accommodation in Southern Africa: The Limits of Independence* (Berkeley: University of California Press, 1973).
12. Little purpose would be served here by a discussion of the complexities of the negotiations aimed at bringing about an internationally acceptable settlement in Namibia. Suffice to say that since 1978, when all the relevant parties accepted UN Security Council resolution 435 as a basis for a settlement, South Africa has continuously prevaricated. Since the arrival in office of the Reagan Administration in the US (which South Africa correctly perceives as more sympathetic to its cause) Pretoria has extracted a series of concessions from the Western Contact Group (objecting in particular to the extent of the UN's proposed supervisory role during an interim, pre-independence period on account of the General Assembly's recognition of SWAPO as the sole legitimate representative of the Namibian people). More critically, however, the extent of its aggression in Angola (which has received the tacit backing by a US Administration mesmerised by the Cuban presence in Luanda) suggests that the apartheid regime has little intention at the moment of relinquishing its control over Namibia under any constitutional arrangement which would allow a significant role to SWAPO. Of course, time and changing circumstances may alter Pretoria's stance, but it is suggested here that this will only occur as a result of far greater pressure than the Western Five are at present willing to exert.
13. The above discussion is based heavily on Richard F. Weisfelder, 'The Southern African Development Co-ordination Conference (SADCC): A New Factor in the Liberation Process', in Thomas M. Callaghy, (ed.) *South Africa in Southern Africa* (New York: Praeger: 1983).
14. Apart from Grundy, *Confrontation and Accommodation in Southern Africa*, see for instance, Ann Seidman and Neva Seidman Makgetla, *Outposts of Monopoly Capitalism: Southern Africa in the Changing Global Economy*, (Westport: Lawrence Hill, 1980).
15. R. H. Green, 'Southern African Development Co-ordination: The Struggle Continues', *ACR Volume 13, 1980–81*, A24–A34.
16. Weisfelder, 'SADCC'.
17. Roger Southall, 'South Africa' in Timothy M. Shaw and Olajide Aluko (eds) *The Political Economy of African Foreign Policy* (Aldershot: Gower, and New York: St. Martins, 1984) 221–62 and Legum, 'South Africa in the Contemporary World'.
18. D. G. Clarke, 'The South African Chamber of Mines: Policy and Strategy with Reference to Foreign African Labour Supply', University of Natal Development Studies, 1977, Research Group Working Paper No. 2.
19. W. Scott Thompson and Brett Silvers, 'South Africa in Soviet Strategy' in Richard E. Bissell and Chester A. Crocker (eds) *South Africa into the 1980s* (Boulder: Westview, 1979) 133–58.
20. L. H. Gann and P. Guignan, *South Africa – War, Revolution or Peace?* (Stanford: Hoover Institution Press, 1978) 58.

21. Thompson and Silvers, 'South Africa in Soviet Strategy'; and Peter Bissell, 'How Strategic is South Africa?' in Bissell and Crocker (eds) *South Africa into the 1980s*, 209–32.
22. For an interesting assessment of US options, see Garrick Utley, 'Globalism or Regionalism? United States Policy towards Southern Africa' (London: International Institute for Strategic Studies, 1979) Adelphi Paper, No. 157.
23. Alex Callanicos and John Rogers, *Southern Africa after Soweto*, (London: Pluto, 1977) 152.
24. Jitendra Mohan, 'Southern Africa: Imperialism, Racism and Neo-colonialism', *Review of African Political Economy*, 11, January–April 1978, 31–9.
25. Ibid, 37.
26. Ibid, 38.
27. P. Thandika Mkandawire, 'Reflections on Some Future Scenarios for Southern Africa', *Journal of Southern African Affairs*, 2 (4), 1977, 427–39; and Heribert Adam, 'Three Perspectives on the Future of South Africa', *International Journal of Comparative Sociology*, 20 (1) 1979, 122–35.
28. Rolef Botha, *South Africa: Plan for the Future – A Basis for Discussion*, (Johannesburg: Perskor, 1978); and F. Van Zyl Slabbert and David Welsh, *South Africa's Options: Strategies for Sharing Power* (Cape Town: David Philip, 1979).
29. For one overview, see Harrison M. Wright, *The Burden of the Present: Liberal-racial Controversy over Southern African History* (Cape Town: David Philip, 1977).
30. Michael O'Dowd 'South Africa in the light of the stages of economic growth', in Adrian Leftwich (ed.), *South Africa: Economic Growth and Political Change* (London: Allison & Busby, 1974) 29–44.
31. Heribert Adam, *Modernising Racial Domination: The Dynamics of South African Politics* (Berkeley: University of California Press, 1971).
32. Donald G. Baker, 'Retreat from Challenge: White Reactions to Regional Events Since 1974' in J. Seiler (ed.) *Southern Africa Since the Portuguese Coup* (Boulder: Westview, 1980) 155-67.
33. Heribert Adam, 'Minority Monopoly in Transition: Recent Policy Shifts of the South African State', *Journal of Modern African Studies*, 18 (4), December 1980, 611–26.
34. Ibid, 617.
35. Ibid, 625.
36. Ibid, 624.
37. For one elaboration, see Kenneth Good, 'Settler Colonialism: Economic Development and Class Formation', *Journal of Modern African Studies*, 14 (4) December 1976, 597–620.
38. Mohan, 'Southern Africa' 33.
39. *Sechaba*, September 1980.
40. Ruth First, 'After Soweto: A Response', *Review of African Political Economy*, 11, January–April 1978, 93–100.
41. Timothy M. Shaw, 'International Stratification in Africa: Sub-

Imperialism in Southern and Eastern Africa', *Journal of Southern African Affairs*, 2 (2), 1977, 145–66.
42. Samir Amin, 'The Future of South Africa', *Journal of Southern African Affairs*, 2 (3), 1977, 355–70.
43. Ibid, 369.
44. Ibid, 369.
45. Ibid, 369.
46. Chester Crocker, 'Current and Projected Military Balances in Southern Africa', in Bissell and Crocker, (eds) *South Africa into the 1980s*, 71–106.
47. Gann and Duignan, *South Africa*, 21–35.
48. Crocker, 'Current and Projected Military Balances in Southern Affairs'.
49. Adam, 'Minority Monopoly in Transition', 611–12.
50. R. W. Johnson, *How Long Will South Africa Survive?* (London: Macmillan, 1977).
51. John S. Saul and Stephen Gelb, *The Crisis in South Africa: Class Defense, Class Revolution* (New York: Monthly Review Press, 1981). (Citations from 144–6).
52. For an excellent recent discussion, see Sam C. Nolutshungu, *Changing South Africa: Political Considerations* (Manchester: Manchester University Press, 1982).

6 The Future of EurAfrica

JOHN RAVENHILL

'Prophecy is the most gratuitous form of error'
– George Eliot, *Middlemarch*

For the last century (many would argue 'for longer') the political economy of Africa has been determined primarily by European actors. As the centennial of the Congress of Berlin approaches, and African states begin fully to comprehend the potentialities and limitations afforded by political independence, it is an appropriate time to question whether there are indications that Europe's predominant position in the political economy of its southern neighbour will significantly diminish before we enter the twenty-first century.

George Eliot's dictum notwithstanding, this chapter will attempt to predict the future course of Africa's multilateralised relations with Europe, obviously but one dimension of the relationship between the two continents. In hazarding a prediction about the future of EurAfrica, it is tempting to resort to the behaviouralist's equation which asserts that the best predictor of the situation at $t + 1$ is t. Indeed, the conclusion to this chapter might suggest that this has been the course adopted by the author. For despite considerable diversification of economic links by African states in the two decades since independence, Europe remains the most significant economic partner for most of Africa.[1] In the absence of viable alternatives, it is likely to continue to remain so.

Sources of potential change in the future of EurAfrica might be found in four areas: the international system, the dynamics of Europe's own political economy, the institutionalised relationship between the two continents and in Africa itself. Obviously, the four areas are highly interconnected. As relatively weak actors in the international economic and political systems, the behaviour of African states has occurred principally in response to external impulses. It is appropriate, therefore, to begin a consideration of the possible alternatives that will be available to Africa in the future with a review of potential changes in the international system.

THE FUTURE INTERNATIONAL SYSTEM

The last twenty years have seen a remarkable transformation in the structure of the international economic system. American hegemony has been eroded as a result of the successful reconstruction of the economies of Western Europe and Japan. More recently, a small number of developing countries have emerged as significant economic actors, either as a result of their success in manufacturing for export (the NICs) or because of their successful exploitation of their oligopolistic control of critical raw materials.

For weak actors, these developments have had both postiive and negative repercussions. On the positive side, the number of potential commercial partners has been increased. On the other hand, the erosion of American hegemony has led to instability within the international economic order, an instability which has been exacerbated by the shocks emanating from OPEC. A slowing of growth in the industrialised countries, accompanied by high levels of inflation, has created an economic environment in which it is politically difficult for Western governments to seek domestic adjustment in order to accommodate increased exports of manufactured goods from LDCs.

Inflation of the prices of manufactured goods from the West, plus the effects of the dramatic increase in oil prices, has placed great strain on the balance of payments of most African countries (with the notable exception of oil exporters) a problem which has been compounded by a decrease in demand for industrial raw materials as a result of the recession in the world economy. For many African countries, future growth prospects would appear to depend heavily on the state of the international economy; in this matter there is a harmony between African needs and the interests of the industrialised world.

In the forseeable future, a continuation of present trends in the international economic system might be anticipated. The present NICs can be expected to continue to enjoy relatively high rates of growth, while a small number of other countries, for instance, Argentina, Venezuela, and India, might graduate to that status. Accordingly, the way will be opened for a continued diversification of Africa's economic links. New trading partners may be able to offer the intermediate technology that is suited to Africa's factor endowments.

Economic relations will not be on a different basis – the NICs and OPEC have demonstrated already that they are unlikely to be any more charitable towards the less fortunate LDCs than have been the industrialised countries of the OECD. Here it is necessary to examine in further detail the nature of the economic links that might be expected to develop between Africa and the NICs. There is little to suggest that these countries will be willing to open their markets to labour-intensive manufactures from Africa. Neither are they likely to have any significant interest in Africa's tropical agricultural products. Rather, their interest is likely to lie in Africa's mineral resources, especially fuels.

New competition for Africa's resources may be expected to enhance bargaining capability with MNCs. But it is extremely doubtful whether Africa will reap a significant benefit from any future scarcity of primary products. Again, the obvious exceptions are the producers of petroleum and of uranium. Some of the more exotic minerals found in Zimbabwe and South Africa will continue to command high prices unless substitutes are developed. But for many other producers of such minerals as copper and iron, the exploitation of the resources of the seabed will probably weaken their economies even further.

There seems to be little potential for future cartelisation among the producers of most of Africa's raw material exports. Oil seems destined to remain the exception, with a few minor products – uranium, bauxite – with the potential to prove the rule. Neither can African governments anticipate significant benefits from international commodity agreements; econometric work has demonstrated that gains to producers will accrue in substantial quantities only to exporters of tropical beverages, Western governments are unlikely to provide the resources necessary to sustain a meaningful Common Fund; other potential donors with the necessary resources appear equally unwilling to make a commitment.[2]

Attempts to diversify economic links will undoubtedly include new relations with the 'second' world. But, again, the potential for such diversification appears limited. To date, Africa's economic relations with the member states of COMECON and with China have been a source of disappointment. None of these countries are likely to provide significant markets for Africa's current and potential exports. COMECON members have their own interests in the production for export of the type of labour-intensive manufactures that appear the most feasible alternatives to the current heavy reliance by African states on raw material exports. Neither will the second world become a significant source of technology for African states, given its own heavy dependence on the West. Unless a significant liberalisation of COMECON occurs, enabling the convertibility of member states' currencies, trade with Africa is likely to continue to be conducted primarily on the basis of long-term barter arrangements – not necessarily the most advantageous form of economic partnership for the African states. The absorptive capacity of second world markets will remain limited.

In brief, the future development of the international economic system will permit African states to continue to diversify their commercial relations. But there are few grounds for believing that the system will present dramatically different opportunities for African states in the form of new markets, new sources of technology, or new sources of financial aid. Diversification will occur but it will be gradual, and constitute only a limited reduction of dependence on Europe as the principal commercial partner.

DEVELOPMENTS IN EUROPE'S POLITICAL ECONOMY

One of the most salient questions to ask of Europe's contemporary political economy is whether the 'New Protectionism' will turn into an old mercantilism. Here, again, future policy options for Africa are highly dependent on developments in the international economic system. Two scenarios may be posited, neither of which are particularly favourable for the future of Africa's economic relations with Europe.

In the first scenario, the international economy escapes from the present stagflation to attain the rates of growth experienced in the 1950s and 1960s. European industries successfully adjust to the challenges presented by the NICS and concentrate on exports of high-technology goods. Labour-intensive stages of manufacturing in Europe are phased out, primarily in favour of the NICs which provide an expanding market for European exports of capital goods and high-technology products.

African states, in this scenario, simply decline in relevance for the EEC, so that the latter loses interest in maintaining the 'special relationship'. The Community, under pressure from the NICs, will be unwilling to maintain the trade preferences that African members of the ACP group currently enjoy via the Lomé Convention. European multinationals will be attracted to the more advanced LDCs of Asia and Latin America, which will not only begin to offer a significant domestic market, but also have the advantage over African states of possessing a relatively sophisticated infrastructure, and the promise of greater political stability.

There is some evidence that this scenario is already being realised.[3] EEC trade and strategic interests have increasingly focused on the Arab world; European multinationals have concentrated their investment in the NICs. The preferential access to the European market enjoyed by African countries has been diluted as the Community extended its network of preferential trading agreements. The Community's desire to pursue new political relationships, with the Peoples' Republic of China, for instance, has produced agreements in specific sectors; for example, the granting of quotas for certain textile products, which again remove a share of the Community market which might otherwise have been reserved for African countries.

A second scenario might be posited which is less optimistic regarding restructuring in Europe – in this case the new protectionism is transformed into policies akin to the old mercantilism. The EEC Commission itself has acknowledged the potential difficulties that some member states will face in adjusting to changes in the pattern of international economic relations:

> Generally speaking, Europe seems to lag behind the United States and Japan in adapting to competition from the developing countries and appears more vulnerable to an intensification of this competition in the future because of the trend and pattern of the external trade of most Community countries. They tend to export more and import less of the type of products produced by the developing countries (particularly products with a high unskilled labour content) than Japan and the United States, where the process of adjusting the structure of production and foreign trade to competition from these countries has been under way for longer.[4]

There are, obviously, significant differences between member-states with regard to this vulnerability. Britain, France and Italy, where productive investment has lagged in recent years, have been slow to move out of labour-intensive activities. In a period of prolonged recession and high unemployment, protectionist pressures arising in these countries may become irresistible.

In this second scenario, African countries continue to be of significance to the EEC as protected markets for European capital and consumer goods which are non-competitive in the markets of their technologically more advanced rivals – Japan and the United States – and in those of the NICs. A renewed mercantilism would represent a return to the policies of the colonial era, when, for example, the franc zone consumed a large share of the total output of a number of non-competitive French industries.[5]

Although African countries figure more prominently in this scenario than in the first, the outcome for them may be no more beneficial. In an era of mercantilism, the EEC is unlikely to be any more willing to open its markets to African exports than to those of other low cost producers that also threaten its traditional industries – a tendency that has already been noted in the textiles sector. Expansion of the Community to include Portugal and Spain, countries whose economic growth will depend on their exporting to other EEC members the types of products that African countries might feasibly be able to produce in the foreseeable future, will increase protectionist pressures in the Community. Certainly, in this scenario, African countries will not be devoid of bargaining power; but in an international economy characterised by continued recession and inflation in the West, coupled with regular increases in the price of imported energy, most African economies will be sufficiently weakened to be vulnerable to 'purchase' at low cost by promises of continued European aid. Asymmetries in the vulnerabilities of the partners will preserve Europe's upper hand in the bargaining process.

TOWARDS LOMÉ VI?

Institutionalised relationships between the European Community and Africa have gradually evolved towards a relationship which is less unfavourable for the latter. Provisions in the Treaty of Rome and the Yaounde Conventions facilitated a diversification of trading links between African states and the members of the Community. Gruhn and Zartman are correct in arguing that the Lomé Convention represented a step forward by comparison with the Yaounde Conventions (except in regard to the aid per capita made available to the ACP states).[6] Certainly, the changes introduced in the relationship as a result of the negotiations for Lomé I cannot be ignored. But if Lomé did indeed represent, in Gruhn's words, an 'inching towards interdependence', emphasis must be placed on the word 'inching' rather than 'interdependence'. Lomé remains a very unequal partnership – the ACP are fond of the analogy of the rider and the horse – in which there is an obvious asymmetry in interdependence. As for the dynamic of the relationship, 'inching' is a particularly appropriate term. For those who perceived the negotiations for the first Convention as merely the first tentative steps in an evolving partnership, the Lomé experience has been a bitter disappointment.[7]

Improvements made in the terms of the relationship in the transition from Yaounde to Lomé were largely a matter of the removal of the negative features of the earlier agreements, in particular, the European insistence on reverse preferences. These improvements were achieved at little economic cost to the Community, but were of great symbolic importance in ensuring a successful outcome to the negotiations. Only in the matter of access for ACP sugar was there a major conflict of interest between the EEC and ACP which necessitated costly concessions by the Community (although these were not passed on to the relevant domestic interests in EEC member states).[8]

Implementation of the first Convention exposed several areas in which a genuine conflict of interest exists between the ACP states and the Community. ACP dissatisfaction with a number of the Convention's provisions, and the manner in which they had been implemented, led to demands during the negotiations for Lomé II for substantial improvements in the terms of the Convention. For the ACP, the problem is that the low-cost concessions in the Lomé relationship have been exhausted. Its further extension would involve issues where zero-sum relationships predominate. This is only to be expected: as the EEC Commissioner for Development, Claude Cheysson, noted 'when a development aid policy ceases to be marginal, when it goes beyond financial aid, it becomes a domestic policy in the industrial countries'.[9] But it is the very failure of the Community to promote internal change at the expense of domestic interests, in order to accommodate the logical consequences of its development policies, that marks the limits of the Community's commitment to its ACP partners, and the boundaries beyond which the Lomé relationship will not progress.

If it is to be anything other than a minor insurance scheme for ACP countries, the results in the trade field (the most crucial aspect of the relationship) during the implementation of the first Convention were negligible. To some degree this was to be anticipated: Lomé itself could hardly be expected to bring about a significant transformation of the composition of ACP exports. But more disturbing than the lack of change on this dimension were the indications that the European Community was unwilling to continue to underwrite the terms of the Convention if the ACP took advantage of them to the extent of adding to the problems faced by Community industries.

One of the favourite assertions that the European Community makes regarding the Convention is that it provides security for the ACP since the relationship is 'based on a *de jure* system resulting from a contract freely negotiated between equal partners'.[10] This security would be meaningful for the ACP only if it allowed for a diversification of their exports, particularly into processed and manufactured goods. Community behaviour during the implementation of the first Convention undermined this notion of security. By threatening to utilise the safeguard clause against Mauritian exports of textiles, the Community demonstrated that it was unwilling to treat ACP exports of 'sensitive' products in a manner different from those originating in non-preferred suppliers. The implications of the textiles decision go beyond this one sector: no potential investor in an ACP country can be certain of access for future production to the European market if there is a possibility that such exports might adversely affect European interests.

The Community has announced that it wishes to foster a 'dynamic complementarity' between economic development in Europe and that in the ACP. Community notions of the form that such complementarity will take are extremely one-sided and disadvantageous to the ACP. During the renegotiations of Lomé, Community officials suggested that the problem of conflicts of interests in the industrial field would be ameliorated if ACP states would agree to regular consultations between governments and representatives of economic and social groups of all parties to the Convention. ACP representatives were suspicious of the motivations that underlay these Community proposals – not without good reason. There is a tremendous disparity between the Commission's positive and negative powers in the field of industrial co-operation. While the Commission has the power to cutoff imports (initial action in imposing a safeguard may also be taken unilaterally by a member-state), it has very little that it can offer the ACP on the positive side by way of promoting adjustment within the Community to allow for an increase in and diverisification of ACP exports.

In its recommendations on industrial co-operation in the second Lomé Convention, the Broeksz Report to the European Parliament asserted that:

> It is clear that the Community must do more than simply make available a certain amount of money and technical knowledge. The Community must restructure its own market so as to encourage the manufacture of certain industrial products in the ACP States. The purchasing power which would then be created in the ACP States would also benefit the Community's industry.[11]

It is the very lack of an adjustment policy at the Community level which underlies the disparity between the Commission's positive and negative powers in the field of industrial co-operation. Even at the level of the member-states, only the Netherlands has had a planned policy of restructuring in favour of imports from LDCs, although the Federal Republic has achieved considerable success in promoting industrial adjustment through fiscal incentives. Industrial restructuring policy in the Community remains the prerogative of the member-states – one that is jealously guarded. Germany, in particular, is hostile to the idea of creating a Community-wide industrial policy. Since the Commission lacks the power to enforce adjustment in the member-states (even assuming that a consensus could be achieved within the Commission in favour of this) its proposals for consultations in order to promote 'dynamic complementarity' appeared to the ACP as an attempt to channel ACP development efforts into projects that would not compete with European industry.

Community behaviour since the signature of the first Lomé Convention casts serious doubt on its professed commitment to ACP industrialisation. Contrary to Lynn Mytelka's argument that the first Lomé Convention was intended to facilitate the construction of a new international division of labour, whereas Lomé II marked a move away from this commitment,[12] I have found no evidence that officials at the Community level have ever taken seriously the commitments to ACP industrialisation which were written into the first Convention. Lomé I's chapter on industrial co-operation was inserted at the request of the ACP, the result of their initiative at the Kingston negotiating meeting in July 1974. In fact, the actual content of the Convention's chapter is remarkably similar to the ACP proposals, written by a Nigerian academic, except that all mention of commitments to specific targets was removed.

As Commissioner for Development Cheysson later acknowledged, these provisions 'lacked operational content'. There can be little doubt that this was not accidental. Co-operative efforts in the industrial field were to be focused on the creation of the Centre for Industrial Development (CID), which has become the scapegoat for the failure to realise the objectives specified in the Convention's chapter. The Community, however, has always had a very limited conception of the role that the Centre should play – essentially as a liaison between entrepreneurs and governments in ACP states, on the one hand, and the European private sector, which, the Commission believes, must be the principal agent in bringing industrial expertise to the ACP.

Considerable delay occurred before the Centre was established and became operational; subsequently it has been handicapped by inadequate funding. Conflicts between the ACP and the Community have arisen over its objectives, and disputes occurred between the Centre and the Commission's Directorate-General for Development over their respective jurisdictions, culminating in the dismissal of the Centre's first Director. As far as the Community is concerned, the Centre's role should be limited to promoting co-operation to assist import-substitution by ACP states – one of the sources of conflict between the Centre and the Commission was the former's support for projects in the textiles sector and for ACP efforts to establish free trading zones.

Community control of the purse-strings has enabled it to limit the role that the Centre can play. ACP representatives have argued that if the objectives of the industrial co-operation chapter are to be achieved, then a Fund for Industrial Co-operation must be established which would assist directly in the financing of projects identified by the Centre. Community response to this proposal has been cool – although, as a token gesture to the ACP in order to complete the negotiation of Lomé II, a commitment was made to appoint a group of experts to study the matter. The heart of the problem is the issue of control over the proposed funds, a matter which has implications behind this issue in that it illustrates the limited extent to which the Community is willing to go beyond rhetoric in its commitment to an 'equal partnership'. Fundamental to this dispute was the Centre's position as the only jointly-administered institution in the Lomé relationship (until the creation of a Technical Centre for Agricultural and Rural Co-operation in Lomé II). Quite simply, the Community is unwilling to contribute money to a fund which would be jointly managed and which would be able to make independent investment decisions.

Similarly, the Community has not taken the commitment to an equal partnership in the trade field seriously. Free access to the Community market was given willingly as long as there was no significant conflict between ACP exports and European interests. Where this occurred – as in certain CAP products, sugar, and rum – exceptions to the principle of free access were written into the Convention. Several senior Community officials that I have interviewed states bluntly that there was never any intention of giving ACP states *carte blanche* as regards access to the European market; this notion is reinforced by a number of internal Community memoranda which suggest that the EEC will have to re-evaluate its commitment to the ACP if some of the latter gain the capacity to become significant exporters of manufactured products.

For this reason, the EEC has insisted on the maintenance of a safeguard clause in the Convention. Although the ACP were successful in the renegoatiation of the Convention in adding a rider that the safeguard clause was not to be used for protectionist purposes, this has little meaning, given the ability not only of the Commission but also of the member-states to act unilaterally (as was the case with Mauritian textiles where Britain threatened to act outside the Community framework in imposing a safeguard action). Again, the asymmetry in the management of the 'equal partnership' is evident.

As Helleiner argued, prior to the negotiation of Lomé II, it is unrealistic to expect that the EEC would abandon the safeguard clause since every international trade treaty contains escape clauses. Nevertheless, there was 'a real opportunity for the Lomé Convention to lead the world in the development of appropriate terms for the use of safeguard clauses, well in advance of any likely major utilisation thereof'.[13] Even the threat of imposition of trade barriers is sufficient to generate welfare losses for exporting countries as a result of the uncertainties created.[14] Helleiner's very reasonable suggestion – that the Lomé Convention should implement the GATT principle that when the principle of market access enshrined in the agreement is violated then compensation should be offered for the resulting losses – would have dramatically changed the relationship in the direction of a more equal partnership. But here one encounters another paradox of the 'special relationship': the EEC is unwilling to make any commitments in the context of the Lomé relationship which might be seized upon by the 'Group of 77' as setting a precedent for concessions in the global North–South dialogue. Thus, at the time of the re-negotiation of Lomé, the EEC was adamantly refusing to compromise in the MTN discussions on defining potential limitations on the imposition of safeguard clauses. Not only is the 'special relationship' limited by the Community having one eye on domestic interests, but its other eye will always be on the implications of the Lomé provisions for the Community position in other international forums.

In the future there is little likelihood of a significant improvement in the Lomé provisions on trade. A commitment to total free access for ACP agricultural products would threaten Community producers in what are already sensitive areas, and which will become more problematic with the enlargement of the Community. Rather than an extension of the advantages enjoyed by the ACP from the trade preferences, one can anticipate a further reduction. Commission officials appear commited to the gradual elimination of the preferential margins enjoyed by the ACP by virtue of Lomé. The most likely scenario is that the Community's Generalised System of Preferences will be enlarged to include most duty-bearing products of interest to the ACP, and, at some stage in the future, the trade provisions of the Convention will be subsumed under a new GSP whose benefits will be limited primarily to low-income states.[15]

There have already been several indications of a movement in this direction. In extending its GSP offers in the last five years, the Commission has paid little attention to ACP complaints that their interests were being adversely affected. Most officials of the Community as well as academic commentators acknowledge that the level of preferences currently enjoyed by the ACP is insignificant. Cheysson has commented:

> Preferences are being eroded and if we are to give partners – who need to develop their external trade – the sort of advantage that will enable them to develop this trade properly, we will have to do more than grant customs preferences.[16]

According to the Commission, the principal advantage which is given to the ACP is secure access to the Community market, but as has already been noted, this security has been undermined by Community protectionist actions. Neither is the Community prepared to sponsor ACP states' industrialisation to the extent that they will receive significant benefits. The inevitable conclusion is that the trade provisions of the Convention will diminish in importance for Africa.

If Lomé provides few benefits in the trade field in the future then it will be reduced to a partial insurance arrangement for the ACP, rather than constructing a relationship which holds the promise of promoting economic transformation and growth. The aid provisions of the Convention will increasingly be its most significant feature, but on these dimensions also, there is little prospect for a major improvement, largely for the same reasons that block forward progress in the trade field.

Lomé's scheme for the stabilisation of export earnings (STABEX) was hailed as its most original chapter. Although the system continues to retain the support of the ACP, largely because of the absence of any preferred alternative, its very limited contribution to resolving the problems faced by primary product exporters was exposed during the course of Lomé I. As the Court of Auditors of the European Communities commented:

> apart from the ten or so special cases observed during a specific year, the final impact on the economies of the recipient ACP states was probably slight. Sporadic transfers cannot have lasting effect, and the amount of financial resources involved is usually too small.[17]

Principal among STABEX's limitations are its selective product coverage (which is confined to materials in their raw state or which have undergone only limited processing) its failure to cover (with the exception of states whose traditional export markets lay outside the EEC) earnings from exports other than those directed to the European Community, its confinement to nominal export earnings and the limited financial resources available to the system. This last problem became particularly evident during the first year of implementation of the second Convention when the year's allocation of resources from the system were exhausted: rather than pledging additional funds, the Community decided to make a proportional reduction in the transfers for that year.

The likelihood of a correction of these weaknesses is slight. The EEC is unwilling greatly to increase the system's product coverage either because it will encroach on the Community's Common Agricultural Policy (in the case of certain currently-excluded primary products (1984), and for a number of processed agricultural products such as tinned fruit) or because of concerns that the system will be subject to manipulation by multinationals (in the case of minerals) or because of the potential cost (again, primarily with respect to minerals). Neither will the Community be willing to extend the system's coverage to include export earnings to all markets. Community spokesmen have stated quite bluntly that they regard STABEX as an aspect of the 'privileged' bilateral relations between the ACP and the EEC, which excludes the latter from responsibility for ACP relations with other economic actors. In one respect, Lomé II marks an improvement on this dimension since it allows for the possibility of extending the system to include an ACP country's exports to another ACP state (subject to approval on a case-by-case basis by the Council of Ministers). A globalisation of system coverage on the other hand will probably occur only if agreement is reached in the future on a world STABEX – which, of course, would remove the system from the Lomé relationship.

Modification of the system to cover the real value of export earnings is unlikely on two grounds: (i) the costs involved and (ii) the unwillingness of the Community to create a precedent in the Lomé relationship which might then be utilised by the 'Group of 77' in the wider North–South dialogue as a signal by a group of industrialised countries of acceptance of the principle of indexation. Again, the Lomé relationship is constrained by Community concerns regarding its demonstration effect.

In the absence of these improvements, STABEX will remain a truncated scheme, certainly of some value to particular recipient states, but far short of the claims that enthusiasts have made for it. SYSMIN, the insurance scheme designed to maintain ACP production and export of minerals to the Community market introduced in Lomé II, is a clear indication of the evolution of Community thinking on raw materials issues. Unless a major change occurs in the bargaining power of African exporters (which, as the earlier part of the chapter indicated, is highly unlikely) the trend in commodities issues within the Convention will be towards measures aimed at meeting Community concerns regarding the security of supply of raw materials.

These tendencies within the Lomé relationship suggest that it is rapidly regressing towards a mere aid relationship. Again, the importance of the resources transferred through the European Development Fund should not be completely discounted, least of all for the poorest ACP countries, among which African states are disproportionately represented. But what can Africa expect from the EDF in the future? As has been true of bilateral aid from most donors, the EDF has failed to keep pace with the rate of inflation – a problem exacerbated by its continued slow rate of disbursement. Unless the European economy experiences a marked recovery in the future, the trend towards a decreasing real value in EDF aid per capita of the population of ACP states is likely to be maintained, and may be exacerbated if the EEC adopts a more 'globalist' perspective in its development policies.

One other trend within the EDF should not noted. Increasingly, the Commission has placed emphasis on a 'basic needs' approach as the central focus for its commitments. While a poverty-oriented focus in itself is difficult to crticise, this new orientation within the EDF has been used to justify the continuation of an old policy of unwillingness to fund directly productive projects within recipient countries. Infrastructure continues to receive the lion's share of EDF funding, while manufacturing remains the poor cousin and is likely to continue to do so given the EEC's belief that the responsibility for promoting the growth of manufacturing and the transfer of technology should reside with the private sector.

This rather depressing overview of the Lomé relationship and the likely direction in which it will develop gives little reason to suggest that it will become significantly more attractive for African states in the future. The question is not one of whether a dramatic transformation of the relationship will occur, but whether the 'partnership' will be maintained at all. A crucial consideration here is whether attractive alternatives to this outward orientation will emerge within Africa itself.

AFRICA: TOWARDS THE YEAR 2000

In the uncertain world of prophecy one of the least risky predictions regarding the future of Africa is that increasing disparities will occur between the rates of economic growth on the continent.[18] This makes it all the more dangerous to speak in terms of 'Africa's' future. Options available to the more successful states will obviously be more numerous than for those who fail to improve on the average continental performance in the two decades since independence. For in this period, only nine countries have experienced a 'relatively substantial' increase in per capita incomes.[19] Only a handful of African countries have enjoyed growth in per capita incomes in excess of the annual rate of 3 per cent achieved by middle-income and industrial countries – the gap between Africa and the rest of the world is increasing in relative as well as absolute terms.[20] Africa's performance in comparison with the rest of the Third World is particularly poor in the food sector where increasing crisis, exacerbated by continued high rates of population growth, can be anticipated in the next two decades.[21]

Nothing discussed so far in this chapter suggests that substantial help for African countries will be forthcoming from the international economic system. There is little evidence, either, that there will be many internally-generated alternatives to the present pattern of participation in the world economy. To be sure, some countries will discover and exploit additional raw materials. There will be continued progress towards increasing the value added locally to exports of raw materials. But even the more successful states will continue to resemble Tawney's description of the predicament of the peasant as sitting in a river, up to his neck in water. Little latitude will be available for the faster-growing states within a region to offer side-payments to their weaker neighbours to induce them to participate in regional co-operation projects. I stand by my earlier gloomy prognosis on the potential for regional economic integration to serve as a partial alternative to the present outward-orientation of African economies.[22]

Several commentators have suggested that disillusionment with the growth rates achieved under present economic strategies, coupled with the apparent closing-off of the potential for a strategy based on export-led manufacturing under the Lomé Convention, will lead African governments to move increasingly towards a self-reliant strategy.[23] There are a number of factors, I would suggest, which cast doubt on these conclusions. First, there will be a continued demonstration effect from countries that are successfully pursuing export-led development – especially the NICs but from many other developing countries also according to the World Bank, by 1975 there were forty LDCs whose manufactured exports totalled over $100m.[24]

Second, these commentators overestimate the importance of the Lomé provisions for gaining access to the European market. Certainly, the textiles decision destroyed any notion that the Lomé Convention would guarantee access for any manufactured product, but even within the restricted definition of 'dynamic complementarity' that the EEC is promoting, there will be options available for African states to pursue. Since the tariff advantages enjoyed under the Lomé Convention are generally insignificant, particularly for manufactured goods, their potential disappearance will probably not be a major factor in the competitiveness of African exports.

Indeed, if the present trend towards restricting the benefits of the GSP system to the poorest countries is carried to its logical conclusion, African states may actually be net beneficiaries from the changes in the Community's external economic policies. I am not arguing that any African state can anticipate making major strides towards industrialisation through manufacturing for export to the European market: rather, the argument is that opportunities will continue to exist in sufficient quantity as to maintain this option as an attractive policy alternative to African governments, particularly given the ever-present need to earn foreign currency.

A third factor militating against the adoption of a self-reliant strategy is its relative unattractiveness. If externally-oriented strategies have proved relatively unsuccessful in the last two decades, those states inclined towards the self-reliant strategy have few role models which would suggest that this alternative might be a more desirable option. Self-reliance is no panacea, as the experience of as disciplined a country as Tanzania illustrates.[25] For African élites – the present principal beneficiaries of the externally-oriented development models – few incentives are present to warrant the risk of moving to an alternative strategy.

Self-reliance is a difficult strategy to impose on a population when there are few grounds for believing that it will produce the results that publics with inflated expectations are demanding. But, the argument goes, continued disillusionment with outward-oriented strategies and corrupt élites will produce revolutionary pressures to sweep away the *ancien regime*. These 'Marxoid arguments', to use the felicitous term of Nicholas Demerath,[26] with their tendency to equate a violent change of government with a social revolution, demonstrate a lamentable ignorance of the nature of successful revolutions and their preconditions.[27] Contrary to Fanon, the lumpenproletariat appear to have little revolutionary potential. Rather than a series of social revolutions, the political future of Africa is more likely to be marked by a continuation and, indeed, exacerbation of the political instability characteristic of the continent in the last twenty years.[28] In these circumstances, one will be unlikely to see the emergence of disciplined party organisations with a commitment to self-reliance, and with the necessary legitimating ideology and organisation to carry the aspiration into practice.

Since neither collective nor national self-reliance will figure prominently as viable alternatives available to or pursued by African states in the foreseeable future, external links will remain important. Barring any radical upheaval in the world economy, Europe will remain predominant in these external links. But will the Lomé Convention be maintained?

Zartman, in his own attempt at predicting the course of African development towards the year 2000, asserted that the second Lomé Convention would be the last.[29] I believe that he is mistaken, if only because of the important bureaucratic interests that exist on the part of both the European Community and the ACP in its maintenance.

That is not to say that the Convention will continue in its present form. I have already indicated that I foresee the phasing out of the preferential trade advantages accorded the ACP by the Convention. This itself will have important implications, especially for those states which originally sought 'partnership' with the Community for defensive reasons, fearing a loss of markets if the enlarged Community discriminated against their exports (which appeared to be the dominant motive for Kenya, Uganda and Tanzania, at least at the time of the negotiation of the Arusha Convention). If equivalent trade benefits become available through the GSP then a number of states may wish to opt out of the Lomé relationship, which still bears the taint of neo-colonialist overtones. Here, much will depend upon whether or not the Community can induce Mozambique and Angola to participate – if they continue to disdain the proffered partnership then they may form the nucleus of a group of 'rejectionist' states.

A second significant factor will be the extent to which the ACP institutionalises itself, for it has no logical claim to existence outside the Lomé relationship. If the ACP Secretariat is successful in its plans to launch an ACP Development Bank then the longevity of the relationship may be ensured.

Continued interest in Lomé on the part of the Caribbean and (to a lesser extent) the Pacific States will depend in large part on future arrangements for the export of their sugar to the Community. While the recent events at Tate and Lyle may be the thin end of the wedge for ACP sugar, it is difficult to see how the Community can renege on its commitment, much as it might like to do so.

If Lomé is renewed in 1985 (and I believe that this will occur, *faute de mieux* from the ACP perspective) it will happen amid considerable bitterness at both the disappointing results of the first two conventions, and at EEC unwillingness to extend the relationship and its concentration on matters of greatest interest to the Community itself. But Lomé will survive, because, if nothing else, it offers not inconsiderable sums of aid to a number of the world's poorest states. If present trends are projected, the multilateralised relations between Europe and Africa may be reduced to being solely an aid-relationship. But for a number of African countries, in danger of becoming 'ghettos of benign neglect', the benefits may be worth the stigma of continued close association with an organisation of former colonial powers.

NOTES

1. Steven Langdon and Lynn K. Mytelka 'Africa in the Changing World Economy', in Colin Legum *et al*, *Africa in the 1980s: A Continent in Crisis* (New York: McGraw-Hill, 1979) Table 3.
2. See, for instance, Jere R. Behrman, 'International Commodity Agreements: An Evaluation of the UNCTAD Integrated Program' in William R. Cline (ed.) *Policy Alternatives for a New International Economic Order* (New York: Praeger, 1979).
3. Lynn K. Mytelka and Michael Dolan 'The EEC and the ACP Countries' in D. Seers and C. Vaitsos (eds) *Integration and Unequal Development* (London: Macmillan, 1980).
4. Commission of the European Communities, Directorate-General for Economic and Financial Affairs, 'Structural Change in the Community: Outlook for the 1980s' (Brussels, December 1979).
5. Pierre Moussa, *Les Chances Economiques de la Communauté Franco-Africaine* (Paris: Libraire Armand Colin, 1957).
6. Isebill V. Gruhn 'The Lomé Convention: Inching Towards Interdependence' *International Organization* 30 (2) Spring 1976, 241–62; and I. William Zartman 'Europe and Africa: Decolonization or Dependency?' *Foreign Affairs* 54 (2) January 1976, 325–43.
7. John Ravenhill, 'Asymmetrical Interdependence: Re-negotiating the Lomé Convention', *International Journal* 35 (1) Winter 1979–80, 150–69.
8. In one sense, the Community did impose costs on domestic producers by refusing to allow them to satisfy the total Community demand for sugar.
9. Quoted in Corrado Pirzio-Biroli, 'Foreign Policy Formation within the European Community with Special Regard to Developing Countries', 249.
10. EEC Spokesmen's Group, *Information Memo* Number p-92, October 1979, 1.
11. 'Report on the Negotiations for a New Lomé Convention' (Broeksz Report) *European Parliament Working Documents* 487/78, 1 December 1976, 19.
12. Lynn K. Mytelka, 'Africa: A Primary Producing Hinterland for Europe', *Conference on Europe and Africa*, Department of State, Washington, DC, April 1981.
13. Gerald K. Helleiner 'Lomé and Market Access' in Frank Long (ed.) *The Political Economy of EEC Relations with African, Caribbean and Pacific States* (Oxford: Pergamon, 1980) 185.
14. Jagdish N. Bhagwati 'Market Disruption, Export Market Disruption, Compensation and GATT Reform' in Bhagwati (ed.) *The New International Economic Order* (Cambridge: MIT Press, 1977).
15. One factor which might delay this is a conflict of bureaucratic interests within the Commission – the GSP is administered by the External Affairs Directorate (DG I), and Lomé by the Development Co-operation Directorate (DG VIII). But whether or not a formal merger of the two

systems occurs, the net result is likely to be the same – the ACP being placed on the same footing as GSP beneficiaries.

16. Quoted in Ellen Frey-Wouters, *The European Community and the Third World* (New York: Praeger, 1980) 47.
17. COM(80) 211 fin, Appendix p. 20.
18. Timothy M. Shaw, 'From Dependence to Self-reliance: Africa's Prospects for the Next Twenty Years', *International Journal* 35 (4) Autumn 1980, 821–44; and I. William Zartman, 'Social and Political Trends in Africa in the 1980s' in Legum *et al*, *Africa in the 1980s*, 67–119.
19. Adebayo Adedei, 'Africa: The Crisis of Development and the Challenge of a New Economic Order' quoted in Shaw 'From Dependence to Self-reliance', 826.
20. See data in *World Development Report* (Washington, DC: World Bank, annual).
21. Shaw 'From Dependence to Self-reliance', 829 and Zartman 'Social and Political Trends in Africa in the 1980s' 80–1.
22. John Ravenhill, 'Regional Integration and Development in Africa: Lessons from the East African Community', *Journal of Commonwealth and Comparative Politics* 17 (3) September 1979, 227–46.
23. Langdon and Mytelka 'Africa in the Changing World Economy' and Shaw 'From Dependence to Self-reliance'.
24. *World Development Report, 1980.*
25. Thomas J. Biersteker 'Self-reliance in theory and practice in Tanzanian trade relations', *International Organization* 34 (2) Spring 1980, 229–64.
26. Quoted in Victor T. LeVine, 'African Patrimonial Regimes in Comparative Perspective', *Journal of Modern African Studies* 18 (4) December 1980, 669.
27. Theda Skocpol, *States and Social Revolutions* (Cambridge: Cambridge University Press, 1979); and Kenneth Jowitt, 'Scientific Socialist Regimes in Africa: Political Differentiation, Avoidance and Unawareness' in Carl G. Rosberg and Thomas M. Callaghy (eds) *Socialism in Sub-Saharan Africa* (Berkeley: Institute of International Studies, University of California, 1979) 133–73.
28. Colin Legum, 'Communal Conflict and International Intervention in Africa', in Legum *et al*, *Africa in the 1980s*, 21–66.
29. Zartman, 'Social and Political Trends in Africa in the 1980s', 105.

Part III
The Continental Condition

7 Possible Futures for the OAU in the World System

AMADU SESAY and
OROBOLA FASEHUN

INTRODUCTION

'If we could first know where we are, and whither we are tending, we could better judge what to do, and how to do it.' – Abraham Lincoln[1]

Notwithstanding V. S. Naipaul's widely quoted statement that 'Africa has no future,[2] Africanist scholars are still committed to identifying and advancing possible futures for the continent. In short, it is not true that Africa has no future. Admittedly, the prophecy that Africa has no future must have been inferred from the continent's poor performance in economic and political matters. But that itself stems from Africa's inheritance and is not immutable.

LEVELS OF ANALYSIS

This chapter is not concerned with a discussion of the Organisation of African Unity's (OAU) superstructure *per se.* Although any discussion of the Organisation necessarily entails an examination of such things as the secretariat and other pertinent bodies, we have concentrated on the substructure – modes of development on the continent and their impact on the OAU in the past, present and future. In short, we have decided against presenting yet another orthodox analysis of the OAU because we believe that the futures of the institution in particular, and those of the continent as a whole, will be decided by economic issues; for instance, whether Africa should continue following its present (1984) predominantly capitalist developmental model which has left the continent powerless, uninfluential and increasingly excluded from the world's 'high table', yet ineluctiably incorporated into the periphery of the capitalist economic system. We believe that Africa still has a choice to adopt what we can call self-reliant or transformationist development strategies that would leave the continent more self-sufficient economically and politically.

A discussion of possible futures for the OAU also requires some clarification. First, the OAU exists within a certain environment. The African environment in which it operates is at the level of the superstructure characterised by (i) interstate and intra-state conflicts and (ii) conflicts over decolonisation, development and human rights. These conflict types have resulted in challenges to the integrity of the state or the regime in many African countries.

Second, at the level of the substructure, the African milieu is dominated by dependence, reverse or stagnant growth, and underdevelopment. The African environment, then, is embedded in a global context of which Africa along with its regional organisation is peripheral and dependent. As such, any analysis of OAU futures should clearly recognise the continent's dependence.

Third, the Organisation is composed of fifty-one or so members with different and conflicting economic, political and cultural systems. That being so, there is really no such thing as, say, an 'OAU policy' on decolonisation or an 'OAU future'. What is often discribed as 'OAU policy' is nothing more than the distillation of the positions and strategies of member-states on specific issues of either continental or global import.

When we talk about OAU futures in this chapter, then, what we mean essentially is that we will examine alternative strategies of African states in some of the issue areas identified and then make prognostications as to the impact of such strategies on the Organisation. In short, whatever futures we can identify for the OAU between now and the year 2000 cannot and should not be divorced from the futures of its fifty-one members. After all, these members collectively and individually, make the OAU what it is today and what it will be in the future.

The structure of the rest of the chapter reflects two broad but interrelated concerns. First, an account of the OAU's present and past performance is undertaken in four issue areas: (i) decolonisation, (ii) strategic issues, (iii) development and (iv) human rights. Second, possible futures for the OAU in the world system are identified with regard to these four issue areas.

PAST AND PRESENT PERFORMANCE

Decolonisation

The OAU's past performance on decolonisation is an indication as to its future role in the decolonisation of Namibia and the attainment of black majority rule in South Africa. A useful lesson can be learned by taking stock of the OAU's record on decolonisation and projecting this into the possible futures of the Organisation. Most OAU members attained their independence through negotiated constitutional talks which transferred power to national bourgeois elements. The experience of peaceful political decolonisation influenced the strategy and tactics which most of the new states in the OAU have adopted in their quest to liberate the remaining pockets of colonisalism in Africa.

These strategies are divisible into two although they have at times been pursued simultaneously. The first strategy involves the imposition of diplomatic sanctions against colonisers and regimes of the white redoubt. The second strategy is the absence of social and trade intercourse with the pariah regimes. It was and is hoped that such strategies would force the affected regimes (now only Namibia and South Africa) to decolonise and accept black majority rule.

Many OAU members, especially those pursuing a dependent capitalist development path have not fully implemented the OAU strategy of social and economic sanctions against South Africa. It is, of course, true that no African state – save Malawi – has established formal diplomatic relations with the outcast regimes. But many African states maintain surreptitious diplomatic and trade links with one or all of them. Zaire maintains secret links with South Africa while Nigerian governments found ready markets in Portugal from 1963 until 1971.[3]

The failure of 'soft' strategies to effect the peaceful transfer of power to blacks made reliance on the tougher and harder strategy of armed struggle through liberation movements mandatory. Accordingly, in 1973 the OAU re-endorsed armed struggle through liberation movements. But it was neither the OAU's re-endorsement of armed conflict nor its diplomatic and social sanctions that led to the independence of Luso-African territories in 1975 and 1976 and of Zimbabwe in 1980. The reasons for the Organisation's ineffectiveness are myriad. We shall only document two here.

First, the OAU, reflecting its membership's poverty, is a materially-poor Organisation. Its 1980 annual budget was a mere $US17.6m. Given the record of non-payment of funds, it is quite unlikely that the members will pay even this paltry sum.

Second there has been a continuing ideological conflict between its Liberation Committee and the total OAU membership. The Committee, a co-ordinating body for Africa's assistance to the liberation movements, is based in a transformationist state. Tanzania. Not surprisingly, it has generally been more militant than the parent Organisation. As such, conservative capitalist states have been rather distrustful of the Committee; they have expressed their dissatisfaction against the Organisation by holding back contributions to the Liberation Fund. Starved of monies, the Committee and its clients are forced to turn to non-OAU sources for financial support.

Strategic Issues

Since the flush of independence on the continent in the 1960s, intra- and inter-African disputes have become a common feature of African international relations. By 1963, then, African leaders were well aware of this trend. Accordingly, they devised safeguards against such disputes recurring among OAU members. First, the Charter deemed members to be sovereign and equal. Second, it preached against intervention in the affairs of others and upheld their territorial integrity. Third and finally, all African states were implored to settle their disputes through mediation, conciliation and arbitration. In short, African leaders were determined to impose order on the continent. But despite its rather elaborate superstructure and procedure, the OAU has not succeeded in preventing inter-African conflicts.[4]

Several factors are responsible for this poor performance. We will mention just a few here: (i) The Commission (on mediation, conciliation and arbitration) which was set up in 1964 lacked mandatory jurisdiction; (ii) African disputes are highly politicised and thus not amenable to legal solutions and (iii) the majority of African states regard arbitration as an extremely unfriendly act against a sister state. Not surprisingly, the Organisation has been quick to improvise new methods of conflict resolution more in tune with contemporary international relations on the continent. These techniques can be broadly categorised into two types: formal and informal. Under the former there are: (i) conference diplomacy; (ii) *ad hoc* committees of heads of state and/or prominent Africans; and (iii) 'good offices' committees whose members are normally heads of state.

These methods, like their counterparts under the Commission, have their own drawbacks. Conference diplomacy seldom settles anything. The conference room is not a congenial setting for quiet diplomacy which is a prerequisite for the pacific settlement of most conflicts. However, summit diplomacy sometimes puts a dispute 'on ice' thereby allowing tempers to calm down until an appropriate mode of settlement can be found. The more successful of the 'new breed' of conflict resolution apparatuses in the OAU's laboratory are *ad hoc* committees and 'good offices' committees.[5]

Closely related to this system is what we have called 'Presidential mediation'. Influential African heads of state often put their influence and prestige to the test by offering to mediate in inter-African disputes with the hope of finding permanent solutions to such conflicts. This technique is perhaps the one most widely used today. The most celebrated case of Presidential mediation is still the Algero–Moroccan conflict of 1963–4. President Modibo Keita and Emperor Haile Selassie of Ethiopia succeeded not only in bringing the disputants to the conference table but also in separating them on the battlefield. The conflict was then frozen for nearly nine years until it was finally resolved by President Boumedienne and King Hassan in 1972.

There are myriad reasons for the prominent role of OAU's informal channels of conflict management. First, the Organisation lacks material and ideal resources; finance, qualified personnel, logistical support and so forth. Second, at the moment (1984), the OAU does not have a mobile police force. Such a force must be able to take-off at very short notice and quell successfully, not only smouldering conflicts but also those which have broken out into open hostilities. Third, the OAU has not been seen by many disputants as 'impartial'. The absence of salience perhaps explains why King Hassan has been reluctant to face the Organisation's *ad hoc* Committee on Western Sahara.

The OAU is perhaps the poorest – as well as the largest – regional organisation of its kind in the world. Not only is its budget minuscule, neither does it have any single state or group of states who could bail it out of its perennial financial insolvency. This situation was vividly demonstrated in 1980 when the Organisation attempted to raise a peace-keeping force to separate the warring factions in the Chadian civil war. It could not raise the required $US40m. Consequently, the peace-keeping force of Nigerian, Senegalese and Zairean troops were largely supported by French and American aid. Such reliance clearly undermined the OAU's claim to maximising regional autonomy through self-regulation.

Finally, despite the total support which its members seem to give to it, the OAU's standing in the continent and elsewhere is dwindling because most of its decisions are not backed by effective sanctions.[6] This has been so for most of the Organisation's pronouncements on inter-African disputes. In this chapter, we shall discuss briefly only three examples: the Tanzania-

Uganda, the Chadian and the Western Sahara conflicts. All three fall within our conflict genre: threats to the integrity of the state, threats to the integrity of the regime and ideological and personality incompatibility.

The Tanzania–Uganda dispute broke out in 1971 after the overthrow of Milton Obote (President Nyerere's personal friend) by the head of the former's armed forces, Idi Amin. Thereafter, there were continual complaints by both sides of harassment and aggression, which sometimes claimed the lives of innocent citizens of the two countries. The OAU's *ad hoc* committee on the Tanzania–Uganda conflict could not impose a solution on the two disputants. When the dispute was eventually settled in 1979, it was through military victory by Ugandan exiles supported by Tanzanian regulars. By the time the sixteenth summit met in Monrovia, the Tanzanians had achieved a *fait accompli* in the neighbouring state, with Amin's overthrow and forced exile in Saudi Arabia.

The Chadian conflict also brought to light the OAU's impotence in tackling intra-African disputes. Although an *ad hoc* committee of African heads of state was set up in 1977 to find a permanent solution to the crisis, it did not succeed in doing so. Besides this, the Organisation's peace-keeping force in Chad was unable to enforce the peace amongst the warring factions in the troubled country.

Our final example is the ongoing conflict (1984) over control of Western Sahara. Again, like the other two conflicts, the OAU was able to set up an *ad hoc* committee on Western Sahara in 1978 during the Khartoum summit. But the committee has been subjected to a series of rebuffs by King Hassan of Morocco. It was not until September 1980 that he allowed his representatives to sit at the same conference table as the Saharan people: the Polisario Front. So far, the OAU has not been able to impose a solution on Morocco or censure its monarch. This failure has led to a lot of resentment amongst the socialist and radical members of the Organisation and has tended to polarise its membership ideologically still further. The radicals' disappointment was expressed forcefully by Zimbabwe and Mozambique at the seventeenth summit in Freetown in July 1980.[7] Both countries accused the King of intransigence, colonialism and imperialism and called upon the OAU to recognise an independent Saharan Democratic Republic (SADR). We shall consider the implications of this ideological cleavage in detail in the next section of this chapter, on futures.

In concluding the discussion on strategic issues, a number of points have emerged. First, lack of resources has hindered the OAU's capacity to resolve inter-African disputes amicably in the past and continues to do so today. Second, there is no provision for mandatory sanctions in the charter against a recalcitrant member. Third, the combined effects of the above factors have resulted in some loss of prestige by the OAU not only in the eyes of its members but also in those of outside observers.

Development

> The very existence of some of our nations is being critically threatened by adverse economic forces and natural disasters. It will take years before we in Africa can exercise our right to full equality and effective participation in the current international economic system.[8]

> Sub-Saharan Africa has the most disturbing outlook . . . its growth rate in 1985–90 would be a meagre 1 per cent per person . . . average incomes would actually be lower in 1990 than they were in 1980.[9]

One of the rationales for creating the OAU at the flush of independence in the early 1960s was to harmonise and co-ordinate the development strategies of the continent so as to accelerate the economic and political well-being of its members and their peoples. It was hoped that rapid economic development would also make political independence more meaningful and so enhance Africa's influence and standing in the world system.

However, after two decades of political independence, Africa in 1981 is neither economically developed nor technologically advanced. In the past, the OAU devoted almost all its resources and time to superstructural matters such as decolonisation and strategic issues on the continent. The substructure – economic development and social welfare – were neglected in spite of the creation of Specialised Commissions charged with responsibility for such issues.[10]

This situation is due to a number of factors. First, the question of political instability. This has been a prominent feature of the continent and continues to plague most independent African states. Second, ideological-cum-personality incompatibility amongst African states and their leaders, which has hampered co-operation at the inter-state level. The problem of Africa's poor economic growth has been made much worse by the presence of comprador classes in control of many African states. These ruling classes maintain dependent and interwoven economic and social linkages with their counterparts in the erstwhile colonial metropoles and have resisted moves towards inter-African economic co-operation, which they see as weakening such linkages. A third point relates to what we can call the African continent's overall diversity which has been vividly described by Ali Mazrui.[11] This socio-cultural fractionalisation continues to hold back meaningful and practical co-operation amongst the Africans. In the meantime, the continent remains on the periphery of the world economic, political and military systems. And, of course, the gloomy predictions about the future continue unabated.[12]

In addition to sluggish and/or zero growth, mounting foreign debts, growing oil bills and a general fall in the living standards of their populations, most African states have also had to contend with a worsening food situation as a result of a general increase in population. At present, African cannot feed itself. The Sahelian drought and disaster and the chronic problem of starving refugees are examples of the urgent need for the continent to map out clear-cut strategies with a view to responding more effectively in future to such natural or man-made disasters.[13] The major responses so far have been from extra-continental actors, mainly those in the industrialised West. On the other hand, such a situation only increases the incorporation of African states into the periphery of the world capitalist system.

The OAU has taken a number of measures in the past to arrest the continent's deteriorating economic and food situation. Up to the early 1980s, a series of international seminars and conferences have been organised by the Organisation and/or in conjunction with the Economic Commission for Africa (ECA) to find permanent solutions to these twin problems. The most notable have been the Monrovia futures seminar of 1979 and the special Lagos economic summit of 1980.[14]

More accent is now being placed on development but not just for its own sake. Rather, inthe 1980s, the new approach seems to emphasise development of the people and for the people; that is, less stress on the superstructure, more on the substructure. There is growing appreciation also that salvation for Africa in particular and for the Third World in general lies in self-reliance both individually and collectively. But the success of these interrelated strategies would involve a lot of sacrifice by the continent's ruling classes.

At the moment the few countries which have pursued self-reliance policies are also those whose élites and bureaucrats are willing to forego their privileged economic and social positions for the good of the masses in their own societies. These countries have accordingly pursued socialist transformationist economic policies. But for the majority that practice the capitalist path of economic development, domestic inequalities continue to grow as a result of their increasing absorption into the orbit of the developed North – the OECD nexus.

Human Rights

The need for a Human and Peoples Rights Charter in Africa is a pressing one. Twenty years after the first wave of political independence, the continent's human rights record is not enviable. Besides that, although economic development and prosperity are still elusive prospects for the majority of African states, if and when they do join the club of wealthy industrialised countries of the world, the wealth would be meaningless for the continent's masses unless their right to life, decent living and property, freedom of speech etc, are guaranteed by a pan-continental human rights document. The history of post-independence Africa is dotted with atrocities committed against individuals and/or communities by states and governments. There have been instances of genocide against communities and ethnic groups either because they belonged to the wrong side of the power configurations within their respective states, or simply because they held religious or political views at variance with those of the leadership. Besides such cases, there has also been civil strife in which thousands and, in a few cases even millions, of innocent African lives have been lost: the Sudanese civil war, the Nigerian civil war and the communal strife in Burundi and Rwanda in the late 1950s, the early 1960s and the early 1970s. Finally, the first two decades of Africa's independence have also witnessed the emergence of dictators who have slaughtered thousands of their citizens during their reign of terror. The three most notorious are: Idi Amin of Uganda, Jean Bokassa of the former Central African Empire and Macias Nguema of Equatorial Guinea. All three were an embarrassment not only to their own countries but to the continent and the world at large. Bokassa was personally responsible for the murder of some 200 schoolchildren in 1978 whilst Amin and Nguema were both responsible for the annihilation of hundreds of thousands of their citizens in cold blood.

Despite these dastardly crimes, the OAU watched silently and powerlessly. When for instance, Amin, Bokassa and Nguema were eventually ousted from power in their respective countries, the removals were undertaken either by domestic elements alone or in collusion with external forces.[15] In the Ugandan case, not only did the Organisation turn a blind eye to the murderous reign of Amin, but the Ugandan leader was at the height of his brutality when he hosted the twelfth annual summit in Kampala in July 1975. Apart from Julius Nyerere of Tanzania and Kenneth Kaunda of Zambia, many other African leaders simply trooped into the Ugandian capital and pretended that 'all was well' in that country. Moreover, Amin routinely became Chairman of the OAU for the next twelve months during which time he also served as Africa's chief spokesman and representative. As this post conferred some legitimacy on the dictator's brutal administration, much of the verbal attacks on his regime and personality subsided somewhat during his tenure as OAU chairman.

A number of factors are responsible for the OAU's nonchalant attitude on human rights violations in the past. First, is the stoic adherence by its members to principles of sovereign equality and non-interference in the affairs of others. The all-embracing protective shield which the latter, in particular, gave to African states explains in large measure the deafening silence of the OAU on human rights issues. Finally, at the time of the OAU's creation, most African leaders were concerned primarily with political order and stability within their newly-inherited political kingdoms. Consequently, they were hypersensitive to challenges to the integrity of either their persons, their regimes or their states. Thus human rights issues were ignored.

Belatedly, however, there has been increasing demand for a human rights charter for Africa. In part, this call has been inspired by the violent record and gross violations of human rights by the independent African states. It is also a result of the realisation by African leaders that anti-human rights activity in their countries is neither an insurance against violent overthrow of their regimes, nor does it guarantee continued tenure in office. Thus, at the sixteenth annual summit in Monrovia in June 1979, African leaders unanimously agreed to commission a group of experts to draw up an African Human Rights and Peoples Charter. By July 1981 when the OAU held its eighteenth summit in Nairobi, the African Charter was ready and was unamimously adopted by the Assembly of African Heads of State and Government (AHG). The Charter covers many crucial areas including: (i) equality before the law and equal protection of the law, (ii) right to receive and disseminate information, (iii) right to free association and (iv) right to existence and self-determination. In addition, there is a call to all African states to 'eliminate all forms of foreign economic exploitation, particularly that practised by international monopolies, so as to enable their peoples to benefit fully from the advantages derived from their natural resources'.[16]

The successful implementation of the Charter would mark the beginning of a new era for human rights on the continent. Never the less, there are many problems ahead. Some of them we will explore in the following section on futures. Suffice it at the moment to say that some of these problems would arise from the interpretation of the Charter. One such area relates to the proviso on freedom to receive and disseminate information. Who, for example, is to determine whether national constitutional limits have been transgressed by individuals in pursuit of such rights? Surely, governments would still find ways and means of suppressing information to opponents on spurious constitutional grounds? Again, how would offenders – especially former heads of state – be brought to book if they had already left their countries and were in exile either on the continent or overseas? These and other salient questions will be tackled in the section on futures to which we now turn.

POSSIBLE FUTURES FOR THE OAU IN THE WORLD SYSTEM

Decolonisation

The two major and dialectical developmental perspectives in Africa – the peripheral capitalist development path as against the transformationist self-reliant way – have each been advocated in the past to influence OAU policy on decolonisation. Future OAU policy on decolonisation will be determined by whichever of these two developmental models emerges dominant in the continent. As such, two scenarios for OAU decolonisation are possible.

The first and perhaps most probable – even if it is not preferred – is the emergence of a group of states with sufficient energy and other resources to transform themselves into veritable regional and sub-imperial and semi-industrialised states. These states will form the core in the African periphery and will prefer a decolonisation strategy that will usher in regimes that will pursue a capitalist mode of development in the former colonial territories, including colonial South Africa. The transfer of power to black capitalists in South Africa is rather crucial to these states since a black capitalist South Africa can be expected to be a source not only of capital but also of technology to the other regional powers in the continent. Although support will continue to be given to the liberation movements, the preference will be for a negotiated settlement that will hold intact the class structure of South Africa shorn of apartheid and officially-sanctioned racism. It can be reasonably expected that Western capitalist states with heavy capital investments in South Africa will support the strategy that poses the least risk to their investments and guarantees the continued existence in power of interests that are dependent on them.

The alternative scenario is predicated on the emergence of an OAU dominated by transformationist states: states that seek to decouple themselves from the world's capitalist system to reduce linkages which are not beneficial to the generality of Africans. This group of states situated at present (1984) in Southern Africa – Angola and Mozambique – and in Central and Western Africa – Ethiopia, Tanzania and Guinea Bissau – would not only want power transferred to blacks but rather to those blacks with a materialist perspective on social relations. An OAU dominated by these states would not only fully support the armed struggle to dislodge the white capitalist minority regimes but also to destroy the apparatus of capitalism and South Africa's sub-imperial expansion. Such states may view a socialist South Africa as the nucleus of a truly African socialist federation that could serve not only as the engine of growth but of development; one that would cater to the human needs of Southern Africans in particular and Africans in general. The same scenario with minor modifications – given the territory's special legal status – would hold for Namibia.

Strategic Issues

The futures of the OAU in strategic issues – defined here to mean intra- and inter-African disputes and external intervention – would depend on which of the two ideological blocs identified earlier controls it and, indeed, the entire continent between now and the year 2000. Our first scenario, then, is centred on an OAU dominated by transformationist states and with particular reference to the issue of external intervention in Africa. There would either be no intervention at all, or much less. Sub-imperial African states would also not be able to intervene directly or indirectly to rescue their tottering colleagues as was the case during the two Shaba crises in the late 1970s. Besides that, they would find it increasingly difficult to collude with capitalist Western powers.

But for the radicals to be able to ward off such incidents of external intervention, they would have to strengthen the organs of the OAU. This would involve (i) creation of an African High Command and (ii) increased powers for the Secretariat. The Secretary-General would have to be given more executive powers to respond swiftly and effectively in times of crisis. There must also be a state or group of socialist states both willing and able to bail the organisation out of its present financial insolvency. South Africa under a revolutionary black government could, perhaps, play this critical role. There are bound to be risks in this sort of arrangement in the sense that dominant states would be tempted to 'victimise' the minority. But such temptation would be less for the transformationist than for the sub-imperial regimes. In sum, the combined effects of radical control over the OAU would be the emergence of a continent which would be increasingly inward-looking. The OAU would be more effective in controlling not only intra-African conflicts, but also all incidents of external intervention on the continent. African problems in general would also be disposed of within an exclusively African context.

The scenario for sub-imperial states is quite the opposite of that for the transformationist countries. Under their aegis, external intervention would increase. Moreover, the OAU would be ineffective in controlling it. Besides that, its response would depend on two factors (i) the identity of the aggressor and (ii) the identity of the victim of aggression. The regional capitalist states would, as we have argued, be quite eager to collude with Western countries either to restore order in their client states, or to restore their colleagues to power. On the other hand, the same states would condemn vehemently any intervention by socialist states even if such action is in pursuit of legitimate OAU objectives such as the liberation of Namibia and South Africa. They would see any incursions into the region by the radical states and their associates as a threat to their own economic and political interests since successful overthrow of the white redoubt would be likely to result in the installation of a radical black regime. This strategy explains their preference for a negotiated settlement to the conflicts in the region by potential sub-imperial states – Nigeria, Zaire, Ivory Coast, and Kenya.

Development

How would the ascendancy of either of these two dominant modes of development in the continent affect the OAU in the future? We suggest five possible scenarios. The first relates to the concept of non-interference in the affairs of other states. An OAU dominated by sub-imperial states would see the gradual abolition of this principle for the following reasons (i) the sub-imperial semi-industrialised capitalist states would increasingly need extra markets for their finished products in neighbouring countries; (ii) they would also need regular supplies of raw materials (and probably cheap labour) to feed their rapidly expanding industrial machine; and to ensure that such markets are kept within their spheres of influence, the regional powers would (iii) undertake policing and peace-keeping duties in their sub-regions in particular and in the continent as a whole, in much the same way as the US has been doing in Latin America. In short, we envisage an OAU which would be more or less like its 'first cousin' in the Americas: the Organisation of American States (OAS). There would be no doubt that relative order would prevail on the continent, but such order would be at the expense of the less fortunate members of the society of

African states. Its main objective would be to make the largely 'agrarian' African societies more amenable to economic exploitation.

The second picture is one that involves increasing economic, political and military penetration of the continent by extra-regional powers. The penetration would, however, be much more indirect than it is today and the OAU would be powerless to do anything about it. This is because the intervention would be done through regional powers acting as Trojan horses for their counterparts in the developed North. Although the sub-imperial African states themselves would not be able to compete with the Western half of the developed North on an equal footing with the rest of the world for influence, they would, never the less, be powerful enough regionally and sub-regionally to prevent 'independent' action by extra-continental actors. The overall effect would be the incorporation of the OAU system and the continent into the periphery of the capitalist system. Such development would paralyse the Organisation's capacity to protect its weaker members, one of its *raisons d'être*.

Our third scenario concerns the emergence of relatively powerful and radical transformationist states on the continent. They would obviously oppose the economic incorporation of the continent into the mainstream of monopoly capitalism, and consistent with their domestic economic strategies, they would challenge the collaborative, and indeed destructive, role of the sub-imperial states on the continent. The radical states prefer an economic strategy which would utilise Africa's resources at home and so free the continent from its unequal embrace with the capitalist countries. They would want to see an OAU that is able to respond more effectively to the challenges posed by extra-continental states. The socialist African states would also try to redirect the OAU's development strategy with more emphasis on self-reliant economic policies within a continental context. This scenario envisages some radical modifications to the Lagos Plan of Action, to purge it of all its neo-colonial elements, and the rejection of the World Bank's 'Agenda' for Accelerated Development in Sub-Saharan Africa, which recommended the continued incorporation of Africa into the world capitalist system.

Such a puritanical ideological posture by the radicals would polarise the Organisation and serves to lead to our fourth scenario. This is the widening ideological gulf between the capitalists and the socialists (who would probably be in a minority). The latter would, as a result, form a caucus within the OAU, to protect their interests as a first step on the road to the formation of their own regional organisation. We noted earlier the increasing frustration of the radicals over the OAU's handling of issues which are close to their hearts at the Freetown summit in July 1980. For example, the speeches of Zimbabwe and Mozambique on the Western Sahara issue are a pointer to what is to be expected in the future. Their disenchantment is bound to increase further as economic inequalities sharpen within and between member states. A radical caucus would conceivably also cut across racial, linguistic and religious barriers to embrace 'southern' as well as 'northern' elements in the continent. This prognosis assumes the emergence of a relatively prosperous and militarily powerful and revolutionary South Africa which is willing to provide leadership for the radicals.

Our fifth and final scenario envisages the breakdown of the OAU along racial and cultural lines. The Africans may yet leave the institution *en masse* to form one which would be exclusively black. This could come about as a result of black African frustration over Arab contributions to Africa's development efforts – Arabs both inside and outside the continent.[17] Closely related to this is the fact that Arabs are so far the only people that have a caucus within the OAU. In other words, they act as a single bloc on most issues before the Organisation. This was especially pronounced before the split in their ranks over Egypt's peace initiative with Israel. This inter-Arab political warfare – if not actual bloodletting – is causing a lot of anxiety amongst the black African members. Much of Organisation's business was hampered because of the boycott of Egypt by the Arab 'rejectionist' front which is opposed to peace with Israel. This has led to several walk-outs against Egypt, as well as a boycott of Egyptian officials at the OAU Secretariat by the rejectionists, to the annoyance of many black African states. Given the above, then, the Africans would be compelled at sometime in the future to make a cost-benefit analysis of keeping in or expelling the Arabs from the OAU. Such a decision would be influenced by two crucial developments (i) if the Arab north fails to implement the Lagos Plan by evolving a regional organisation which would facilitate the creation of an African Common Market by the year 2000 and (ii) if a free Namibia and a South Africa purged of its radical discrimination should emerge before a permanent peace is found for the Middle East. This prognostication would remove the most resilient bond of identity between the two radical groups: anti-imperialism and anti-racism, the latter implying being anti-Israeli for the Arabs.

Human Rights

The OAU's futures for human rights, like those for decolonisation, strategic issues and development, are tied up with the ongoing struggle in the continent between the radical and capitalist countries. The ascendancy of veritable regional, sub-imperial and semi-industrialised states would encourage the disregard of what we can all the political and economic rights of their citizens. First of all, there are bound to be increasing domestic inequalities in these states: the few at the upper echelons of the political and economic ladder will become increasingly richer, whilst the masses suffer increasing deprivation, both political and economic. Their economic picture would resemble that of the 'Brazil 1976 model'.[18]

The extreme poverty of the masses will lead to demands for reform of the political and economic systems in the sub-imperial countries, a situation akin to that in many Latin American countries. However, such unrest would only lead to increasing political and military repression and, of course, to violations of the economic and human rights of the ordinary citizens – arbitrary arrests of political opponents, murder and/or 'mysterious' disappearance of dissidents and/or their families and friends. Under such circumstances, there would be freedom neither of speech nor of the press; nor, for that matter, the right to receive and disseminate information as guaranteed under the Human Rights Charter of the OAU. This scenario, then, is one in which the industrialised capitalist states would figure prominently and regularly before an African Commission for Human Rights to answer various charges of human rights violations.

We are not arguing that there would not be any human rights infringements in transformationist regimes. On the contrary. But such charges would arise from different sources (i) political dissidents would through their activities violate their national constitutional rights but would then receive support from the sub-imperial states and (ii) charges of human rights transgressions would be trumped up by the capitalist states to discredit the social and economic gains made by the socialist countries. Again, such activities would be carried out in the guise of 'promoting the cause' of so-called 'prisoners of conscience'. Such a campaign would perhaps be reminiscent of that between the East and West in the cold-war period. The effectiveness of the OAU in redressing human rights infringements would thus depend on the integrity of the Human Rights Commission and of course, the determination of individual Africans – especially the legal experts – to ensure that no state or leader gets away with serious violations of human rights as is the case at present. In that connection, Mazrui's call for an All African Supreme Tribunal is especially pertinent. Such a court should be empowered to try not only malevolent incumbent leaders but also those who might have lost power and are still living either in their respective states or in exile. Under Mazrui's scheme:

If a former President were to be captured in his country the succeeding

> regime would hand him over to the custody of the Chairman of the OAU until judicial proceedings could get under way. A former President who managed to escape to another African state would be handed over to the custodian authorities of the All African Tribunal.[19]

The advantage of this system is that it would enable the OAU to sign extradition agreements with both African and non-African countries. That way, an African Commission on Human and Peoples Rights could bring before it anybody charged with human rights violations. Such provision would make it difficult for malevolent ex-heads of state or their close aides to retire in relative security and comfort. Surely, the arrangement would make it rather difficult, if not impossible, for future Amins and Bokassas to get a hiding-place in the continent or elsewhere.

SUMMARY

The fruition of any of the possible futures for the OAU which we have conjectured in this chapter,[20] would largely depend on which of the predominant developmental paths is able to gain pre-eminence on the continent. The chances are that it is more probable for regional capitalist powers to emerge. The effects of such ascendancy on the OAU and the continent at large have already been conjectured. What we can say with some degree of certainty is that irrespective of the scenarios we have painted, the OAU as we all know it in 1984 will (i) continue as an inter-state organisation in the mid-term future, and (ii) will not be the same in 1990 or, indeed, in the year 2000.

NOTES

1. Abraham Lincoln, quoted by Andrew M. Kamarck 'Sub-Saharan Africa in the 1980s: An Economic Profile' in Helen Kitchen (ed.) *Africa: From Mystery to Maze* (Lexington: Lexington Books, 1976) 167.
2. V. S. Naipaul, *New York Times Book Review*, 15 May 1979, 36.
3. It is interesting to note, though, that even OPEC Gabon with the highest income per capita in black Africa has also received loans from South Africa for the construction of the Trans-Gabon railway system.
4. For a more detailed discussion of these and related issues, see Amadu Sesay, 'The OAU and Continental Order' in Timothy M. Shaw and Sola Ojo (eds) *Africa and the International Political System* (Washington: University Press of America, 1982) 168–225, and Orobola Fasehun

and Amadu Sesay 'The OAU and Conflict Control' in Timothy M. Shaw and Ralph I. Onwuka (eds) *Africa and World Politics: Independence, Dependence and Interdependence* (London: George Allen & Unwin, forthcoming).

5. For details see Fasehun and Sesay, 'The OAU and Conflict Control'.
6. The exception so far has been the brief collective ostracisation of the new regime of Master Sergeant Doe of Liberia. He came to power after assassinating William Tolbert who was President of Liberia and Chairman of the OAU. For details see Amadu Sesay, '*Le coup d'état au Liberia: facteurs internes et effets régionaux*' *Politique Africaine* 11 (7) September 1982, 91–106.
7. See *West Africa*, 14 July 1980, 1269, for the speeches of Robert Mugabe and Samora Machel.
8. Address by President Shehu Shagari of Nigeria at the thirty-fifth Session of the UN General Assembly, October 1980, in *Daily Times* (Lagos) 14 October 1980.
9. *World Development Report, 1980* (Washington: World Bank, 1980) 6.
10. For more details, see Sesay 'The OAU and Continental Order'.
11. See Mazrui's graphic description of the diversity in Ali Mazrui, *The African Condition* (London: Heinemann, 1980) 92.
12. Albert Tevoedjre (Rapporteur) in *What Kind of Africa by the Year 2000*? (Addis Ababa: OAU, 1979) 15.
13. She needs at the moment some $560m. to cover the immediate needs of Africa's refugees. So far, the only significant African contribution is $3m. from Nigeria. On the other hand, the US has committed $285m, the EEC $68m, Saudi Arabia $30m, Britain $13m. and France $2m. See *West Africa*, 20 April 1980, 849–50.
14. For a detailed discussion, see Sesay 'The OAU and Continental Order'.
15. All three dictators were ousted between 1979 and 1980. Amin fled Uganda after an 'invasion' led by Tanzanian soldiers and Ugandan exiles in 1979. Nguema was overthrown by his own soldiers in 1979 while Bokassa was overthrown by his army in a coup engineered by France in 1980.
16. For details see *The African Charter on Human and Peoples Rights* (Addis Ababa: OAU, 1981).
17. For details on the effects of the oil crisis on Afro–Arab relations, see Sola Ojo 'The Oil Crisis and Afro–Arab Relations', *Nigerian Journal of Political Science* (Zaria) (forthcoming) and Timothy M. Shaw and Olajide Aluko, 'The OAU, Arab League and the EEC', *Conference on African–Arab–OECD Trilateral Co-operation*, Bellagio, Italy, May 1980.
18. For more on the 'Brazil 1976 model', see Philippe Lemaitre, 'Who Will Rule Africa by the Year 2000?' in Kitchen (ed.) *Africa*, 272.
19. Ali Mazrui, 'The Anatomy of Violence in Contemporary Black Africa', in Kitchen (ed.) *Africa*, 73.
20. For a more orthodox discussion of the OAU's futures, see Claude Welch, 'The OAU' in Kitchen (ed.) *Africa*, 215.

8 The Future of Food and Agriculture, or the 'Greening of Africa'–Crisis Projections and Policies

CYRIL KOFIE DADDIEH

'Agriculture began in what is now called the Third World. The ancestral homes of the world's most important crops are in Third World countries: rice, wheat, maize, potato, cassava, sweet potato, surgarcane, soybeans, pulses, numerous vegetables, most fruit trees, cotton and other fibres, many forage grasses and legumes, and numerous forest trees including most hardwood species.' – Dr M. S. Swaminathan, Director-General of the International Rice Research Institute[1]

'Two generations ago, the banana was a luxury; oranges were seasonal fruit only; the use of tobacco was far less; a century ago tea and coffee were luxuries for the rich alone, and cocoa unknown. Today, bananas, oranges all year round, tea, coffee and cocoa in the humblest domestic budget in North America and Great Britain . . . Man and beast are fed increasingly from tropical countries. Industry demands rubber in quantities undreamed of 30 years ago, and other "colonial" raw materials are increasingly in great demand.' – Royal Institute of International Affairs, 1932)[2]

INTRODUCTION

Few developments are likely to have more profound consequences for Africa's socio-economic and political mid- to long-term future than the continued stagnation, in some cases even relapse, of the continent's agricultural sector and the attendant imperative of having to spend scarce foreign exchange earnings on imported food to feed growing urban as well as the increasingly marginalised and impoverished rural populations. This is because farming remains the dominant economic activity of the majority of the continent's population; some 85 to 95 per cent of the work force is estimated to be engaged in agriculture.[3] And despite the elusiveness of industrialisation and the current deteriorating trends in agriculture, Africa's peasants have always been vital to the socio-economic and political interests of their states – particularly to their ruling classes – since they have directly produced the surpluses without which much of what has passed for economic development would not have been possible.[4]

Africa's current agrarian crisis became apparent in the early 1970s when a series of droughts claimed thousands of human lives and decimated herds of livestock. Indeed, the 1972–3 drought in the Sahel provided the most immediate but largely convenient backdrop against which the continent's agrarian crisis began to be evaluated. A decade later, the crisis has intensified as well as spread to encompass virtually all of the continent's ecological zones, making many of the comfortable assumptions underpinning much of the orthodox explanations of the crisis suspect as well as untenable; that is, we are led to search for alternative explanations to drought as the cause.

It is also interesting to note that the crisis has impacted state capitalist and state socialist countries alike. Moreover, both civilian and military regimes have succumbed to the political repercussions of their inability to mediate the crisis: the combination of food shortages and high food prices has proved volatile, inducing working-class and student activism in Ghana, Ivory Coast, Liberia, Nigeria, Sierra Leone, Zambia, and Zaire, among others, and providing both the cause and pretext for military intervention.[5] The interrelatedness of food shortages, the high cost of food, and the concomitant social discontent and political activism recall the militance of urban consumers and the rise of nationalism resulting from the global inflation and the intransigence of colonial firms and the colonial state to grant requests for wage increases. As Robert Bates has observed:

> Not only have consumer interests remained militant; governments have remained vulnerable to consumer disaffection. The colonial regimes were not the last governments to lose power in part because of increases in the cost of living. The fate of the Busia government in Ghana is illustrative.[6]

The food component of the high cost of living and the food shortages attendant upon the combined stagnant or declining rates of production and bottlenecks in the distribution system are only two of the persistent manifestations of the current crisis. A more complete synthesis will have to include (i) levels of emergency food aid that are solicited or delivered; (ii) the magnitude of food in the overall import bill; (iii) the incidence of rural poverty and relative levels of rural outmigration; (iv) infant body weights and (v) illicit cross-border trade coupled with (vi) the under-utilisation of plant capacity caused by shortages of raw materials and/or lack of spare parts – both of which usually reflect foreign exchange difficulties.

The significance as well as urgency of the current crisis in contrast to that of the nationalist period is that on this occasion Africa's rural population has been just as badly hit as its urban counterpart: growing numbers have been turning increasingly to the market in order to secure their requirements of rice and bread (itself made from imported wheat). To be sure, the presence of rice and bread in the consumer basket of rural populations is partly reflective of the degree to which tastes have become homogenised: imported urban tastes have been 'transferred' or have they merely trickled down?) to the rural areas. This is symptomatic of the deepening and widening crisis, though it is by no means clear yet whether and when this conjuncture will engender revolutionary pressures in the countryside that might fuse with urban militancy.[7]

What is certain is that the current agrarian crisis has become truly continental in scope, affecting both urban and rural populations and a variety of regime types, recognising, of course, that there exist variations in the levels of affect. Moreover, it has become enough of a concern that scholarly interest, publications and debate are growing rapidly. This renewed interest and debate is manifested no less keenly in the recent flurry of diplomatic activities at the continental level starting with the Freetown Declaration of the Ministers of Agriculture in November 1976 which resulted in the publication of the FAO *Regional Food Plan for Africa* (1978) and culminating in the OAU *Lagos Plan of Action* (1980) in which the African leaders collectively proposed to transform both the continent's inherited economy and its place in the world system by cultivating the 'virtue of self-reliance'.[8] Instead of extroverted growth, the *Plan* asserts that:

> Africa's huge resources must be applied principally to meet the needs and purposes of its people; Africa's almost total reliance on the export of raw materials must change ... Africa ... must map out its own strategy for development and must vigorously pursue its implementation.[9]

I shall return to the perspective of the *Plan* particularly as it relates to the agrarian crisis. First, however, it is my contention that these 'semi-official' declarations contain some sober reflections that merit serious evaluation if further refinements in critical analysis and praxis are to be achieved. The objectives of this chapter are quite modest: it is intended to evaluate past and recent trends in Africa's food situation and the projected future performance in agriculture. It identifies some of the explanations advanced for Africa's deteriorating condition and the policy prescriptions resulting from these explanations and projections. However, it goes much beyond these to point to some of the ways in which these prognoses might be made more relevant through the identification of the underlying causes of the agrarian crisis.

THE FOOD SITUATION: PAST AND RECENT TRENDS

Africa's performance in food production in recent years has been rather lacklustre. Between 1970 and 1977 the average annual rate of growth was only 1.3 per cent as compared with 2.7 per cent for the period 1961-70. Per capita production was even more disappointing – it deteriorated from its low annual average of 0.3 per cent in 1961-70 to −1.4 per cent in 1970-7.[10] Table 8.1 gives the indicative figures for this pervasive decline.

TABLE 8.1 *Growth of food production in Africa*[1]

	Average Annual Growth Rate			
	Total Food Production		*Per Capita Food Production*	
Subregion	*1961–70 %*	*1970–7 %*	*1961–70 %*	*1970–7 %*
Northern Africa	3.0	2.1	0.7	−0.7
Western Africa[2]	2.1	1.1	−0.3	−1.5
Central Africa	2.6	1.0	0.1	−1.3
Eastern and Southern Africa	2.8	1.9	0.4	−0.9
AFRICA	2.7	1.3	0.03	−1.4
MSA in Africa	2.7	1.2	0.4	−1.4

[1] Based on FAO Indices of food production
[2] Includes Sahel

SOURCE FAO *Regional Food Plan for Africa*, 3.

For the continent as a whole there has been a sharp deterioration in cereal self-sufficiency from 96 per cent to 83 per cent, although meat showed some improvement from 98 per cent to 105 per cent in the decade 1962–4 to 1972–4. It is important to note that while these aggregate indicators are revealing, they may understate the extent of the crisis in some cases. To be sure, there are significant subregional variations in the demand and supply of food that may easily be obfuscated by aggregate data.[11] Not surprisingly, the Sahel has showed the greatest deficit in cereals. The Sahel's deficits in rice and millet were of the order of 413 000 and 269 000 tons respectively. A deficit was recorded for the subregion's pulse production while its meat surplus increased substantially.

In West Africa the self-sufficiency ratios (SSR) for cereals, meat and milk showed a decline but increases were recorded for oilseeds and sugar. The 1972–4 deficit in wheat (728 000 tons) and rice (372 000 tons) represented a threefold and 50 per cent increase respectively over the 1962–4 level. Central Africa recorded a decline in all commodity groups except pulses. There was a general increase in the deficit for milk, meat and cereals (wheat and maize) although it maintained its surplus in sugar, oilseeds and pulses. The Eastern and Southern African subregions fared much better, according to these estimates, enjoying generally higher and more stable SSRs. Whilst they suffered deficits of the order of 620 000 and 359 000 tons of wheat and rice respectively in 1972–4, their meat output improved markedly, yielding a surplus of some 245 000 tons.[12]

Several different dimensions of Africa's agrarian crisis have been summarised rather succinctly:

> The growth of food in the 1970s has slowed and lagged behind the growth of population; and there has been a pronounced decline in calorie self-sufficiency in nearly all subregions. Dietary energy supplies in relation to the requirements have declined in all subregions except Northern Africa . . . The lagging growth of food production in the face of high population growth and even higher rates or urbanisation has led to a dramatic increase in the imports of cereals, particularly wheat, and has caused a heavy drain on the scarce foreign exchange resources.[13]

The dire consequences of these deteriorating trends have been collectively admitted by African leaders:

> Hunger, malnutrition and starvation afflict more and more people every year. Today, in Africa, the food available to each person, on average, is 10 per cent less than a decade ago. The dietary energy supply per person has fallen below requirements.[14]

THE FUTURE PROJECTED

If the current African condition is paradoxical and gives more than sufficient cause for concern, the future is no more promising. Whilst *The Global 2000 Report to the President* has projected that overall world food production will increase more rapidly than world population with average per capita consumption increasing by about 15 per cent between 1970 and the year 2000, in the Third World, unhappily, food production is expected barely to keep ahead of population growth. In sub-Saharan Africa per capita food consumption is actually expected to decline while population is unlikely to decrease either proportionately or absolutely. Consumption deficit of more than 20 per cent below the FAO minimum required standard is forecast for central Africa barring a recrudescence of the drought.[15]

On the basis of existing trends, the *Regional Food Plan* has projected that:

> unless policies change and there is a great improvement in agricultural performance, the rate of growth of production will lag behind the growth in demand for all commodity groups (except rootcrops) from 1972–4 to 1985. As a result, the self-sufficiency ratios would show a decrease (usually a substantial one) for nearly all commodities.[16]

Even assuming breakthroughs in the way in which land and water resources are managed, coupled with better disease and pest control, the *Regional Food Plan* expects only modest improvement by 1990. In general it is anticipated that a more than 100 per cent self-sufficiency in rootcrops will be achieved by 1985 an in pulse by 1990. These increases will not represent exportable surplus from Africa but will fill the gaps left by the deficits in cereals and meat which are expected to continue. The situation with regard to the decline in milk self-sufficiency may, however, be arrested by 1990.[17]

To summarise briefly, it is projected that the falling trend in cereal self-sufficiency will be reversed, with progressive improvements up to 1985 and 1990 but the protein deficit is not likely to be made up as fish consumption is expected to decline in 1985 and again in 1990. Thus, the *Regional Food Plan* cautions that whilst the projected modest improvements may very well lead to a reduction in the levels of food imports, especially cereals, from extra-continental sources, food imports will continue to feature prominently in the import bill in the mid-term future. On the basis of existing trends, the *Regional Food Plan* has estimated that the annual rate of growth in demand for cereals would increase from 2.9 to 3.1 per cent; for pulses from 2.4 to 2.6; for meat from 2.2 to 4.4 per cent; and for milk from 2.9 to 3.9 per cent. The projected rate increase in production which was already below the demand growth rates, except for meat and fish, does point to a dismal performance except perhaps for cereals, milk and rootcrops.[18] Table 8.2 illustrates the problem further.

TABLE 8.2 *Projected trend self-sufficiency levels and demand and production growth rates for the major commodity groups in Africa between 1962–4 and 1972–4 and 1985*

	Self-sufficiency ratios (SSR)			*Annual growth rates* 1972–4 – 1985	
Commodity	*1962–4*	*1972–4*	*1985*	*Production*	*Demand*
Cereals	96	83	76	2.2	3.1
Rootcrops	101	100	100	1.8	1.8
Pulses	110	107	90	1.2	3.1
Meat*	98	105	84	2.4	4.4
Milk	93	85	76	3.0	4.0
Fish	93	101	87	1.7	3.0

* Including 'other meat' (game, etc.)

SOURCE *Regional Food Plan*, 12.

FOOD IMPORTS

In the past, food deficit African states had relied upon food imports to meet local demand. Figure 8.1 illustrates the character and extent of the food import situation for selected African countries as a result of stagnant or declining food production. Characteristically, wheat is an important component relative to the proportions of other imported foods; so, too, are rice and sugar.[19] This composition of staple food imports is reflective of the major interests that are served by state food policy, which is generally urban-biased even if, as suggested earlier, the rural populations are becoming equally dependent upon the same imported food items.

It is worth noting that the imported food has been largely paid for out of the proceeds from the sale of export cash crops. In recent years this strategy of concentrating on commodity exports in order to meet the food needs of the African continent has become untenable. This situation

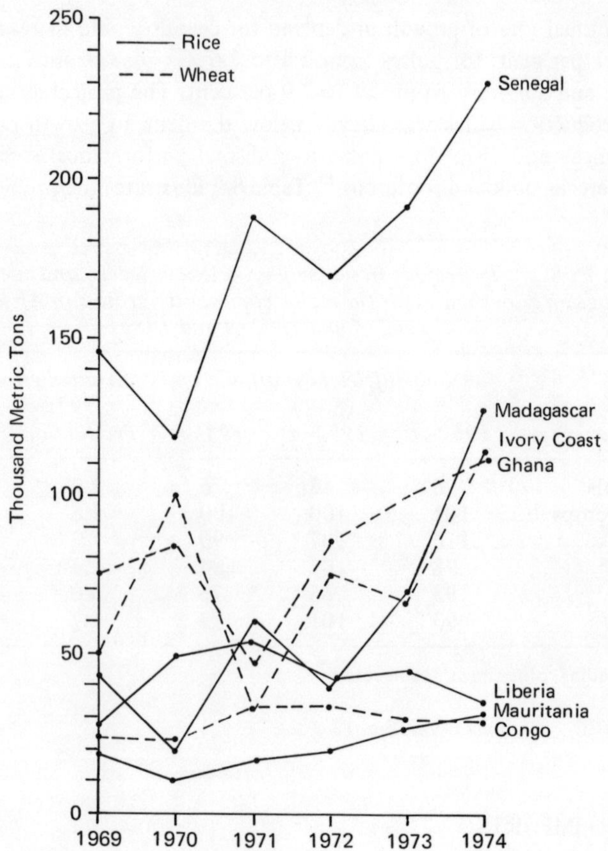

FIGURE 8.1 *Selected major food imports by countries of Tropical Africa 1969–74*

SOURCE W. B. Morgan, 'Food Supply and Food Imports of Tropical Africa', *African Affairs*, 76 (303) April 1977.

has developed for reasons which Yash Tandon characterised as a 'conspiracy of four factors' (i) the near depletion of world food resources by 1972/3 as a result of the decision by the major grain-exporting countries (US, Canada, Australia and Argentina) to reduce the area devoted to food production; (ii) the entry of the Soviet Union into the world grain market in the same year with the purchase of enormous quantities of grain at low prices in order to build up its reserves and to avoid having to slaughter livestock, (iii) the serious famine that occurred in several African states as a result of the severe drought of 1973–4 and, finally, (iv) the energy crisis exploded the prices of food grains and inputs (such as fertilisers) and exacerbated the plight of oil-importing low-income countries as nothing else had done before.[20] Tandon contends that:

> It was this fourth factor, more than any other, that made the most important impact on countries like Tanzania. By overnight depleting its foreign exchange the oil crisis reduced the ability of these countries to purchase food from abroad as and when the situation demanded.[21]

Like the entry into the grain market of more economically solvent food-deficit states and deliberate state policies to encourage the withdrawal of cultivable grain lands from cultivation, the energy crisis was a serious contingent factor that undoubtedly exacerbated an already growing continental food crisis. But combining as they did in the early 1970s, this set of contingent factors placed severe constraints on the ability of African states to maintain a competitive bidding for grains on the world market: they did not determine the food crisis. If so, then the critical issue related at the contingent level to 'market failures' and at the more structural level to (unequal) terms of exchange, with implications for the kinds of strategies that can be designed to counter both of these problems. The fundamental dilemma, as Michael F. Lofchie and Stephen K. Commins have so succinctly summarised, is that:

> countries which have pursued an aggressive strategy of emphasis upon agriculture have often experienced failure in its bitterest form. Their earnings from agricultural exports have fallen far short of national needs, and they have been consistently unable to enter the grain market on anything remotely resembling an adequate scale.[22]

The market for Third World agricultural commodities is so highly competitive that entry of a single new producer or the harvest of a bumper crop in one country or, for that matter, fabricated news about a bumper crop can depress prices below levels necessary to sustain development and other expenditures. Second, it is overdetermined by a handful of powerful transnational corporations (TNCs) such as General Foods, Nestlés, Lipton, Cadbury, and Brooke Bond, so that:

> If tropical commodities appear expensive on the shelves of Western supermarkets, the reasons have less to do with the rate of return to producer countries than with the ability of these processing and trading

> firms to engage in the time-honoured tradition of purchasing cheap and selling dear.[23]

Finally, this unequal strength between agri-business and the tropical producer is further reinforced by the elasticity of consumer demand for tropical raw materials as well as by the availability of synthetic or substitute products that enhance the ability of individual consumers to alter their consumption patterns in response to price fluctuations.[24]

These findings help to situate the continental food crisis within its broader and proper context. They also suggest a need to go beyond drought as cause. Nicole Ball has argued that what is required is for attention to be focused on the factors that undermine the ability of eco-systems and populations to cope with the impact of natural phenomena and a determination as to why adequate protective mechanisms and infrastructure have not been made available to disaster-prone regions. In the case of the former French colonies, the energetic research by Jean Suret-Canale and Claude Meillassoux has revealed that forced production of export cash crops by the peasantry, unequal terms of trade between Europe and Africa and economic recessions and inflation in Europe and North America have been prominent causes of starvation. Faced with that kind of evidence Ball has concluded that:

> A drought, like all other 'natural disasters', should properly be viewed as resulting from a combination of social, political, economic and environmental factors. The interaction of these elements, over the long term can seriously reduce the ability of a system to cope with new and/or suddenly intensified stresses.[25]

Similarly, Nicholas Cohen and Rene Dumont have argued in a recent provocative study that 'the division of the world into contrasting regions of hunger and relative plenty is not a matter of chance nor does it depend solely on the national fortunes of climate and soil'.[26] Instead, they point to the exploitation of the agricultural producer in the producing Third World countries and unequal exchange between the Third World and consuming nations as major constraints on agricultural improvements in the Third World.[27] In other worlds, they, too, point to socio-economic and political forces shaping food and agricultural policies, priorities and consequences.

The problem may be put in its proper perspective by recalling that before World War Two all the developing countries were cereal exporters; today they are all major importers. Figure 8.1 reflects this shift from surplus to deficit, from relative self-sufficiency in food to dependence on food imports. The growth in per capita food production in the Third World as a whole has narrowed from 0.7 per cent per annum in the 1950s to 0.2 per cent in the 1960s. This represented a yearly gain of only 400 grams per capita whereas the gain in the industrialised countries over the same period was nearly thirty times greater and averaged 11 250 grams.[28]

FACTORS AFFECTING PRODUCTION AND CONSUMPTION

The growing literature on African and Third World agriculture contains a plethora of factors that are commonly associated with the current food crisis. Population increase and pressures on the land available for food production, increased urbanisation, the diversion of labour from agriculture to other forms of economic activity, the loss of child labour with the growth in elementary school education, the cheapness of imported grains (rice, for example) in coastal towns are just a few of the factors that are frequently mentioned. To these must be added aging farm populations, aging trees (in the case of cash crops), the intensive exploitation of crop land that is fit for extensive use only and post-harvest losses that have been growing steadily in Africa and which reflect a lack of storage facilities and a breakdown in or difficulties of transportation. Space does not permit a detailed examination of these factors. Suffice it for me to suggest that the factors that affect food production and consumption are of two kinds. The factors enumerated above not only fall into the first kind – the more immediate or contingent set of factors – but they may also be categorised as land, labour and technico-managerial constraints.

Juxtaposed against the more immediate and contingent factors are more long-term structural or systemic factors such as the continued cultivation of export cash crops to the detriment of the food-crop sector. A number of analysts have recognised the positive correlation between export cash crop production and food deficits and, hence, of the politico-economic roots of the current crisis. As Carl K. Eicher has argued, colonial approaches to development placed a high premium on facilitating the production and extraction of surpluses from the African countryside – copper, gold, iron, bauxite, cocoa, coffee, cotton, etc, for external markets. Colonial officials not only neglected to pay attention to investments in human capital, research on food crops, and the strengthening of internal market linkages but in many cases they deliberately hastened the destruction of internal linkages through labour legislation and taxation policies.[29] Eicher contends that:

the effects of colonial policies on contemporary land ownership patterns and agricultural research and training institutions are important contributors to the current food production and poverty problems. Many colonial regimes focused their research and development programs on export crops and the needs of commercial farmers and managers of plantations.[30]

Viewed from the above perspective, the current food crisis becomes the logical outcome of the failure of post-colonial African states to make a marked departure from the crop, research and training priorities of their predecessor, the colonial state. It has been charged that African states have assigned a low priority to investments in agriculture and to increasing food production over the past two decades. No matter what their ideological predisposition – capitalism, socialism or humanism – African political leaders have tended to view agriculture, peasant agriculture in particular, as a 'backward' sector from which surpluses must be extracted – in the form of taxes and labour – to finance industrial and urban growth.[31] This orientation to agriculture has dictated the shifting of the burden of economic growth and development on to the shoulders of the peasants through the mediation of state monopoly buying and pricing policies. The World Bank's *Agenda for Action* has estimated that, taking into account the effect of the overvalued currency and the net tax burden, producers in thirteen sub-Saharan African states received less than half of the real value of their export crops over the 1971–80 period.[32]

If agriculture in general is assigned a low priority, food production is given rhetorical encouragement – Operation Feed Yourself (OFY); Operation Feed the Nation (OFN) – but not the serious attention it deserves in terms of research, investments in infrastructure (storage facilities, feeder roads, transport vehicles) and incentives. Rather, African states are all too tempted to intervene in the market to insure low cost food to city dwellers given, as suggested before, the latter's propensity to engage in militant action to prevent the erosion of their purchasing power. The concern of African political leaders was best summed up by the Nkrumah government's *Seven Year Development Plan*:

> In the periods when the imbalance between the supply and demand for food has been most acute and food prices have risen most sharply – such as 1947–8, 1950–1 and 1961–2 – the threat to the standard of living of the people has given rise to a great deal of social tension.[33]

The fact that African states remain important employers of wage labour makes intervention in the food sector as a way of mediating antagonistic contradictions between urban workers and the state even more tempting.

Meanwhile, food and agricultural policies in many African states (both capitalist and socialist; civilian and military) have been generally supportive of plantations, state farms, land settlement schemes and the replacement of private traders and money-lenders with government trading corporations, marketing boards and credit facilities.[34] In this regard, it is the state farms or large-scale plantations and individual bureaucrats, wealthy, hence progressive, farmers and members of co-operative societies who, given their connections with the state, have absorbed the lion's share of state expenditures in agriculture.[35] Yet it is the neglected peasant producer who is relied upon to produce the bulk of the export as well as food crops. Whilst the level of peasant productivity has been much maligned and used as a pretext for initiating large-scale mechanised ventures, the evidence thus far make it clear that peasant farm productivity is comparable, even superior, to productivity on large-scale mechanised farms. State-supported marketing boards and state farms have been plagued by a variety of woes including over-staffing, over-centralisation, managerial incompetence and/or corruption and high marketing costs.

On further reflection, the continuing crisis of food and agriculture is at the same time a crisis in gender relations (see next chapter). This becomes self-evident if we conceptualise the export cash crop and food crop production dialectic in terms of encroachment. The successful expansion of export cash crop production leads to encroachments on land normally used for food production. But where there is a bifurcation between the producers of food crops (women) and cash crop producers (men) as in much of Africa, the continued exploitation of the most fertile arable lands represents an indirect assault or encroachment on women's use rights. With women being relegated to less fertile, hence less productive, lands and/or having lost the labour services of younger dependents and even their husbands to the cash-crop producing heads of their households, the dialectic between food and cash crop has turned, in the final analysis, on gender relations. The difficulties of finding food as well as wood-fuel to prepare the available food are having very serious adverse consequences on the African family or household as reflected in the increase in the number of female heads of households, divorces, and female preference for loose forms of conjugal association.[36]

The current predicament relates as well to the issues of class and social equity or social justice. After all, the level of disposable income – effective entitlement – enjoyed by individuals and households mediates the content as well as extent of their food consumption. As Eicher has observed,

'The hunger and malnutrition problem is caused by poverty – that is, even in areas where per capita food production is not declining, the poor do not have the income or resources to cope with hunger and malnutrition'.[37] According to a 1965 sample survey of agricultural income, 60 per cent of the farming households in Nigeria saved nothing. The average income of a farmer was a paltry £20 per annum. It is suggested that the prosperous farmers who save tend to invest in urban areas or in the education of their children rather than reinvest in the rural sector.[38] In a situation of skewed distribution of income the availability of food may be no consolation to those who cannot afford it. Amartya Sen is particularly emphatic on this point. He cautions that:

> Moving food into famine areas will not in itself do much to cure starvation, since what needs to be created is food entitlement and not just food availability. Indeed, people have perished in famines in sight of much food in shops. Since famines reflect a collapse of entitlement, famine relief has to take the form of generating entitlements through other channels.[39]

The interconnectedness of income distribution and food consumption – effective entitlement – is receiving greater attention. Ferdinand Monckeberg has drawn attention not only to the need for increased production in future, but also the need to streamline distribution to benefit the poor. Undernourishment results, he reckons, not necessarily because individuals do not know what to eat or because they lack an adequate variety of food, but, most importantly, because:

> they lack the necessary economic means to assure an adequate daily diet. In developing countries, there is a direct relationship between income and amount of calories consumed. With higher incomes, caloric consumption increases and the quality of the diet also improves by greater animal protein intake.[40]

POLICY PRESCRIPTIONS

Although effective policy prescriptions for arresting and reversing the current trends in food and agriculture can only be made with the concrete situation of particular African countries in mind, the general requirements are clear: there is the need to transcend Africa's inheritance by reversing the trend toward increasing amounts of cropped land being devoted to cash crops to the detriment of food crops. The income position and purchasing power of the rural poor is in urgent need of improvement if increased food production is to be stimulated. The time when African states could extract food surpluses from the countryside without adequate infrastructural or monetary compensation may be fast waning. As Aluko, Eicher and others have argued, the incentive structure for farmers is in need of overhaul. Increased farm income must be adopted as an important goal of social policy in the 1980s. 'Moreover, increasing incentives to farmers is a strategic policy lever for attacking poverty and promoting rural employment'.[41] Not only must the flow of resources to food and agricultural production, and hence to the countryside, be elevated to higher levels, but the small farmer must receive deservedly special attention.

In addition to taking the side of the small farmer, the concern with food production and consumption dictates that attention be focused on the role of women and gender relations. In many areas of the continent women not only produce the bulk of the food but they also bear the responsibility for feeding their households. Research, as the *Plan* has concluded, must be focused not only on how best to minimise post-harvest losses but also on developing appropriate tools to make rural work more productive and less onerous.[42]

The relentlessness of the current situation may well require unorthodox schemes such as those advocated by Okello Oculi. He contends that:

> The other villager that needs direct large-scale investment from Government in Nigeria is the rural cow, the rural goat, the rural sheep, rural donkey, rural camel and rural bushmeat. The last group, rural bushmeat, has so far been divorced from the domain of food policy and assumed to fall under the non-nutritious domain of tourist items. Yet it is obvious from the prices roadside food sellers charge that this is a food area of high consumer appreciation, in spite of a chaotic mode of production . . . Centres for domesticated bushmeat production in villages under the direction of a national bushmeat corporation would be an invaluable means of boosting the protein resources of rural areas, and also a source of income for villagers who have surplus to sell to the urban areas.[43]

CONCLUSIONS

A few things have changed at least superficially since the Royal Institute made its poignant assessment of world agriculture in 1932. Agriculture, as the Institute implied, and the *Plan of Action* emphasises, is not only the direct source of livelihood for the majority of Africans as well as the mainstay of African political economies, but it also provides the principal means through which the continent participates in the world capitalist system. Africa's position within this system has progressively deteriorated and its future is unpromising.

Whilst it is doubtful that in the decades ahead, especially given a contraction in economic growth in the north, 'neo-colonial' raw materials will be increasingly in great demand except for a few critical ones, the fundamental structural dependence relationships and unequal exchange to which the Royal Institute's assessment pointed have become exacerbated.

The process leading to unequal distribution of and access to available supplies of food, as I have shown, can only be comprehended within the context of both the economic and political structures which determine relationships between rich and poor. A critical contributing factor has been the removal of control over production from those who work the land into the hands of those who speculate and profit from it.

Against the real likelihood that the 'political will' which the *Regional Food Plan* and the *Plan of Action* regard as the prerequisite for resolving Africa's food crisis will prove elusive, Cohen and Dumont have set the ultimate strategy of the peasants taking command if their situation is to change, if a restructuring of social and political relationships in their countries is to be achieved.[44] This imperative, the most revolutionary of all revolutionary strategies for Africa's future, is also the hardest to achieve. But to think that this is impossible to achieve, especially given the increasing contradictions in Africa's political economies, is to engage in the politics of despair and not in 'a new politics of food and agriculture'.

NOTES

1. Dr M. S. Swaminathan, 'Agricultural Progress – Key to Third World Prosperity', *Third World Quarterly*, 5 (3) July 1983, 553.
2. Royal Institute of International Affairs, *World Agriculture: An International Survey* (London, 1932), cited in Gail Omvedt, 'The Political Economy of Starvation', *Race and Class*, 17 (2) Autumn 1975, 115.
3. See Harvey K. Flad, 'Africa and the Problems and Paradoxes of Food Production and Distribution', in Robert W. Brown *et al*, *Africa and International Crisis* (Syracuse: Maxwell School of Citizenship and Public Affairs, 1976) 59. See also Colin Leys, 'African Economic Development in Theory and Practice', *Daedalus*, 3 (2) Spring 1982, 99–124.

4. Bob Shenton and J. P. Olinger, 'Decolonisation and the West African Peasantry', *Centre for African Studies* (Dalhousie University, 1981).
5. For further elaboration on this interrelatedness of food problems, coups and diplomatic weakness, see Carl K. Eicher, 'Facing Up to Africa's Food Crisis', *Foreign Affairs*, 61 (1) Fall 1982, 151–74. See also Emmanuel Hansen, 'Public Policy and the Food Question in Ghana', *Africa Development*, 6 (3) July–September 1982, 99–115 and Okello Oculi, 'Food Imperialism and African Diplomacy in the 1980s', *Africa Development*, 6 (3) July–September 1981, 63–73.
6. Robert H. Bates, *Markets and States in Tropical Africa: The Political Basis of Agricultural Policies*, (Berkeley: University of California Press, 1981) 30–1.
7. The literature on the revolutionary potential of Africa's peasantry is growing. For a sampling of that debate, see Claude Ake, *Revolutionary Pressures in Africa* (London: Zed, 1978); Frantz Fanon, *The Wretched of the Earth* (New York: Grove 1968); John Saul, 'African Peasantries and Revolution', in his *The State and Revolution in Eastern Africa* (New York: Monthly Review, 1979) 297–338 and Ken Post, '"Peasantisation" and Rural Political Movements in Western Africa', *Archives Européenes de Sociologie*, 13, 1972, 223–54.
8. OAU *Lagos Plan of Action for the Economic Development of Africa* (Geneva: International Institute for Labour Studies for OAU, 1981) 8, hereafter referred to as the *Plan.*
9. Ibid, 8.
10. *Tenth FAO Regional Conference for Africa* (Arusha, Tanzania, September 1978) ARC/785 July 1978, 3. Hereafter referred to as *Regional Food Plan.*
11. Ibid, 8. For more on this useful reminder, see Shlomo Reutlinger and Marcelo Selowsky, *Malnutrition and Poverty Options* (Washington, DC: World Bank Occasional Paper No. 23, 1976). See also S. J. Burki and T. J. Goering, *A Perspective on the Foodgrain Situation in the Poorest Countries* (Washington, DC: World Bank, 1977). Staff Working Paper No. 251.
12. FAO, *Regional Food Plan*, 8–9.
13. Ibid, 11.
14. OAU *Lagos Plan*, 8.
15. *The Global 2000 Report to the President: Entering the Twenty-first Century. Volume 1* (Washington, DC: US Government Printing Office) 17.
16. FAO, *Regional Food Plan*, 12.
17. Ibid, 13–14.
18. Ibid, 12.
19. See W. B. Morgan, 'Food Supply and Staple Food Imports of Tropical Africa', *African Affairs*, 76 (303) April 1977, 170–3.
20. Yash Tandon, 'New Food Strategies and Social Transformation in East Africa', *Africa Development*, 6 (2) April–June 1981, 88–9.
21. Ibid, 89. See also Flad, 'Africa and the Problems and Paradoxes of Food', 63–5. The oil crisis may have been a blessing in disguise for African agriculture especially if it has succeeded in discouraging

costly and inappropriate farm technology imports which tended to benefit the large-scale producers rather than the peasant smallholder. See Robert E. Clute, 'The Role of Agriculture in African Development', *African Studies Review*, 25 (4) December 1982, 1–20.

22. Michael F. Lofchie and Stephen K. Commins, 'Food Deficits and Agricultural Policies in Tropical Africa', *Journal of Modern African Studies*, 20 (1) March 1982, 11. For more on the misgivings about 'comparative advantage', see Clute, 'The Role of Agriculture', 1–2.
23. Ibid, 11. For a lament from the leader of one of these countries, see 'Ivory Coast. Houphouet's gloomy forecast', *West Africa* 3443, 8 August 1983, 1850.
24. Lofchie and Commins, 'Food Deficits and Agricultural Policies in Tropical Africa', 12.
25. Nicole Ball, 'Understanding the Causes of African Famine', *Journal of Modern African Studies*, 14 (3) September 1976, 520. See also Hector Gambarotta, 'The Sahel Region: Splendor Yesterday, Famine Today: What Will Happen Tomorrow?' *Africa Development*, 5 (1) January–March 1980, 5–38. See also Claude Meillassoux 'Development or Exploitation: Is the Sahel Famine Good Business?' *Review of African Political Economy*, 1, August–November 1974, 27–33.
26. Nicholas Cohen and René Dumont, *The Growth of Hunger: A New Politics of Agriculture* (London: Marion Boyars, 1980) 27.
27. Ibid, 6.
28. See Jan Tinbergen *et al*, *RIO – Reshaping the International Order: A Report to the Club of Rome* (New York: Dutton, 1976) 28–9.
29. Eicher, 'Facing Up to Africa's Food Crisis', 157.
30. Ibid, 157.
31. Ibid, 158. For further commentary on this continuity with colonial state policy, see Hansen, 'Public Policy and the Food Question'. See also Clute, 'The Role of Agriculture in African Development'.
32. World Bank, *Accelerated Development in Sub-Saharan Africa: An Agenda for Action* (Washington, DC, 1981) 55.
33. Ghana, *The Seven-Year Plan for National Reconstruction and Development: Financial Years 1963/64–1969/70* (Accra: Planning Commission, 1964) 56.
34. See Eicher, 'Facing Up to Africa's Food Crisis' and Clute, 'The Role of Agriculture in African Development'. And also Saa Dittoh, 'Green Revolution or Revolution? The Case of Independent African Countries', *Africa Development*, 6 (3) July–September 1981, 49–62.
35. See Frances Hill, 'Experiments with a Public Sector Peasantry: Agricultural Schemes and Class Formation', *African Studies Review*, 20 (3) December 1977, 25–41. For an alternative view, see Jan Kees van Donge, 'Politicians, Bureaucrats and Farmers: a Zambian case study', *Journal of Development Studies*, 19 (1) October 1982, 88–107.
36. See Nancy J. Hafkin and Edna G. Bay (eds), *Women in Africa: Studies in Social and Economic Change* (Stanford: Stanford University Press, 1976). Also Jane I. Guyer, 'Food, Cocoa and the Division of Labour by Sex in Two West African Societies', *Comparative Studies in Society and History*, 22 (3) July 1980, 355–73.

37. Eicher, 'Facing Up to Africa's Food Crisis', 151.
38. See S. A. Aluko, 'Rural Economic Development', in Maxwell Owusu (ed.) *Colonialisation and Change; Essays Presented to Lucy Mair* (The Hague: Mouton, 1975) 242.
39. Amartya Sen, 'The Food Problem: Theory and Policy', *Third World Quarterly*, 4 (3) July 1982, 45. A similar situation occurred in Ghana in 1974 and 1977 when officials denied that there was famine in the Upper Region. Official denial resulted in delays in getting food aid to the affected areas. The food was held up in Bolgatanga. See Andrew Shepherd, 'Farming and Drought in the North-east', *West Africa* 3157, 16 January 1976, 97. Shepherd asks rhetorically, 'It is surprising, in view of this history, that villagers have refused to pay taxes and to register as electors for the coming referendum?'
40. Ferdinand Monckeberg, 'Food and World Population: Future Perspectives', in Philip M. Hauser (ed.) *World Population and Development: Challenge and Prospects* (Syracuse: Syracuse University Press, 1979) 139.
41. Eicher, 'Facing Up to Africa's Food Crisis', 160. See also Aluko, 'Rural Economic Development' and OAU *Lagos Plan of Action*, Annex I, 10.
42. OAU *Lagos Plan of Action*, 98.
43. Okello Oculi, 'Dependent Food Policy in Nigeria 1975–1979', *Review of African Political Economy* 15/16, May–December 1979, 72. Oculi also recommends the setting up of a *National Grass Corporation* and a collective *Pan-African Grass Corporation* to insure grass production to feed livestock (73).
44. Cohen and Dumont, *The Growth of Hunger*, 27. For an extended review of this stimulating and timely work, see Daddieh, 'Toward a New Politics of Agriculture', *International Journal*, 36 (2) Spring 1981, 389–91.

9 The Changing Position of Women in the African Labour Force

MAJORIE MBILINYI

This chapter analyses changes which are taking place in the position of women within the peasant sector and in wage-employment. Underlying these changes is the deepening incorporation of African producers and neo-colonial states into the world-wide capitalist system. Although they have been separated here for purposes of analysis, the peasant and wage employment sectors are integrally related to each other. The nature of their relationship is a subject of intense debate which cannot be explored here. Suffice to note that the productive and reproductive activities of peasant women are the epitome of this dynamic relationship.

THE PEASANT SECTOR

Historical Factors

The organisation of the labour process varies according to (i) the specific commodities being produced and sold and (ii) the degree of differentiation and monetisation in production itself. Although a division of labour by sex and age has historically characterised all peasant production systems, it is now changing in response to class differentiation and monetisation. It is, therefore, impossible to generalise about the sexual division of labour in peasant production. Concrete investigation is necessary to explore the changes taking place in the labour process in specific class categories and localities in each African country.

Certain historical tendencies do emerge however. During the colonial period, men produced most of the industrial crops as a result of crop specialisation within the peasant economy or wage employment on company plantations, white settler farms or *kulak* farms. Female labour was also depended upon in all forms of industrial crop production. At the same time, women were left to carry the burden of food production, processing and storage almost single-handed or with minimal input of male labour. This was particularly true in labour reserves and industrial-crop-growing areas.

The colonial sexual division of labour was only partly the result of nineteenth century pre-capitalist property relations, in which the male head of clan or household or the chief controlled the allocation of land, livestock, labour and labour product. Production was organised in most groups according to a sexual division of labour whereby wives produced food and other goods services also necessary for the labour force, and they produced offspring. Men produced exchange goods like ivory, game meat or livestock and certain crops like millet or bananas. The sexual division of labour varied, however, depending on the extent of differentiation and commoditisation which had developed, and the class or class category of the persons themselves. Hence, in feudal or semi-feudal chiefdoms, male and female slaves and commoners produced surplus which was appropriated by the rulers (women and/or men) and also provided labour services directly to the rulers and their spouses in cooking, toting water, etc (see Mbilinyi forthcoming).

Capitalist penetration transformed pre-capitalist *relations*, although particular *forms* of organising production and reproduction resemble the old relations. Capitalist marketing relations began to undermine the peoples of Tanzania by the sixteenth and seventeenth centuries. However, colonial conquest and the establishment of the colonial state unleashed the full violence of capitalist social relations. Colonial states taxed men – from 15 years of age upwards in Tanganyika. Agriculture extension services and production inputs were oriented to export crops and not to subsistence food crops, and focused specifically on male progressive farmers as a part of the transformation approach. The monetisation of bridewealth was reinforced by the colonial laws and court system, which required a statement about the amount of bridewealth promised and paid in marriage registration forms of several countries. The state fostered the concept of male head of household in its practices with respect to land tenure systems, schooling, guardianship of children, etc. Wherever land tenure was transformed into an individualised system of private property, a male 'owner' was sought, even if he was a young unmarried son of the effective producer, his mother. Marketing co-operatives only recognised male heads of household as members despite the reliance on female labour in cash-crop production. Where settlement schemes were created, 'the settlers' were defined as male household heads who were given juridical land ownership. One condition for being accepted as a settler in neo-colonial Tanzania, for example, was that the settler be married and settle *with* his wife, in recognition of the absolutely essential labour input of women in peasant agriculture. Women refused the terms of settlement in some schemes and left them, leading to their collapse (Brain, 1976).

In these and many other ways, the state introduced sex specificity into the commoditisation process. Sex specificity was *not* a mere perpetuation of 'traditional' divisions of labour and ownership relations. The allocation of minimal education to women and the restriction of its content to 'domestic science' courses was and is extremely significant in reinforcing the new social relations in the making. Given the historical role of women producers in food production, the emphasis on domestic science in schools, community development and adult education programmes represents the effort by the state to construct *new* sexist ideologies and to match skills and knowledge to the sex segmentation being developed in the labour market.

Differentiation of Peasants and Deterioration in Family-based Peasant Agriculture

A major change which has occured in the 1970s and early 1980s is the way poor women peasants are now compelled to engage in different forms of commodity production and/or often seasonal wage-labour to supplement the cash incomes of their husbands and other male relatives as well as to supplement their own subsistence production. This takes the form of food processing in Northern Nigeria (Simmons 1973); beer brewing in Ethiopia (Kebeb) 1978), Botswana (Kerven 1979a, 1980), Kenya (Kenya 1978, Kayongo-Male and Walji 1980, Monsted 1977), Tanzania (Bryceson and Kirimbai 1980, Kirimbai 1981, Mbilinyi 1982a, Sachak 1979, 1980) and Zambia (Jiggins 1980); or migrating to towns in search of wage labour, or other forms of employment in Tanzania (Sachak 1979, 1980), Botswana (Kerven 1979a, 1979b, 1980), Kenya (Bujra 1975) and Zambia (Jiggins 1980).

Accompanying the increasing involvement of women in market-oriented commodity production and/or wage labour is their increasing cash contribution to the maintenance of the family. Not only are women producing food needs of the family, they are now purchasing food, clothes, medical services, hiring labour to substitute for absent family male labour, and paying school fees (see MacCormack, 1979, on Sierra Leone; Monsted,

1977, on Kenya; Bryceson and Kirimbai, 1980, Mbilinyi, 1981a and Sachak, 1980, on Tanzania; Cuyer, 1977 and Henn, 1978, on Southern Cameroon and Kerven, 1979a and 1980, on Botswana).

These developments are often interpreted both by women peasants themselves, and by social scientists, as examples of women's oppression by men. It is argued that women are now providing cash purchases formerly provided by men and the men are diverting their cash income to personal consumption (much of it for beer or homebrew consumption). Yet this is an inadequate explanation of what is taking place. In order to understand the phenomenon itself, it is necessary to examine two related issues (i) that of peasant differentiation and (ii) that of the absolute deterioration of peasant agriculture, especially of poor peasants.

Differentiation of peasants has escalated in relation to commoditisation of production and reproduction and the development of capitalist relations in agriculture, embryonic though they may be. The majority of rural producers are poor peasants who subsist on the basis of farm or livestock production and are (i) increasingly forced to supplement their farm or livestock incomes by selling their labour power on a seasonal basis to rich peasants or capitalist farmers, (ii) by migrating, or (iii) by engaging in non-farm petty commodity production like brewing beer, processing food, etc. A certain amount of crop or livestock production is oriented to the market, in order to acquire the cash necessary to purchase subsistence needs (including producer goods like hoes and hybrid seeds as well as consumer goods and services). Labour still represents a major constraint on production, but it is increasingly accompanied by a growing scarcity of land, depleted herds, soil deterioration, and lack of access to the cash or credit necessary to purchase farm inputs or to hire labour.

A separate class category are the landless rural proletariat, representing a growing proportion of the population in highly commercialised agriculture areas in different countries such as Kenya (Monsted, 1977; Okeyo, 1980), Lesotho (Mueller, 1976), and Botswana (Fortmann, 1980). The landless subsist on the basis of hiring out their labour power, brewing beer, processsing food, prostitution, remittances from relatives, and/or charity from neighbours.

The sexual division of labour is very different for different classes of peasants. For example, Kirimbai (1981) found that female and male poor peasants jointly engaged in subsistence food production in *Dodoma villages of Tanzania*. The wives traded the product of their joint work in order to acquire the cash necessary for subsistence. They also separately or jointly engaged in seasonal forms of wage labour, or brewing beer, or took turns to migrate to Dodoma town in order to seek employment.

At the same time, women were primarily responsible for domestic labour such as cooking, pounding grain, toting water or collecting firewood, although children also contributed their labour to these activities regardless of sex.

In rich peasant households, the stereotyped sexual division of labour has been prevalent. Women provided nearly all the family labour in subsistence food production, which was supplemented to varying extents by hired labour. Men engaged in livestock production and tomato cultivation for the market, and relied on hired labour. The men controlled all the major cash resources of the household, thereby placing their wives in a dependency relationship for access to major cash purchases. Women were able to substitute hired labour or cash purchases in place of their own domestic labour in pounding and water-toting. Other women were hired to pound millet, sorghum or maize. One segment of the 'rich peasants' category was composed of female household heads who accumulated on the basis of hired labour in brewing beer.

Among poor peasants in *Kakamega District, Kenya*, the intensification of female labour in production on the subsistence or cash-crop plot was due to the increasing pressure on the whole family to intensify labour in order to survive (Monsted, 1977). This affected children as well, who were likely in poor peasant families to contribute more labour to production and to domestic labour before and after school as well as on weekends and holidays. At the same time, men rarely worked in subsistence production, whereas in the Kisii area the men did help out in cash-crop production. Where one crop was cultivated both for subsistence and for the market, there were major disputes between husbands and wives over allocation of the grain store, particularly when it got low. In Kakamega and Bungome districts, traditional forms of communal labour or the assistance of relatives supplemented family labour until children were old enough to work. Elsewhere, hired labour had completely supplanted these forms of assistance. In general, in poor peasant households the wives provided all the food needs and daily necessities, and also contributed to major costs like school fees from cash earnings derived from marketed crops, beer-brewing, or casual labour. Husbands sought casual employment in house-building, fencing and ploughing especially in the more commercialised areas. They contributed a certain amount of cash each month to cover costs of farm labour, school fees, farm inputs like seeds, fertiliser and ploughing.

The middle to rich peasant households in Kakamega District tended not to have a division between subsistence and commercial plots. Where the division existed, it was often a mechanism to force wives to produce food subsistence needs without draining cash from the husband. In such cases, the wife also supervised and contributed daily labour on the commerical farm with her children. Casual labour was relied upon during peak labour seasons to supplement female and child family labour. All farms of more than four acres used hired labour. In polygamous households, one of the co-wives was usually in charge of keeping a shop owned by the husband. Polygamous husbands did not cultivate at all; instead they 'supervised' the labour force consisting of wives, children, and hired women, men and children. Domestic labour inputs were nearly as demanding for these women as for poor-middle peasants, though lessened by the use of rain-barrels to collect water, and charcoal instead of firewood for cooking. In these households, as in the Dodoma case investigated by Kirimbai, the rich peasant wives were completely dependent on the husbands for cash income. Moreover, they often lived and worked like poor peasant wives, and were not sharing in the wealth to which they had contributed through their own production. In such cases, Monsted (1977) argues, it is correct to talk about the appropriation of surplus by the husband.

Kakamega landless husbands and wives were both forced to seek some form of wage employment. In the late 1960s, the male labourer received 40/= a week and maize flour twice a week along with one half pint of milk daily, but paid rent for a house provided by the farm (10/= to 15/= K.sh. per month) and was sometimes provided with less than one-eighth of an acre for gardening. The wives worked as casual labourers during the peak seasons for 2/= to 2/50 K.sh., per day or engaged in petty trade. Families could not afford to send their children to school. As soon as they were old enough they became hired farm labourers (girls and boys from 13-14 years) or herders (boys). Monsted notes, 'It is not possible for the husband to detach himself from the family economy as all resources which can be generated by any member of the family are needed for food and daily necessities' (Monsted, 1977, p. 306).

The growing impoverishment of poor peasant households in Africa is partly due to general inflation – which hits rural areas even harder than the urban areas – and to declines in the real incomes which men have historically derived from sale of export crops. Because of changes in settlement patterns and land tenure systems, and growing state and market pressure to intensify labour and land use, the old slash and burn cultivation systems can no longer be followed. Soil fertility is deteriorating and producing lower yields as a result. The means to offset soil deterioration require cash inputs like fertilisers, and enough land to allow for crop-rotation, which poor peasants cannot afford. The decline in the capacity of poor peasant agriculture systems to reproduce the family forces male and female children as well as the husbands and wives to seek casual labour or to migrate elsewhere in search of wage or other non-farm employment. This leads to a reduction in the labour force available to produce on the family farm, leading to lower levels of output and often to real declines in productivity (see Kerven, 1979a, 1980; Jiggins, 1980). This process of deterioration in agriculture threatens the welfare and lives of peasant women, men and especially children.

For example, in Rwanda 60 per cent of the rural population was below the absolute poverty level compared with 30 per cent of the urban population in 1975 (UNDP 1980). In a 1971 survey by WHO, 45 per cent of the under-fives population exhibited signs of pre-clinical malnutrition, and 10 per cent suffered from marasmus or kwashiokor. Kwashiokor did not exist a few decades ago in Rwanda (UNDP 1980:84), any more than in other areas of Africa. The majority of the rural population lack safe water or permanent housing, and only 6 per cent of the children are reached by health nutrition centres. Similarly in Zambia, malnutrition and anaemia are especially high in Luapula, North-west and Northern Provinces where there is also high outmigration of men, and major agricultural decline. In Luapula Province, 50 per cent of the children suffered from protein – energy malnutrition in 1974 (Jiggins, 1980:26). In a 1972-3 survey of food consumption, 48 per cent of rural and 23 per cent of urban households had insufficient food intake (Jiggins, 1980:28-29). An increasing proportion of households could not subsist on the land. All the female household heads in one Northern village and all but two in another sought piece-work casual labour where the labourer was paid the day's food supply as a daily wage.

> Many claimed to eat nothing except a snack of boiled or roasted cassava some days, feeding the younger children on boiled cassava or bean leaves to stop them crying. Beer drinking too, was used as a soporific and deadened the pangs of hunger (Jiggins 1980:38-39).

The situation worsened during seasonal periods of food shortage. In a 1980 survey of three villages, up to 50 per cent of men were undernourished, 71 per cent of women and 65 per cent of children. The same phenomena of declines in food output and in real income levels, and heightened levels of malnutrition, differentiated for different peasant classes or class categories, is found throughout the continent.

The deterioration in poor peasant agriculture is the result of capitalist transformation in agriculture. It is not the product of 'backward' precapitalist production systems but rather the destruction of pre-capitalist social relations and the growing subjugation of peasant producers to the demands of capital for cheap labour and/or cheap commodities. In the absence of alternative employment opportunities, the demise of peasant agriculture threatens the survival of millions of people in Africa. The growing reliance on food imports and food aid to feed peasants illuminates the problem.

THE WAGE EMPLOYMENT SECTOR

The largest proportion of wage labourers (male and female) work in unskilled low-paying jobs in the 'modern' organised sector or in what is called the 'informal' sector. The majority of women workers are relegated to these jobs. Moreover, women often have access only to seasonal, casual or temporary labour leading to even lower pay and irregularity of income. Very few women have formal wage employment (for example, less than 15 per cent of the modern wage sector in Kenya, Ghana and Zambia are female [Akerele, 1979a]). Given the sex segmentation in the labour force conditioned by very high rates of male and female employment, women are usually allocated to 'dirty' manual work like processing cashew nuts, or shrimps, sorting and cleaning coffee, and the processing or manufacture of cotton, textiles, knitted garments, buttons, tobacco, and shoes (see Akerele 1979a and 1979b; Bryceson 1980; Haile 1980; Kenya, 1978; Meghji, 1977; Mgaya, 1976; Mihyo, 1981; Shields, 1980 and Swantz and Bryceson, 1976). So long as women are employed in the organised sector, their workers' rights to a minimum wage and other benefits are protected by the law and backed up by the labour unions.

However, in the informal sector, where most women are employed, workers lack such protection and work under extremely high rates of exploitation. Seasonal employment is particularly prevalent in the rural areas, and absorbs not only a 'neighbouring' labour force but also migrants from other rural areas. However, both the modern and the informal sector employ seasonal labour; for example, in processing factories or on large capitalist farms or plantations.

In Kenya, for example, the proportion of women casual agricultural labourers ranges from one fifth in some provinces to a large majority in Central Province (Kenya, 1978). In Botswana, women mainly hire out to farmers from December to July; or in January and February (Kerven, 1980). They are paid 1.4 bags of grain under the *Majako* contract. Alternative jobs are not available for women. For example, in Kgatlang, Botswana, the proportion of women migrant labourers in South Africa dropped from

18 per cent in 1971 to 11 per cent in 1978. The majority worked as domestic servants, and are now affected by the South African reorganisation of the labour force which is reducing the numbers of foreign labourers.

In the one large-scale capitalist fishing industry with a monopoly in Liberia, one-third of the labour force are women. However, women represent 60 per cent of the labour force in the shrimp-processing factor. The employers prefer to hire women because they believe they are more careful, patient, and manually dexterous (Akerele, 1979b). These are the usual explanations given by the multinationals in Asia, Latin America and Africa for their preference to hire young, often illiterate, women to do routine, boring, manual and low-paying work. More of the women in the fresh fish processing sector are seasonal, unskilled workers. The industry also depends on the labour of 'fish mammies' who sell the fish products through agents. Although they resemble self-employed traders, these women are equivalent to wage-labourers paid a piece-rate, in that their income depends on their sales and in some cases a commission. They face seasonal fluctuations in employment and the market, and work a much longer, self-propelled working day typical of the informal sector.

A recent study of a large capitalist farm enterprise in Senegal financed by a consortium of a private Brussels-based company, the World Bank and the Senegalese government clarifies the process of sex segmentation (Mackintosh, 1979). Wage employment was differentiated on the farm according to skills and sex. A total of 2000 workers were employed during the height of the season but the total fluctuated according to the agriculture season and market. All the skilled and semi-skilled work was done by men, mainly migrant, though 99 men were permanently employed. Women were concentrated in melon- and pepper-packing, which was unskilled, least paid and seasonal. The women bean-pickers were the least stable workforce, paid on a price-rate basis and hired by the day. Nearly all the women workers were living in nearby villages. They accepted such exploitative conditions because of the decay in agriculture in the wet season which forced them to seek wage employment of any kind in order to provide for themselves and their families.

Women workers receive consistently lower wages than men, even when they have the same amount of education and work experience (see Table 9.1 for the Botswana case). Statutory sex differentials in wages exist in Kenya (Kayongo-Male and Walji, 1980; Kenya, 1978). Elsewhere, these differentials are the result of the way women are specifically allocated to unskilled low-paying jobs. The creation of sex segmentation in the labour market is one mechanism of maintaining a reserve army of cheap labour, to be drawn in and thrown out of employment according to the labour

TABLE 9.1 *Annual wage rates (Rand) in rural areas and Gaborone, categorised by education in Botswana*

	Rural	Gaborone Peri-Urban	Gaborone Urban Excluding Peri-Urban
Males			
No Education	366	494	755
Standard 1-3	436	375	764
Standard 4-7	709	707	829
Form 1-5	–	1074	1279
(Form 1-3)	1249	–	–
(Form 4-5)	2156	–	–
Higher Education	1201	863	1333
Females			
No Education	131	204	185
Standard 1-3	145	–	386
Standard 4-7	365	272	424
Form 1-5	–	846	815
(Form 1-3)	704	–	–
(Form 4-5)	–	–	–
Higher Education	917	–	1465

SOURCE Lucas 1979 cited in Kerven, 1980, Table 2, p. 14.

demands of employers. The lower wage received by a specific group – in this case women workers – contributes to the lowering of the wage for all workers. Sex segmentation is also related to the hierarchisation of skills in the labour force and in education. It is not natural or accidental that women have had less access to higher level skills and technology. The allocation of women and men to different levels and content of education is a mechanism which contributes to the process of sex segmentation and skills differentiation in the labour force itself.

In Kenya, the average monthly wage in the private sector in 1976 was 614/= for men and 525/= for women, in the public sector, 863/= for men and 781/= for women (Kenya, 1978). However, the discrepancy is larger within specific segments of the labour force as can be seen in Table 9.2. Table 9.3 shows the degree to which women are allocated to the lowest paying jobs in Tanzania.

Related to wage differentials and allocation to different segments of the labour force are the higher unemployment rates for women, even when the women have the same education and work experiences as the men (Kenya, 1978; Shields, 1980). Table 9.4 provides data on differential unemployment rates in Tanzania.

TABLE 9.2 *Sex differentials in wages in Kenya, 1976 (Kenya shillings)*

	Public		*Private*	
	Male	*Female*	*Male*	*Female*
Casual labourers	294	167	223	148
Unskilled workers	480	383	295	225

SOURCE Kenya, 1978.

TABLE 9.3 *Distribution of urban labour force by income and sector of employment (Tanzania, 1971)*

Income group (Tanzania shillings)	*Wage earners*		*Self-employed*	
	Male	*Female*	*Male*	*Female*
1–25	.4	0	6.7	–
26–100	3.9	13.5	3.3	47.4
101-199	17.9	29.3	32.8	29.5
200–300	40.7	24.8	14.8	14.7
301–600	24.9	20.3	12.9	6.3
601–1000	5.9	6.1	4.9	2.1
1001–3000	6.1	6.1	10.5	0.0
Over 3000	.6	0	4.1	0.0

SOURCE Shields, 1980, Table 3.5, p. 40.

TABLE 9.4 *Seven towns – unemployment rates by sex and education (%) in Tanzania*

	Active job search	*Including passive job search*
Males		
None	3.5	4.9
Standard 1–4	4.8	5.8
5–8	5.6	10.7
Form 1–4	4.4	4.6
5+	0.0	0.0
Females		
None	16.6	29.9
Standard 1–4	18.1	35.2
5–8	32.0	43.0
Form 1–4	9.2	11.2
5+	0.0	0.0

SOURCE Shields, 1980, Table 4.7, p. 71.

IMPLICATIONS FOR THE FUTURE

The future for women and men in Africa will depend upon the outcome of the struggle for national liberation and socialist democracy in each country and on the continent as a whole. The form these struggles will take depends on the concrete set of social forces in each country as well as worldwide, including the gender aspect of class relations. The specific movements of international capital, its compradorial allies and embryonic national capital will contribute to the shaping of these social forces in each country.

Major changes have occurred in the international division of labour, with specific effects on female members of the labour force in Asia, Latin America and Africa. One way that big capital has sought to overcome the economic crisis of the 1970s and 1980s is to lower production costs by shifting industry to Third World countries where a massive reserve of cheap labour is steadily accumulating. The deterioration of peasant agriculture is one of the fundamental preconditions for the creation of this reserve of cheap labour.

There has been a major growth of manufacturing industries like textiles, garments, leather goods and electronics organised by multinational corporations for export back to the developed capitalist countries. These have so far been concentrated around Bantustans in South Africa as 'border industries' in order to take advantage of the reservoir of cheap female labour. Export industry has begun to take hold elsewhere, however, including Ivory Coast and Kenya. Far more significant for many countries has been the movement of transnational agri-business into Africa to produce food and industrial raw materials for export. International agencies like the World Bank and international financial bank consortiums are instrumental in financing joint business ventures in agriculture, manufacturing and mining involving national governments and local and foreign capitalists.

The exapansion of industry (import-substitution and export-oriented) and agri-business will vary depending to a large degree on the extent to which national governments can and will comply with capitalist demands for a cheap, compliant, adaptive and controlled labour force. As shown in this chapter, women represent the cheapest source of labour because of a combination of factors including old pre-capitalist relations, the sexual division of labour in domestic tasks, sex segmentation in the labour force, and sex specificity underlying state intervention in colonial and neo-colonial situations. It is in capital's interests to subordinate women in the family, in education and in the labour force. This is so for several reasons, the more obvious one being that in this way female labour will continue to be cheap and highly exploitable. Another reason is the reliance on unpaid female labour in the household to maintain and biologically reproduce working class and peasant labourers, thereby reducing the overall cash demands for subsistence, and hence the wage or price payments for crops.

It is not likely that more than a small minority of adults will be absorbed into wage employment in the formal sector in the near future. The majority of people in most countries – and women more than men – will continue to rely on steadily-deteriorating peasant agriculture for their subsistence. There is no future in peasant agriculture, however, as this chapter has tried to show. As Frank (1981) argues, what is happening can be likened to a 'lifeboat' policy:

> if the lifeboat is full and more people try to get into it, everyone will drown, so it is better that some drown in order that others may survive. This argument is used to justify a policy of abandoning those people who cannot play any role in the international division of labour: let them go under, literally, through disease, war, famine, and so forth (Frank, 1981, p. 58).

In the face of heightened threats to survival, women workers and peasants have and will become increasingly militant. In mining towns of Zambia in 1981, for example, women demonstrated against higher prices of maize meal and its unavailability and they encouraged the miners to strike. In 1981 Tanzanian women in Dodoma also demonstrated over the poor distribution of fuel needed to keep grain mills going, which led to a redistribution of fuel. Women workers have engaged in independent strike actions, such as that which took place on the large capitalist farm enterprise in Senegal already mentioned (Mackintosh, 1979). When the management imposed a piece-rate system on the female packing-shed workers, who had been on an hourly-wage system, they struck and eventually won their case.

Women peasants have historically struggled over the reallocation of labour and land. They are withdrawing labour from export crops and intensifying food-crop production over which they have more control at household and village level (Mbilinyi, 1982a and 1982b). In Tanzania women peasants are more openly critical of poor government leadership at village and higher levels than men. They are vehemently outspoken about male control over major cash proceeds. Women were often the most enthusiastic supporters of collective production in ujamaa villages because for the first time they were paid in cash or kind for their work.

The increase of female-headed households among peasant and working-class families is partly due to rejection of bourgeois family social relations by women (see Mascarenhas and Mbilinyi, 1983, for discussion of women's class struggles). In short, women peasants and women workers represent a largely unrecognised and unorganised force for revolution and development in Africa.

REFERENCES[1]

Africa (excluding Tanzania)

J. O. Debo Akande (1979) *Law and the Status of Women in Nigeria* (Addis Ababa: UNECA, ATRCW).

Olubanke Akerele (1979a) *Women Workers in Ghana, Kenya, Zambia* (Addis Ababa: UNECA, ATRCW).

Olubanke Akerele (1979b) *Women and Fishing Industry in Liberia* (Addis Ababa: UNECA, ATRCW).

Janet M. Bujra (1975) 'Women "Entrepreneurs" of Early Nairobi' *Cahiers d'Etudes Africaines* 9 (2); 213–34.

Jette Bukh (1978) *The Village Women in Ghana* (Uppsala: Scandinavian Institute of African Studies).

Anna Conti (1979) 'Capitalist Organisation of Production through non-Capitalist Relations: Women's Role in a Pilot Resettlement in Upper Volta', *Review of African Political Economy*, 15–16: 75–92.

Louise Fortmann (1980) 'Women's Involvement in High Risk Arable Agriculture, the Botswana Case', Workshop on Women in Agricultural Production in Eastern and Southern Africa, April, Nairobi.

André Gunder Frank (1981) *Reflections on the World Economic Crisis*, (New York: Monthly Review Press).

Jane I. Guyer (1977) 'The Women's System: The Lekie, Southern Cameroon', Yaounde: National Advanced School of Agriculture.

Daniel Haile (1980) *Law and the Status of Women in Ethiopia* (Addis Ababa: UNECA, ATRCW).

Jeanne Koopman Henn (1978) *Peasants, Workers and Capital* (Harvard University, Unpublished PhD dissertation).

Barbara Isaacman and June Stephen (1980) *Mozambique: Women, the Law and Agrarian Reform* (Addis Ababa: UNECA, ATRCW).

Janice Jiggins (1980) 'Female-headed Households among Subsistence Cultivators in the Central and Northern Provinces of Zambia', Workshop on Women in Agricultural Production in Eastern and Southern Africa, April, Nairobi.

[1] My references include several unpublished mimeographed works which would remain unknown to readers unless noted here. There is a wealth of original descriptive and analytical work produced in Eastern Africa which is only available in mimeograph form due to the lack of publishing infrastructure. Regardless of their unpublished state, they represent the most current knowledge available.

Diane Kayango-Male and Parvian Walji (1980) 'Women in Employment in Kenya', Paper presented to KULU Women's Research Seminar, July, Copenhagen.

Hanna Kebebe (1978) 'Improving Village Water Supplies in Ethiopia: A Case Study of Socio-Economic Implications' (Addis Ababa: UNECA, ATRCW).

Hanna Kebebe (1980) 'Integration of Women in the Agrarian Reconstruction of Ethiopia' Workshop on Agriculture Production, April, Nairobi.

Kenya, Republic of – Central Bureau of Statistics (n.d.) *Educational Trends 1973–1977*, Nairobi.

Kenya, Republic of – Central Bureau of Statistics (1978) *Women in Kenya*, Nairobi.

Carol Kerven (1979a) *Urban and Rural Female-headed Households' Dependence on Agriculture*, National Migration Study, Central Statistics Office, Ministry of Finance and Development Planning and Rural Sociology Unit, Ministry of Agriculture (to be referred to as National Migration Study) (Gaborone, Botswana).

Carol Kerven (1979b) *Botswana Mine Labour Migration to South Africa* National Migration Study (Gaborone).

Carol Kerven (1980) *Rural Urban Migration and Agricultural Productivity in Botswana* National Migration Study (Gaborone).

R. E. B. Lucas (1979) 'The Distribution of Wages and Employment in Botswana' Rural Incomes Distribution Conference, Central Statistics Office (Gaborone).

Carol P. MacCormack (1979) 'Control of Land, Labour and Capital in Rural Southern Sierra Leone' (University of Cambridge, mimeo).

Patricia McFadden (1980) 'The Conditions of South African Women in Non-capitalist Agriculture', Workshop on 'Women in Agricultural Production in Eastern and Southern Africa', April, Nairobi.

Maureen Mackintosh (1979) 'The Men Form a Union, the Women Go on Strike' IDS 'Women Under Subordination' Conference (Sussex).

Margaret Max-Forson (1979) 'Progress and Obstacles in Achieving the Minimum Objectives of the World and Africa Plans of Action: A Critical Review' UNECA, ATRCW, Second Regional Conference on the Integration of Women in Development, Lusaka, December.

Mette Monsted (1977) 'The Changing Division of Labour within Rural Families in Kenya', CDR Project paper A77.4, Centre for Development Research, Copenhagen.

Martha Mueller (1976) 'Women and Men, Power and Powerlessness in Lesotho'.

M. S. Muntemba (1980) 'Women in Agriculture in the Railway Region of Zambia' Workshop on Agricultural Production, April, Nairobi.

C. N. Murithi (1980) 'The Role of Women in Small-scale Farm Production in Kenya' Workshop on Agricultural Production, April, Nairobi.

Harriet Ngubane (1980) 'Feminine Dilemmas in Rural Swaziland', Workshop on Agricultural Production in Eastern and Southern Africa, April, Nairobi.

Achola Pala Okeyo (1980) 'The Foluo Equation', *Ceres* 13 (3) 37–42.

Emmy B. Simmons (1973) 'The Small-scale Rural Food Processing Industry in Northern Nigeria' (Washington, DC: Office of Women in Development, AID).

Zenebework Tadesse (1979) 'The Impact of Land Reform on Women: The Case of Ethiopia', *ISIS*, Spring, 18–21.

Zenebework Tadesse (1980) 'African Women in Industrial Employment', KULU Women's Research Seminar, July, Copenhagen.

UNDP (1980) *Rural Women's Participation in Development*, Evaluation Study No. 3.

United Nations Protein Advisory Group (1979) *Women in Food Production, Food Handling and Nutrition, with Special Emphasis on Africa* (Rome: FAO).

G. Wikan (1981) *Absent Workers and Changes in Subsistence Crop Production* Gaborone, National Migration Study.

Tanzania

Zinnat K. Bader (1975) *Women, Private Property and Production in Bukoba District* (UDM, unpublished MA dissertation).

James L. Brain (1976) 'Less than Second Class – Women in Rural Settlement Schemes in Tanzania', in Nancy J. Hafkin and Edna G. Bay (eds) *Women in Africa* (Stanford: Stanford University Press).

Deborah Fahy Bryceson and Mary Kirimbai (1980) *Subsistence or Beyond? Money-earning Activities of Women in Rural Tanzania* (Dar es Salaam: BRALUP and UWT) BRALUP Research Report No. 45.

Deborah Fahy Bryceson and Marjorie Mbilinyi (1980) 'The Changing Role of Tanzanian Women in Production', *Jipemoyo 2*: 85–116 (Uppsala: Scandinavian Institute of African Studies).

Deborah Fahy Bryceson (1980) 'The Proletarianisation of Women in Tanzania', *Review of African Political Economy*, 17: 4–27.

Mary Kirimbai (1981) *The Impact of Domestic Water Supply Project on the Rural Population and their Role in Production and Reproduction in Dodoma Rural District* (UDM, unpublished MA dissertation).

Ophalia Mascarenhas and Marjorie Mbilinyi (1983) *Women in Tanzania, An Analytical Bibliography* (Uppsala: Scandinavian Institute of African Studies).

Marjorie Mbilinyi (1982a) 'The Unity of "Struggles" and "Research": The Case of Peasant Women in West Bagamoyo, Tanzania' in Maria Mies (ed.) *Fighting on Two Fronts: Women's Struggles and Research* (The Hague: Institute of Social Studies).

Marjorie Mbilinyi (1982b) *The Subjugation of Pre-Capitalist Relations to Capital and the Oppression of Women* (Taamuli (forthcoming): UDM).

Marjorie Mbilinyi (1982c) 'The Health of Children: The Hidden Crisis in Tanzania' in *Basic Needs in Danger* (Geneva: ILO, JASPA).

Marjorie Mbilinyi (forthcoming) 'Wife, Slave and Subject of the King: The Oppression of Women in the Shambala Kingdom', *Tanzania Notes and Records*, 88 and 89.

Mary Hans Mgaya (1976) *A Study of Workers in a Factory* (UDM: Unpublished MA dissertation).

N. Z. Mihyo (1981) 'The Involvement of Women in Small-scale Industries in Tanzania', IDS Seminar, November.

Z. M. H. Meghji, (1977) *The Development of Women Wage Labour* (UDM: unpublished MA dissertation).

Asseny Muro (1979) 'The Study of Women's Position in Peasant Production and their Education and Training: A Case of Diozile Village in Bagamoyo District' (UDM: unpublished MA dissertation).

Marie Antoinette Oomen-Myin (1981) *Involvement of Rural Women in Village Development in Tanzania: A Case Study in Morogoro District* (UDM: Department of Agricultural Education and Extension, Morogoro, Research Monograph).

Najma Sachak (1979) 'Creating Employment Opportunities for Rural Women: Some Issues Affecting Attitudes and Policy', International Political Science Association Congress, August, Moscow.

Najma Sachak (1980) 'The Management of Food Resources under Conditions of Famine' BRALUP, Working Paper No. 1, Workshop on Women in Agricultural Production in Eastern and Southern Africa, Nairobi, April.

Ngwanganga Shields (1980) *Women in the Urban Labour Markets of Africa: The Case of Tanzania* (Washington DC: World Bank Staff Working Paper No. 380).

Marja-Liisa Swantz and D. B. Bryceson (1976) 'Women Workers in Dar es Salaam' (BRALUP Research Paper no. 43).

E. Tobisson (1980) *Women, Work, Food and Nutrition in Nyamurigura, Mara Region, Tanzania*, report presented to Tanzania Food and Nutrition Centre.

Parin J. Virji (1979) 'Summary of Labour Turnover at Friendship Textile Mill – 1978 with Specific Reference to Women Workers', Paper no. 3, BW.

Ulla Vuorela with Jonas Reuben (1981) 'Women's Role in Post-Harvest Food Conservation, Tanzania Case Study', research report to United Nations University.

10 African Development and the Elusiveness of Basic Human Needs: Physical Quality of Life Index and a Case-study of Tanzania

FLORIZELLE B. LISER and
E. DIANE WHITE*

INTRODUCTION

The primary challenge facing sub-Saharan Africa remains fuller development of the region's vast economic potential. Although the region's forty-five states are to varying degrees heterogeneous in their structural characteristics, all share the common problem of poverty. This is not to minimise the progress made on a variety of political, social and economic fronts throughout the continent over the past two decades, but rather to emphasise that the current economic situation in Africa is bleak and future development prospects are limited by a complex set of interrelated problems. Included among these are slow overall economic growth, low agricultural productivity, rapid increases in population and acute balance-of-payments and fiscal problems. In fact, of the thirty-one countries judged by the United Nations to be least developed (LLDC) twenty-one are African countries. The facts underlying the present economic crisis can be seen in the various indices set out in Table 10.2.

Equally distressing are the dim prospects for future African development, particularly when viewed against the backdrop of global economic recession,

* Views expressed are those of the authors and do not represent the views of the Office of the US Trade Representative in the case of Ms Liser or the World Bank in the case of Ms White.

rising energy costs and the pattern of sluggish growth in the industrial countries. It has been projected that in the year 2000, Africa will have about 11 per cent of the global population but will account for only 2.0 per cent of the gross world product, 1.8 per cent of global trade, and only 1.1 per cent of world manufacturing production. In addition, it is estimated that Africa will suffer from a good deficit of some 39 million tons. Average life expectancy and infant mortality will be only 57 years and some 84 deaths per 1000 births, respectively. In fact, it has been estimated that per capita income in most African countries would have to increase at a rate of 3 per cent per annum to attain the present average income levels in Latin America by the year 2000.

Even prior to the onset of the particularly severe economic conditions of the 1970s, dissatisfaction with the results of traditional development strategies which had concentrated primarily on GNP growth as the primary goal or index of development, led to a refocusing of development priorities to include more qualitative goals. In Africa and other developing countries, economic development, while still viewed as an essential condition of development, was no longer regarded as a sufficient condition. More attention was given to providing better nourishment, health, education and employment opportunities to the lower 40 per cent of the population in poor countries. This fundamental redirection of development policy has had important implications for Africa where, as with many other developing countries, increased growth has been distributed unevenly within national boundaries and between socio-economic groups. It was exactly this dissatisfaction with the results of previous development approaches which led several African nations – Tanzania being the best-known case and about which more information is provided later – to adopt development strategies more relevant to meeting human needs.

It is not surprising that up to that point the temptation to search for historical patterns in the development process had led development specialists – African and non-African – to implement strategies based, in many respects, on the experiences of the industrialised Western nations. Though some important lessons could be learned from the Western experience, this approach to development was and still is in many critical ways ill-adapted to the needs of African countries. While Africa's underdevelopment is often viewed as long-term and inevitable, these conclusions are based on the traditional development strategies implemented to date. However, it is clear that this approach has not worked for many developing countries – Africa the least of all. Hence, it is in the interest of African governments to define development in a new and more innovative way which takes into account Africa's economic structures, resource base and political and social realities. This can be done without abandoning the goal of overall economic growth as traditionally defined. Priority, however, must also be given to establishing new growth targets in terms of providing better nutrition, health, housing, education and employment for Africa's increasing poor population.

THE PHYSICAL QUALITY OF LIFE INDEX (PQLI)

In 1977 the Overseas Development Council (ODC) introduced the PQLI, designed to supplement the GNP by providing a more specific measure of what happens to people in situations of underdevelopment. This relatively new index is not all-inclusive and does not measure security, justice, satisfaction, or the general level of development. But it does seek to determine how well societies are able to satisfy certain very elementary needs that are of immediate concern to the very poor.

In the mid-1970s, on a scale of 0–100, Africa had an average PQLI of 32 compared with a Latin American average of 71, a North American average of 95, and a worldwide average of 65. That the PQLI reveals that Africa today is both absolutely and relatively poorer than other developing countries and the industrialised world is no surprise. However, in contemplating Africa's development prospects and future, it is possible to see that through concerted national, regional, and international efforts, Africa could meet the basic needs of its people more successfully than predictions of future GNP and other purely economic indexes would indicate. Thus, depending on one's meaning, Africa could be far more 'developed' by the year 2000 than one would suspect from the current situation and various economic predictions of Africa's futures.

The PQLI was, in fact, developed with the hope of attaining a better evaluation of the performance of, and progress toward, human-oriented development. In addition, the index reflects an increased understanding of the fact that, for many reasons, the traditional GNP indicator of national economic progress – whether recorded as a national total or on a per capita basis – does not tell us much about the quality of life results achieved. The GNP cannot satisfactorily measure the extent to which the human needs of individuals are being met; nor should it be expected to do so, since there is no automatic relationship between GNP and any particular level or rate of infant mortality or literacy, for example.

Also, growth in average per capita GNP does not necessarily improve the well-being of large portions of a country's population, since that income may flow to social groups in very unequal proportions. In many cases, the very poorest groups of a society may not benefit much, if at all. Moreover, even if rising incomes are shared with the poorest groups, there is no guarantee that the increases in income will improve physical well-being.

An increasing awareness of the grave shortcomings of past development approaches has led national and international development planners – African and non-African alike – to focus directly on the fundamental task of developing new approaches to meet the basic health, education and development needs of people, eliminate the worst aspects of poverty within a given time frame (for example, by the year 2000); and to develop new measures that will better assess any national and international progress toward human-oriented development.

Some Criteria for a Basic Needs Indicator and the PQLI

The Physical Quality of Life Index does not address the broadest statement of the basic human needs concept (for example, it does not include employment, transportation, shelter, popular participation, etc.). It does, however, address and meet a special problem in the Basic Human Needs (BHN) debate. If it is noted that a monetary indicator such as per capita GNP cannot adequately measure how well societies are satisfying certain basic needs of their people and that no such measure exists to date, the PQLI does seem to meet many of the criteria for a basic needs indicator.

Even the most elementary and narrowly-defined basic needs index should:

1. avoid measures that are ethnocentric, represent rich-country values or use absolute standards (many developed-country standards, such as those used for housing and nutrition, imply that those standards are universally necessary for a high quality of life when that is not the case);
2. avoid measures that assume that developing countries will inevitably evolve along the paths followed by the countries of Western Europe and North America (hence, an index should exclude inappropriate indicators linked to those paths, such as number of telephones or automobiles per 1000 people);
3. measure results, not inputs, since the intent is to estimate the actual success of a policy, not merely the resources expended in attempts to implement it;
4. be sensitive to the distribution of benefits among the population,

since monetary indicators such as per capita GNP do not indicate whether income is widely distributed or is mainly received by small groups of the population.

In addition, the data on which the index is based should be widely available, the index itself should be simple to construct and to comprehend, and should lend itself to international comparison.

After examining a large array of potential indicators in terms of the above criteria, the Overseas Development Council (ODC) selected three – infant mortality, life expectancy at the age of 1 year, and literacy – that seem to capture many aspects of wellbeing, and the PQLI combines these three indicators into a single composite index. Each of the three components is indexed on a scale of 0 (the most unfavourable performance in 1950) to 100 (the best performance expected by the end of the century). For life expectancy at the age of 1 year, the most favourable figure expected to be achieved by any country by the year 2000 (77 years) is valued at 100, and the most unfavourable performance in 1950 (38 years in Guinea-Bissau) is valued at 0. Similarly, for infant mortality, the best performance expected by the year 2000 (7 per 1000 births) is rated at 100, and the poorest performance in 1950 (229 per 1000 births) is rated at 0. Literacy figures (being percentages) are automatically on a 0-100 scale. The composite index – the PQLI – is calculated by averaging the three component indexes (life expectancy at the age of 1 year, infant mortality, and literacy) giving equal weight to each ofthem.

Any number of factors make life expectancy, infant mortality, and literacy appropriate indicators for measuring physical wellbeing and for assessing progress toward identified targets for the year 2000. Although data on these three social indicators still are uneven in quality – especially in many developing countries – they are widely available. A further major advantage of these indicators is that each measures development results rather than inputs. Because these results reflect more or less universal objectives, they are appropriate standards for performance comparison among countries.[1]

As a composite index, the PQLI recognises that improvements in meeting minimum needs can be achieved in a variety of ways. Better diets, sanitation, medical care, education, etc, are means to an end, and which means are chosen must suit the resources and culture of an individual country. Thus, with the provision that the types of techniques and policies chosen must result in better lives for the poorest people, policy-makers are free to apply any mixture of approaches and policies that will bring about the desired results.

The PQLI: advantages and what it shows

Despite its limitations, the PQLI has many advantages, both in concept and in what it can actually show.[2] Table 10.1 reveals, for example, some of the significant surprises that emerge when the development progress

TABLE 10.1 *Per capita GNP and PQLI*

	Per capita GNP, 1980 ($)	*PQLI*
Low-Income Countries		
(per capita GNP <$400)	225[a]	43[a]
China	290	76
Haiti	270	39
India	240	44
Mali	190	18
Tanzania	260	53
Lower Middle-Income Countries		
(per capita GNP $400–999)	566	56
Egypt	580	54
Liberia	520	37
Peru	930	67
Senegal	450	25
Thailand	670	75
Upper Middle-Income Countries		
(per capita GNP $1000–3499)	1800	68
Brazil	2050	74
Cuba	1410	93
Iran	2030	57
Mauritius	1060	82
Nigeria	1010	31
High-Income Countries		
(per capita GNP >$3500)	8222	93
Australia	9820	96
Gabon	4440	23
Libya	8640	52
Singapore	4480	86
United States	11360	96

[a] Excluding the Peoples' Republic of China.

SOURCE Based on 'Statistical Annexes', in Roger D. Hansen *et al. US Foreign Policy and the Third World: Agenda 1982* (New York: Praeger for the Overseas Development Council, 1982) 160–71. *Agenda 1982* lists the PQLI ratings of all countries.

of countries is viewed not just in terms of per capita GNP but also in terms of the PQLI. Although the levels of per capita GNP and physical well-being are usually closely correlated, a number of exceptions indicate that low income and the worst consequences of absolute poverty need not go hand in hand. Sri Lanka (formerly Ceylon) is a striking case in point. Despite a per capita GNP of only $270 per person, that country has been able to achieve a PQLI rating of 80, which matches or exceeds that of countries with a much higher per capita GNP. The table also shows that relatively high per capita GNP does not necessarily reflect widespread well-being (for example, Iran).

In regard to Africa specifically, the PQLI is helpful in examining the various dilemmas that face many African countries as they try to develop their human and natural resources to their full potential. Consider, for example, Nigeria and Tanzania – more specific information on the latter's development strategy is included later. Despite differing colonial experiences and quite different approaches to development in the past, it is clear that neither country has yet been able to overcome fully the worst aspects of poverty among the majority of their populations. On the one hand, Nigeria is often considered well-off because of its petroleum resources, which provided $16.8bn in export earnings in 1979 and a per capita GNP of $1010 in 1980. Yet Nigeria has an infant mortality rate of 157 deaths per 1000 live births, a literacy rate of 15 per cent, and a PQLI of only 31. Tanzania, in comparison, has a low per capita income of $260. However, despite an infant mortality rate of 125 per 1000 births and a life expectancy of 50 years, Tanzania has achieved a PQLI rating of 53, largely because of its high literacy rate of 66 per cent. Moreover, a close look at Tanzania's infant mortality and life expectancy ratings in comparison with other low-income African countries reveals that Tanzania has fared relatively well (see Table 10.2).

In any case, it is clear that the differing political economic, and cultural backgrounds, the varying population sizes, and the different resource endowments in Africa point to the need for unique and individual national approaches to overall development and to meeting basic human needs. Tanzania (with 19 million people and continuing problems arising out of poor performance in the agricultural sector) cannot go about developing and meeting the needs of its people in the same manner as Nigeria (with 80 million people and petroleum resources). Obviously, development strategies that worked for the Western countries have not been particularly successful in Africa, and the PQLI highlights the need for policies that are generally more aimed at meeting Africa's needs, but that also recognise the individual circumstances of each country. In general, however, most

TABLE 10.2 *Economic and social indicators of development for Africa*

	Population mid-1981 (millions)	Per capita GNP 1980[a] ($)	Per capita GNP (real) growth rate 1970–9 (%)	Physical quality of life index (PQLI)[b]	Disparity reduction rate (DRR) 1960–cur.[c] (%)	Birth rate per 1000[d]	Death rate per 1000[d]	Life expectancy at birth[e] (years)	Infant mortality per 1000 live births[d]	Literacy[e]	Per capita public education expend's 1978 ($)	Per capita military expend's 1978 ($)	Total exports f.o.b. 1979 ($ mill.)	Total imports c.i.f. 1979 ($ mill.)
Low-Income (25) (per capita GNP <$400)	**180.5**	**228**	**–0.8**	**31**	**1.6**	**47**	**20**	**45**	**160**	**25**	**7**	**8**	**5222**	**6693**
*Benin	3.8	300	0.6	29	1.0	49	19	46	149	11	11	3	40	320
*Burundi	4.2	200	1.5	33	0.8	47	20	46	149	25	4	5	105	153
*Cape Verde	0.3	300[g]	4.8[g]	52	n/a	29	8	57	105	37	n/a	6[h]	4	40
*Central African Republic	2.4	300[g]	0.9[g]	23	n/a	42	19	46	190	7	8	4	85[i]	50
*Chad	4.6	120	–2.4	24	n/a	44	21	44	190	15	3	8	58	140
*Comoros	0.4	300[g]	–4.3[g]	44	n/a	40	18	46	148	58	n/a	n/a	25	24
Equatorial Guinea	0.3	390[j]	–4.2	30	n/a	42	19	46	165	20	10	25	n/a	n/a
*Ethiopia	33.5	140	0.3	20	n/a	50	25	39	178	15	3	5	423	576
*Gambia	0.6	250	0.4	17	n/a	48	23	41	217	10	11	0	58	141
*Guinea	5.1	290	0.6	23	n/a	46	21	44	220	20	9	4	280	190
*Guinea-Bissau	0.8	160[c]	–0.6	15	n/a	41	23	41	211	5	n/a	10	14	50
*Lesotho	1.4	390[g]	9.5	50	n/a	40	16	50	114	52	10	0	40	170
Madagascar	8.8	350	–2.5	46	n/a	45	19	46	102	50	13	6	410	600
*Malawi	6.2	230	3.0	34	n/a	52	20	46	142	25	5	4	233	400
*Mali	6.8	190	2.5	18	0.4	52	24	42	210	10	5	4	120	250
Mauritania	1.7	320	–0.7	23	n/a	50	22	42	187	17	16	30	148	259
Mozambique	10.7	270[g]	–5.3[g]	29	n/a	45	19	46	148	11	3	9	100	280
*Niger	5.7	330	–1.2	19	n/a	51	22	42	200	8	3	2	210	290
*Rwanda	5.3	200	1.6	35	n/a	50	19	46	127	23	4	3	90	200
Sierra Leone	3.6	270	–1.2	31	n/a	46	19	46	136	15	9	2	146	270
*Somalia	3.8	140[j]	–0.8	39	n/a	48	20	43	177	60	7	12	110	290
*Tanzania, United Republic	19.2	260[k]	0.8	53	2.5	46	16	50	125	66	12	10	600	1000
*Uganda	14.1	280[g]	–3.5[g]	45	1.2	45	14	52	120	35	10	11	663	180
*Upper Volta	7.1	190	–1.2	19	n/a	48	22	42	182	5	4	14	70	200
Zaire	30.1	220	–2.6	28	n/a	46	19	46	171	15	6	10	1200	620
Lower-Middle Income (17) (per capita GNP $400-999)	**156.3**	**573**	**1.9**	**43**	**1.3**	**46**	**15**	**51**	**121**	**32**	**22**	**40**	**13184**	**16945**
Angola	6.7	470[g]	–9.6[g]	17	n/a	48	23	41	192	5	15	18[l]	1400	830
*Botswana	0.8	910	12.0	48	n/a	51	17	56	97	25	48	22	250	220
Cameroon	8.7	670	3.1	28	n/a	42	19	44	157	19	13	7	1129	1271
Congo, People's Republic	1.6	730	–0.2	39	n/a	45	19	46	180	50	45	23	200[i]	210[i]
Djibouti	0.5	480[g]	–4.9[g]	n/a	n/a	49	22	n/a	n/a	5	n/a	n/a	20	140
Egypt	43.5	580	5.3	54	1.6	41	11	55	90	44	28	91	1840	3837
Ghana	12.0	420	–3.0	40	0.9	48	17	48	115	30	16	5	1050	800
Kenya	16.5	420	2.6	53	1.6	53	14	53	83	45	17	12	1162	1535

[illegible]	[illegible]	[illegible]	[illegible]	[illegible]	[illegible]	[illegible]	[illegible]	[illegible]	[illegible]	n/a	n/a	n/a	27	22
Senegal	5.8	450	0.1	25	n/a	48	22	44	160	10	12	10	320	950
*Sudan	19.6	470	1.5	32	0.7	48	18	46	141	20	4	14	700	1000
Swaziland	0.6	680[g]	4.4[g]	40	n/a	47	19	46	168	50	38	2	160	170
Togo	2.6	410	1.2	34	1.1	49	19	46	121	18	21	8	210	340
Zambia	6.0	560	−1.9	40	n/a	49	17	48	144	39	24	41	1120	650[m]
Zimbabwe[n]	7.6	630	−1.7	47	n/a	47	14	53	129	39	19	31	1154	937[m]
Upper Middle-Income (8) (per capita GNP $1000-3499)	**145.2**	**1412**	**3.8**	**41**	**1.6**	**46**	**16**	**52**	**137**	**29**	**55**	**38**	**41990**	**32113**
†Algeria	19.3	1920	2.8	48	1.5	46	14	56	127	35	115	36	9255	8200
Ivory Coast	8.5	1150	1.3	33	n/a	50	19	46	138	20	64	11	2516	2488
Mauritius	1.0	1060	6.4	82	2.9	28	7	67	34	80	64	2	400	470
Namibia	1.0	1410	0.3	46	n/a	44	15	51	107	38	n/a	n/a	n/a	n/a
†Nigeria	79.7	1010	5.3	31	n/a	50	18	48	157	15	34	28	16800	9692
Seychelles	0.1	1770	3.8	73	n/a	28	7	65	27	58	n/a	n/a	3	55
South Africa	29.0	2290	0.6	62	n/a	36	12	60	97	57	67	80	11250	8370
Tunisia	6.6	1310	5.7	59	n/a	33	8	57	123	62	58	30	1766	2838
High-Income (3) (per capita GNP >$3500)	**4.3**	**7397**	**−0.4**	**50**	**n/a**	**42**	**14**	**54**	**125**	**45**	**334**	**142**	**16640**	**9207**
†Gabon	0.7	4440	5.2	23	n/a	33	22	43	178	12	100	78	1700[i]	530[i]
†Libya	3.1	8640	−1.6	52	n/a	47	13	55	130	50	387	156	14800	7898
Reunion	0.5	3830[g]	−0.9[g]	76	n/a	25	6	65	21	63	n/a	n/a	140	779

NOTES Bold summary lines for each income group are cumulative totals for population, export and import figures, and averages are weighted by mid-1981 populations for all other indicators.

* Considered by the United Nations to be one of the 31 least developed countries (LLDC).

† Member of the Organisation of Petroleum Exporting Countries (OPEC).

a Preliminary data based on 1978–80 weighted average prices and exchange rates.

b Each country's Physical Quality of Life Index (PQLI) is based on an average of life expectancy at the age of 1 year infant mortality, and literacy. For a more extensive discussion of the PQLI, see Morris D. Morris, *Measuring the Conditions of the World's Poor: The Physical Quality of Life Index* (New York: Pergamon for the Overseas Development Council, 1979).

c The Disparity Reduction Rate (DRR) is the rate at which the disparity (or gap) between a country's level of performance in any social indicator and the best performance expected anywhere in the year 2000 is being eliminated. The DRR can be applied either to individual social indicators (such as life expectancy) or to composite social indicators (for example, the PQLI). For more extensive discussion of the DRR concept, its benefits, and its limitations, see James P. Grant, *Disparity Reduction Rates in Social Indicators: A Proposal for Measuring and Targeting Progress in Meeting Basic Needs* (Washington, DC: Overseas Development Council, September 1978) Monograph no. 11.

d For countries with complete or near-complete registration of births and deaths, data are for 1978 or 1979. For most developing countries data are for the period 1975–80, or are the latest available estimates.

e Data are for part or all of the period 1970–9.

f Literacy data are the latest estimates available and generally represent the proportion of the adult population (15 years of age or older) able to read and write, although no uniform definition of 'literacy' has been used.

g Tentative.

h 1976 figure.

i Excludes trade among the members of the Customs and Economic Union of Central Africa (CEUCA) consisting of the Central African Republic, Congo, Gabon, and the United Republic of Cameroon.

j 1979 figure.

k Mainland Tanzania.

l 1975 figure.

m f.o.b.

n Formerly Rhodesia.

SOURCE Based on 'Statistical Annexes', in Roger D. Hansen *et al*, *US Foreign Policy and the Third World: Agenda 1982* (New York: Praeger for the Overseas Development Council, 1981) 160–71.

African nations face obstacles – both economic and political as well as domestic and externally imposed – which limit their ability to develop and implement more African approaches to their development and, more specifically, policies aimed at meeting the basic needs of their people.

OBSTACLES TO AND CONSTRAINTS ON MEETING BASIC NEEDS IN AFRICA

Political

Within the African context, there are a number of political constraints – domestic and international – that hinder the successful implementation of a basic needs strategy. One key constraint revolves around the attitudes of the 'Southern élite'. A basic needs strategy will give priority to growth targets stated in terms of housing, education, nutrition and health. This can be achieved without abandoning the goal of GNP growth but not without some reduction in the growth of certain sectors whose benefits accrue to a small minority. Such a change would involve a fundamental restructuring of existing political and economic relationships which developing country élites are certain to resist because it would threaten their socio-economic status, political power and privileged position.

Further, a basic needs strategy to development will be criticised not only by those developing country élites who perceive the implementation of such a strategy as a threat to their privileged positions at home, but an international Southern élite who will regard the strategy as another manifestation of Northern paternalism. Paternalism because the new strategy is easily seen as another attempt by the North to dictate policy to the South, and to relegate developing countries to a second-class status in the international economy. In other words, now that the trickle-down strategy has failed, Northern developmental economists are back from their drawing boards with a new development strategy emphasising basic human needs. This criticism of the new strategy is not centred on its aim to establish a minimum standard of living for the world's poor, but rather on the perceived absence of dialogue in the development effort.

Finally, African leaders – given the limited economic resources available to them for development generally – are faced with difficult political choices in determining those programmes and projects which will reap political benefits equivalent to the effort and capital expended. With so many indigenous groups typically competing for limited resources yet holding significant political power, African leaders establishing and implementing basic needs strategies will have to be particularly prudent –

perhaps more so than in other developing countries – in determining how and where the products of the programme are distributed.

In terms of international constraints, it must be recognised that the contribution to be made by the international development community to improving the living standards of the poorest segment of the population in developing countries is, in general, limited. The major part of the development effort is and will continue to be shouldered by the poor themselves. None the less, there is a continuing need for external assistance, particularly in Africa which contains many of the world's poor, to support development strategies – both traditional and those more geared towards meeting human needs. There is general consensus in the international development community that the objective of aid is to make it easier for developing country governments to implement 'sensible' development policies. There is less agreement, however, on who – for instance, the development agency or the developing country itself – should make the final decision about what constitutes a sensible policy. Theoretical considerations aside, practical politics dictate that as long as most concessional aid is financed by taxes imposed by Northern governments on their citizens, these governments will have considerable say in how their aid money is used. The question of how much voice is a source of considerable tension between the North and the South.

The 'Northern élite problem' will also prove to be a major obstacle to the successful implementation of a basic needs strategy in Africa. Northern critics of such a strategy will be quick to point out that there is no way to ensure that the target population in poor countries is reached and aid money used wisely. Further, it would be virtually impossible, according to them, to monitor programme performance given that developing countries governments would be unwilling to submit to the degree of intervention in their domestic affairs that such a monitoring function would require. The realities of the domestic political process in the South make it imperative that the government in question should not appear to be bartering the independence of their countries for international aid.

Moreover, other critics of the basic-needs approach from the business and strategic community in aid-donor countries will argue that such a strategy would be too risk-prone as it would require a fundamental restructuring of existing political and economic relationships. This, it is argued, could result in a level of social upheaval and instability incompatible with good business conditions or foreign policy objectives.

These arguments against the adoption of a basic-needs strategy at first glance appear compelling; however, several qualifying remarks can be made. In Africa, in particular, where governments are facing slow overall economic growth, spiralling urban unemployment and growing rural poverty, not to address the needs of the poorest segment of the population may prove to be the more serious threat to the existing political and economic system. Put bluntly, the greatest potential for disruption may, in fact, rest with the forgotten '40 per cent' of the population since they are in the most desperate situation and have the least to lose and most to gain from the demise of the élite structure. Implementation of a programme which provides the absolute poor with a minimum standard of living, while requiring fundamental reshaping of domestic political and economic alliances, may in the longer term provide the existing government with an extended lease on life.

On the international side, while not discounting the performance-monitoring issue, it is at least arguable that a developing country government confronted with the first signs of domestic political unrest might find the prospect of increased aid to finance some of the programmes it has long been promising its constituents not such a bad thing, even at the cost of some unwanted Northern 'intervention' into their domestic affairs. As regards Northern élite fears that a basic needs programme would cause an unacceptable degree of political instability, the contrary would appear to be true. As indicated earlier, instability would seem more likely to result from a continuation of present policies than from the adoption of new policies designed to improve the living conditions of the absolute poor.

Even if convinced of the merits of a basic-needs approach, there remains the question of 'why Africa?', – why focus limited resources on basic needs strategies in Africa as opposed to Asia? Considering that a large percentage of the poorest persons do live in Asia, funds earmarked for basic-needs strategies are more likely to be channelled there. Yet, if one compares development indicators generally or those which might assess basic-needs fulfilment specifically, Africa does not fare as well as Asia. For example, in comparison with average life expectancy of 60 years, and infant mortality rates of 96 deaths per 1000 births for low-income Asian countries, low-income African countries have an average life expectancy of 45 years and an infant mortality rate of 160 deaths per 1000 births. Moreover, the literacy rate of low-income Asia at 52 per cent is more than twice that of low-income Africa with a literacy rate of 25 per cent.[3]

With so many of the UN-designated LLDCs in Africa and with a lower level of development on average than Asia, African leaders will need to make greater efforts to convince the international development community of its plight in order to ensure its receipt of an adequate portion of funds currently earmarked for basic-needs strategies.

Economic

In terms of economic constraints on meeting basic human needs in Africa, the most critical one revolves around the current international recession and slow economic growth in the industrialised nations. This has led to a slowdown in the growth, if not the actual contraction, over the last few years of the funds normally contributed by these nations to international development institutions such as the World Bank. As there are limitations on development funds, choices will have to be made between traditional types of development strategies focusing, for example, on increasing production (that is, GNP) and more innovative strategies largely geared towards meeting the essential needs of people. Because there has been more experience, though not necessarily success, with the former, it is possible that the greatest constraint on implementing basic needs strategies in Africa and other developing countries in the near future will be the limitation of funds for such programmes.

A second economic constraint concerns the problems associated with maintaining basic needs programmes once they have been implemented. As the Tanzania case indicates, one of the most difficult problems which may be faced revolves around recurrent budget financing of programmes and the inability to maintain basic needs services.

CASE STUDY IN A BASIC NEEDS APPROACH: TANZANIA

As an African case study in meeting BHN, Tanzania interestingly reflects many of the political and economic, domestic and foreign-imposed problems that African nations might face in undertaking such a programme. Adoption of the Arusha Declaration in 1967 was groundbreaking in the African context because with it Tanzania became one of the first African states to pursue officially a policy of basic needs fulfilment as the central theme of its rural development strategy. The present economic crisis notwithstanding, Tanzania has made remarkable progress towards providing essential social services to most Tanzanians. This fact is well-illustrated by the PQLI index which increased from 16 in 1960 to 53 in 1983. As will be seen, however, this achievement has not been without considerable costs in both political and economic terms. To the extent that the Tanzanian experience is applicable to other African nations, it can provide insight into some of the problems a basic-needs approach might pose, as well as give some indication of the achievements which can be attained.

Objectives of the Ujamaa Strategy

The Arusha Declaration stressed, among other things, the imperative of rural development, particularly agriculture, as the basis for Tanzanian development, and ushered in the Ujamaa strategy. The basic values embodied in the Ujamaa concept were communal work and overship of land, equitable distribution of basic necessities and respect for the right of each member of the society. With Ujamaa, villages maintained their pivotal position but the approach to their establishment changed. A co-operative agrarian economy was seen as a prerequisite for modernisation in Tanzania, and it was argued that only through the pooling of resources and co-ordination of effort at the local level would Tanzanian farmers be efficient and productive enough to increase their incomes and thereby improve their standard of living. This fundamental transformation of the agrarian economy was to be realised through the creation of co-operative communities called Ujamaa villages.

The Government struck a bargain with rural Tanzania. In exchange for active support of the Ujamaa programme, it would provide rural social services. In the post-Arusha period the Government initiated generous programmes to improve and expand social infrastructure in the rural areas particularly water supplies, schools and health dispensaries. Other government initiatives to induce people to start or join Ujamaa villages took the form of material inducements such as subsidies, famine relief, essential consumer goods, and agricultural inputs. It soon became apparent, however, that the government did not have the resources to deliver fully on all aspects of such an ambitious programme. In short, the government was, within its budgetary and manpower constraints, providing rural social services, but not on the scale or at the pace promised. Moreover, the problem with providing such services as inducements, rather than goals in and of themselves, has been that in most cases they have not worked to improve the productive forces of the Ujamaa villages. Instead, they often created a patron–client relationship between the authorities and the villages in which the peasants began to view themselves as wards of the state. It would perhaps be useful here to review the actual implementation record of the basic needs programme in Tanzania, particularly the provision of basic water supplies, health and education facilities.

Provision of Social Services at the Village Level: Rural Water Supplies

Tanzania's second Five-Year Development Plan stressed the importance of improved water supply as a means of reducing the incidence of disease and labour time required for water collection, thereby increasing the productive capacity of the rural population and, consequently, their contribution to the national economy. Water supply programmes, in addition, served as carrots to induce peasants to produce more in response to Government generosity in supplying a number of social services free of charge.

The objectives of Tanzanian water policy are (i) to provide as a basic free service potable and dependable water within a reasonable distance, not exceeding walking distance (4km) of every village by the end of 1981 and (ii) to provide all villages with access to a public water point at an average distance of 400 metres by 1991.[4]

After ten years of development efforts, the rural water supply situation can be summarised as follows:

1. About 20 to 30 per cent of the 8300 registered villages in Tanzania have been provided with a source of clean, potable water. However, less than 50 per cent of these systems were in working condition in 1980, basically because of lack of fuel, maintenance and repair problems;
2. The rural population will have grown to some 22 million by 1991, which means that more than 1.5 million people need to be provided with water in each of the next ten years to reach the 1991 goal, providing all existing schemes are brought back into operation.

The difficulties in meeting rural water policy goals have revolved around two issues. First, villagisation created a serious and immediate water supply problem by moving many widely scattered farmers into new village sites where between 200 and 400 families would be congregated. Little if any prior planning, particularly for water resource development, was undertaken. As a result, many of the village sites were removed from their traditional sources, lengthening the distance to water supplies. Moreover, the sheer number and concentration of families caused crowding of people around the few water points available. A survey of one region found that villagers' participation in the water programme was limited to sending in petitions to the government during the planning stage and contributing labour during the construction phase. Villages had no say in water source selection, the design of the distribution system or the type of water scheme to install. These decisions were all made by a water engineer, who viewed himself primarily as technician and was little involved in the complex set of social, cultural and environmental factors which affect rural water usage. Kauzeni noted cases where villagers rejected use of new water schemes and continued with the traditional one because their preferences in terms of type of water scheme, location, taste and colour were not taken into account.

Second, a study of rural attitudes towards traditional and improved water supplies in one region of Tanzania (Rukwa) found that respondents reported frequent and long-term breakdowns of water schemes (particularly those fitted with hand pumps) as being among the most serious of the water supply problems.[5] It is not uncommon for pump-operated schemes to become inoperable within a few months, or even weeks after construction. The Ujamaa village programme brought with it government promises of improved water supplies, and rural expectations were further raised by actual water schemes construction. Lack of spare parts and lack of fuel to run the pumps because fuel was unavailable in the district or regional headquarter or was available but villages had no funds to buy it or no means to transport it caused further frustration. An investigation of the water schemes in Rukwa Region in 1979 found that out of twenty-eight pump-operated water schemes, only eleven were functioning.[6]

The purpose of the preceding discussion is not to minimise the strides made in the provision of rural water supplies over the last decade, but to suggest that from the villagers' point of view, implementation of the rural water policy has been far below expectations, and this has contributed to rural Tanzania's general loss of confidence in Government initiatives. This credibility problem is worsened when water-scheme construction does not keep pace with promised targets, when half of the existing schemes are not functioning and when villagers are victims of Government siting errors made in the course of villagisation. The Tanzania experience would seem to support the view that extending social services free of charge and without ties inflates expectations without necessarily making the beneficiaries any more responsive to Government demands.

Health Care

Significant strides have been made in providing health services at the village level in Tanzania over the last decade, including the establishment of rural health centres and dispensaries and the training of health workers and staff for those centres. However, as with the provision of other services such as water, the government was not able to keep pace with promised targets nor to provide services at the level expected by the rural population. Studies have shown that village health posts were often not equipped with essential equipment and drugs. As a result, villagers often sought out district or regional facilities which resulted in excessive travel costs, poor utilisation of peripheral health units and more costly care than the health system was designed to provide. This, naturally, led to the loss of confidence in government initiatives in this regard, and to fill the gap villagers have continued to use traditional 'doctors'.

Education

Among the sweeping reforms usered in by the Arusha Declaration of 1967 were changes in the focus and priorities of the Tanzanian educational system. Nyerere criticised the élitism which characterised education and the system's emphasis on skills and training which were, for the most part, irrelevant to the needs of the rural population. New priorities were outlined in his document *Education for Self Reliance.*

Primary school was no longer to be seen only as a means for selecting the most promising students to attend secondary schools. Instead, primary school was to be a complete preparation in itself which would provide students with the skills and knowledge necessary for productive work in the rural areas.

The Musoma Resolution of 1974 assessed how successfully the policy of education for self-reliance had been implemented and offered guidelines for future development. Political commitment to the goal of universal primary education (UPE) by 1989 was made during the Second Five-Year Plan (1964–9). Following the Musoma Resolution, the target date for attainment of UPE was moved forward to 1977. The first two national literacy tests (1975–7) indicated that illiteracy was reduced from 75 per cent in 1961 to 39 per cent in 1975, and to 27 per cent in 1977. The results of the most recent test indicates adult illiteracy in the 10 per cent range.

UPE, however, has not been achieved without some cost to the quality of education provided. For example, attainment of the goal of increasing textbook supplies from the present ratio of 10 students to 1 text book, to 2 students to 1 book is still a long way off. And while total enrolment figures are high, enrolment of 7-year olds (minimum entry age) in primary school is about 24 per cent. Also because students were supposed to learn Swahili and English, this presented additional teaching problems in areas where children spoke neither language.

In terms of making education at each stage terminal and relevant to the requirements of rural life, the record is mixed. For the most part, though it varies from school to school, the curriciulum is still heavily academically-biased and externally-determined with little regard for the particular needs of the village community. Moreover, while the goal of each student should no longer be solely to pass the Standard VII examination and be admitted into secondary school, this attitude is still deeply ingrained given that school is still viewed as a means to wage employment and sometimes viewed as necessary.

The goal of making schools both 'educational and economic units' is still some ways off. In 1977, self-reliant production activities accounted for only 3 per cent of the recurrent cost of school. Though no small achievement, this figure amounted to 5 per cent by 1980 but must be compared with the goal of 25 per cent.

What emerges, not only in education but in other social services as well, is the problem of effectively maintaining existing facilities and services as well as solving operational problems such as recurrent funding. The point here is not to minimise the progress the Tanzanian government made, but to highlight the setbacks it faced when expectations were high, goals could not be met and the government's credibility was inevitably questioned.

Ujamaa Villages and Operation Vijiji

Such problems meant that the peasantry for its part (with notable exceptions such as the Ruvuma Association) embraced Ujamaa only reluctantly. This was partly because the Ujamaa system of production was imposed from above and peasants felt only limited commitment to its success and partly because it was a mode of production for which the advantages had not been demonstrated. As a result, by 1972 only 14 per cent of the total population was living in Ujamaa villages and Ujamaa as a strategy for transforming the rural economy was in danger of losing its credibility. The general feeling among party and government officials was that villagisation was proceeding too slowly and more official support was required. In response, the government took the initiative in site selection, demarcating the village land areas, choosing village members and participating in the physical movement of people to the new areas. More importantly, in November 1973 Nyerere announced the compulsory villagisation policy known as 'Operation Vijiji' which stated that 'everyone must live in a village by the end of 1976'. By the middle of 1975, over 9 million people (about 60 per cent of the population) were grouped into 6000 villages making Operation Vijiji the largest resettlement effort in African history.

It has, however, been suggested that pressure to come up with development results led many officials to resort to coercion as a managerial approach. What is often forgotten is that with independence, the coercive power of the Tanzanian state apparatus was weakened and the peasant farmers fully expected to be left alone. The new state however soon confronted the peasants with the same demands as had the old state to produce more, to use new techniques, to work harder, etc, and the peasants were not noticeably more responsive to demands from their fellow Africans than they had been to those from colonial officers. Not all peasants were convinced of the advantages of living and working together in Ujamaa villages. Ujamaa involved fundamental restructuring of economic activity in rural areas and subsistence farmers were understandably reluctant to change a way of life that had at least provided for their survival. To limit government interference in their domestic affairs, villagers became quite adept at devising strategies for circumventing government policies and minimising demands on village resources.

It is noteworthy, for instance, that although the party spoke about Ujamaa in terms of class struggle and described better-off farmers as exploiters, ordinary peasants continued to look to this group to play a buffer role between themselves and the government. A study completed by Devries and Fortman in 1974 on the characteristic of village leaders found them to be universally male, generally rich and elderly and often both since it was believed that farmers fitting this description would be best qualified to manipulate the government and the party to the advantage of the village.[7]

None the less, Ujamaa, from the village viewpoint, has had both advantages and disadvantages. Under the villagisation programme, the villages gained new power. A communal field and easily accessible villages were tangible institutions and for the first time higher level party and state officials were directly confronted with a success criterion on which their careers more or less depended. They were understandably worried about the fate of the early Ujamaa villages. Establishment of the Regional Development Fund allowed officials to promise social services and other government help to villages which adopted Ujamaa goals and engaged in some form of communal production. Village power was thus enhanced under the Ujamaa programme because peasant farmers could now retaliate for unkept promises by restricting their own communal production. Von Freyhold described a village in Pangani, for instance, which refused to send its women to the communal *shamba* (farm) until the promised water supply scheme was constructured and later made the beginning of planting contingent upon the receipt of famine relief.

On the other hand, village leaders were under various pressures. They were expected to attend divisional or district meetings where they were briefed on the development directives of the next period and were instructed to pass these orders on below. This function conflicted with the role assigned to them by their electorate which was to protect the village from any demands coming from above.

The preceding discussion is not intended to serve as an exhaustive account of the Ujamaa experience but rather to highlight some of the early problems the programme encountered. In terms of implications for a basic needs approach, several points may be noted. First, the Tanzanian government seemed to overestimate its bargaining position *vis-à-vis* the peasantry. The state required the surplus production of the smallholder to sustain itself but had very little to offer the farmer that was equally essential to him. Certainly, it could improve living conditions in the rural areas by providing schools, health dispensaries, water and roads but these amenities, though desirable, were not critical to peasant survival. To receive the promised social services, rural Tanzania had to commit itself to a programme which entailed a high degree of social and economic restructuring and upheaval for them and, therefore, did so only reluctantly.

Second, without full commitment from the population in the form of self-help activities, the government was bound to fall short of its goals since it did not have the resources to provide fully such amenities on a free basis and should not have been expected to do so. Moreover, the effects of Ujamaa and many years of unfavourable weather conditions combined to disrupt agricultural production. The consequent weakening of the government's tax base made it that much more difficult to deliver the social services promised and to maintain those already in place.

Third, there is, the credibility problem. The inability of the government to provide the services promised while continuing to impose minimum acreage laws and other directives further strained relations between the government and the rural population. Ujamaa remained a system imposed from above. Even though villagers were invited to participate in the development process, their voice was actually muffled since village level development priorities, particularly in the area of provision of social services, were set at the national level by the party, and village plans were simply expected to be in accordance. So even though official government policy was to take rural concerns and priorities more into account in national planning and implementation, peasant farmers remained, in fact, effectively excluded from the national decision-making process.

CONCLUSIONS

A number of things may be concluded from the preceding discussion. First, a great deal both *pro* and *con* has been written about Tanzanian socialism as a 'model' for development. A decade ago Ali Mazrui described the phenomenon of 'Tanzaphilia' – enthusiastic and uncritical support of the Tanzanian experience. By the late 1970s this phenomenon had all but ceased to exist and most observers of the Tanzanian scene had begun to conclude that the Tanzanian experiment in rural socialism had failed. By 1974, the cumulative effects of drought in major food-producing areas, increased oil-prices and world stagflation produced in Tanzania the largest annual trade deficit since independence. Burgeoning government expenditures on villagisation, programmes providing social services, and drought relief all exacerbated a deteriorating situation, leaving the country on the verge of bankruptcy, which was only avoided by massive infusions of foreign aid. Equally important is what some observers have described as the mood of disappointment and demoralisation which has come to characterise the Tanzanian people as a response to years of setbacks. Against this backdrop, why focus on Tanzania when analysing Africa's future and the possibility of meeting BHN there?

Tanzania, the PQLI and Africa's Future in Meeting Basic Human Needs

As noted previously, Tanzania's successes and setbacks must be viewed, on the one hand, in terms of how well this nation has been able to improve the basic living conditions of its people and, on the other hand, how well the provision of such essential services has served as incentives to the populace to participate in overall economic goals such as villagisation and communal agriculture. While the foregoing account of Tanzania's Ujamaa experiment adequately reflects how difficult the latter has been, not enough attention has been focused on the former. In 1960, for example, Tanzania had an infant mortality rate of 190 deaths per 1000 births compared with its current rate of 125, a literacy rate of 10 per cent compared with today's rate of 66 per cent and a PQLI rating of 16 in relation to the current rate of 53. Even more interesting, however, is how this record in meeting basic human needs compares with other developing countries over the same time period. Currently, Tanzania has a PQLI rating similar to that of Egypt (with a 54 rating) and Guatemala (with a PQLI of 59) yet Egypt and Guatemala with per capita incomes in 1980 of \$580 and \$1110, respectively, are considerably ahead of Tanzania with a 1980 per capita income of \$260. Even more interesting, both Egypt and Guatemala had PQLI ratings in 1960 significantly above Tanzania's 1960 rating (that is, 42 and 44, respectively) which would suggest that Tanzania has made far greater strides in meeting the basic needs of its population.

Although it is recognised that much of the progress reflected in Tanzania's relatively high PQLI rating today is a result of the significant progress made in improving literacy in Tanzania, it only emphasises the fact that the PQLI recognises that improvements in meeting minimum needs can be achieved in a variety of ways and that often improving one particular area (such as education) will result in benefits in other areas (such as infant mortality). Tanzania's success also confirms that relatively low income per capita does not necessarily mean that the basic needs of people cannot be met, although it does suggest that there are limitations to how much can be done in such a programme given limited budgetary and other resources. Even given the constraints – political and economic as well as domestic and international – the Tanzanian experience in implementing a basic needs strategy suggests that these obstacles can be overcome, although not easily, and that other African nations who may view the Tanzanian case as exemplary will need to give serious thought to how they implement such a programme given their own political, economic and cultural circumstances. Tanzania's relative success in meeting BHN but its failure to mobilise the rural population in other areas in exchange for providing such basic-needs services suggests, perhaps, that other African nations will simply want to provide such services for their population without expecting significant returns in other areas in the short term. In the longer term, however, the implementation of policies aimed at meeting the BHN of African people will undoubtedly have an effect on other areas, such as productivity in the agricultural and industrial sectors.

While each African nation will continue to face the kinds of problems outlined earlier in adopting and implementing basic needs strategies, each may find it possible in the future to define its own 'development' in a new and unique way which will ultimately ensure that Africa's future is much more hopeful than either the current situation or present predictions would suggest.

NOTES

1. Life expectancy at the age of 1 year and infant mortality rate can be good indicators of important aspects of social progress, since they represent the sum of the effects of nutrition, public health, income, and the general environment. At the same time, the two indicators reflect quite different aspects of social interaction and the quality of life. Preliminary work suggests, for example, that infant mortality is a sensitive surrogate for the availability of clean water, the condition

of the home environment, and the wellbeing of mothers, while life expectancy at the age of 1 year reflects nutrition and general environmental characteristics outside the home. Literacy, too, is a useful indicator, because it is both a measure of wellbeing and a skill that is important in the development process.

2. The PQLI has some limitations that must be recognised. First, it cannot and does not presume to capture the wide range of characteristics suggested by the term 'quality of life', such as justice, political freedom, a sense of paticipation, and happiness. In addition, it does not measure strictly 'economic' development (which remains best expressed by GNP); neither does it measure 'total' welfare. Finally, the PQLI is only as good as the data upon which it is based. For a more extensive discussion of the PQLI concept, its limitation, and its many uses, see Morris D. Morris, *Measuring the Condition of the World's Poor: The Physical Quality of Life Index* (New York: Pergamon for the Overseas Development Council, 1979). For an earlier presentation, see Morris D. Morris and Florizelle B. Liser, 'The PQLI: Measuring Progress in Meeting Human Needs' (Washington, DC: Overseas Development Council, 1977) Communiqué no. 32.
3. For current PQLI ratings as well as its components for all countries, see 'Statistical Annexes', in *US Foreign Policy and the Third World: Agenda 1982* (New York: Praeger Overseas Development Council, 1982) 160–74.
4. Stahl, Sachak and Mkusa, 'A Socio-Economic Study of Water-Related Problems in Northern Nkombe' (Dar es Salaam: University of Dar es Salaam, 1979) BRALUP Research Paper no. 54, 4.
5. A. S. Kauzeni, 'Villagers Expectations and Attitudes Towards Traditional and Improved Water Supplies' (Bureau of Resource Assessment and Land Use Planning, University of Dar es Salaam, 1981) Research Report no. 50, 35.
6. Ibid, 36.
7. Devries and L. Fortman, 'A Study of Ujamaa Villages in the Iringa Region', (UNDP/FAO Planning Team for the Iringa Third Five-Year Plan, 1974).

Selected Bibliography on the Future of Africa

Adedeji, Adebayo, 'Africa: Permanent Underdog?', *International Perspectives*, March/April 1981, 15–20.

'Africa 2000: special number', *Issue* 8 (4), Winter 1978, 1–63.

Allison, Caroline and Reginald Green (eds) 'Accelerated Development in sub-Saharan Africa: what agendas for action?' *IDS Bulletin* 14 (1) January 1983.

Aluko, Olajide, 'Nigerian foreign policy in the year 2000' in Timothy M. Shaw and Olajide Aluko (eds) *Nigerian Foreign Policy: Alternative Perceptions and Projections* (London: Macmillan, 1983) 191–204.

Amin, Samir, 'A critique of the World Bank report entitled "Accelerated Development in Sub-Saharan Africa"' *Africa Development* 7 (1/2) January/June 1982, 23–30.

Arnold, Guy, 'United in Words, Divided in Deeds: the African Economy in the 1980s' *Africa Guide, 1981* (Saffron Walden: World of Information, 1980) 15–19.

Bissell, Richard W. and Chester A. Crocker (eds) *South Africa into the 1980s* (Boulder: Westview, 1979).

Carlsson, Jerker (ed.) *Recession in Africa* (Uppsala: Scandinavian Institute of African Studies, 1983).

Dey, Jennie, 'Is Food Security in Africa No More Than a Dream?' *Africa Guide 1982* (Saffron Walden: World of Information, 1981) 37–42.

Economic Commission for Africa, *ECA and African Development, 1983–2008: Preliminary Prospective Study* (Addis Ababa, April 1983).

Edwards, John, 'African Commodities: Grim Prospects for the 1980s', *Africa Guide 1981* (Saffron Walden: World of Information, 1980) 62–5.

Faruquee, Rashid and Ravi Gulhati, 'Rapid Population Growth in sub-Saharan Africa', *World Bank Staff Working Paper*, No. 559 (Washington, 1983).

Gaudier, Maryse, 'Africa 2000: An Analytical Bibliography on African Proposals for the 21st Century' (Geneva: International Institute for Social Studies, 1982). Bibliographic Series No. 5.

Harvey, Charles, 'The Economy of Sub-Saharan Africa: A Critique of the World Bank's Report', in Colin Legum (ed.) *Africa Contemporary Record, Volume 14, 1982* (New York: Africana, 1981) A114–A119.

Hilling, D., 'Alternative Energy Sources for Africa: Potential and Prospects', *African Affairs* 75 (300) July 1976, 359–71.

Kitchen, Helen, (ed.) *Africa: From Mystery to Maze* (Lexington: Heath, 1976). Critical Choices for Americans, Volume XI.

Legum, Colin, I. William Zartman, Steven Langdon and Lynn K. Mytelka *Africa in the 1980s: a continent in crisis* (New York: McGraw-Hill 1979). Council on Foreign Relations 1980s Project.

Mazrui, Ali A. and Hasu H. Patel (eds) *Africa in World Affairs: The Next Thirty Years* (New York: Third Press, 1973).

Meerman, Jacob and Susan Hill Cochrane, 'Population growth and food supply in Sub-Saharan Africa', *Finance and Development* 19 (3) September 1982, 12–17.

OAU *Lagos Plan of Action for the Economic Development of Africa, 1980–2000* (Geneva: International Institute for Labour Studies, 1981).

Sandbrook, Richard, 'Is There Hope for Africa?' *International Perspectives* January/February 1982, 3–8.

Scandinavian Institute of African Studies, 'Conference on Africa: Which Way Out of the Recession?' (Uppsala, September 1982).

Shaw, Timothy M., 'On Projections, Prescriptions and Plans: A Review of the Literature on Africa's Future', *Quarterly Journal of Administration* 14 (4) July 1980, 463–83.

Shaw, Timothy M., 'From Dependence to Self-reliance: Africa's Prospects for the Next Twenty Years', *International Journal* 35 (4) Autumn 1980, 475–502.

Shaw, Timothy M., 'The African Condition: Prophecies and Possibilities', *Year Book of World Affairs, Volume 36* (London: Stevens, 1982) 139–50.

Shaw, Timothy M. (ed.) *Alternative Futures for Africa* (Boulder: Westview, 1982).

Shaw, Timothy M., 'Debates about Africa's Future: the Brandt, World Bank, and Lagos Plan Blueprints', *Third World Quarterly* 5 (2) April 1983, 330–44.

Shaw, Timothy M., 'The African Crisis: Alternative Development Strategies for the Continent', *Alternatives* 9 (1), Summer 1983, 111–27.

Shaw, Timothy M., 'Africa Projected: Dependence, Disengagement or Dialectic?' *Journal of General Studies* (forthcoming, 1984).

Shaw, Timothy M., 'Unconventional Conflict in Africa: Nuclear, Class and Guerrilla Struggles, Past, Present and Prospective', *Jerusalem Journal of International Relations* (forthcoming, 1984).

'Special Double Issue on the Berg Report and the Lagos Plan of Action', *Africa Development* 7 (1/2) January/June 1982, i–206.

Stevens, Christopher, 'Will Famine Stalk Africa in the 1980s?' *Africa Guide, 1981* (Saffron Walden: World of Information, 1980) 21–6.

Stevens, Christopher, 'Nigeria: Economic Prospects to 1985, After the Oil Glut' (London: Economist Intelligence Unit, 1982). Special Report No. 123.

UNITAR/IDEP, 'Conference on the Future of Africa', Dakar, July 1977 (CS/2796).

US Department of Agriculture, *Food Problems and Prospects in Sub-Saharan Africa: The Decade of the 1980s* (Washington, DC: Government Printer).

World Bank, *Accelerated Development in Sub-Saharan Africa: An Agenda for Action* (Washington, 1981).

Zartman, I. William, 'Coming Political Problems in Black Africa', in Jennifer Seymour Whitaker (ed.) *Africa and the United States: Vital Interests* (New York: New York University Press, 1978) 87–119.

Zartman, I. William, 'Issues of African Diplomacy in the 1980s', *Orbis* 25 (4) Winter 1982, 1025–43,

Zimbabwe's First Five Years: Economic Prospects Following Independence (London: Economist Intelligence Unit, 1981). Special Report No. 111.

Index